ORAL POETRY AND SOMALI NATIONALISM

AFRICAN STUDIES SERIES 32

The African Studies Series is a collection of monographs and general studies that reflect the interdisciplinary interests of the African Studies Centre at Cambridge. Volumes to date have combined historical, anthropological, economic, political and other perspectives. Each contribution has assumed that such broad approaches can contribute much to our understanding of Africa, and that this may in turn be of advantage to specific disciplines.

To Sofia and Delmar

ORAL POETRY AND SOMALI NATIONALISM

The case of Sayyid Maḥammad 'Abdille Ḥasan

SAID S. SAMATAR
Assistant Professor of History, Rutgers University

CAMBRIDGE UNIVERSITY PRESS

CAMBRIDGE
LONDON NEW YORK NEW ROCHELLE
MELBOURNE SYDNEY

CAMBRIDGE UNIVERSITY PRESS
Cambridge, New York, Melbourne, Madrid, Cape Town, Singapore, São Paulo, Delhi

Cambridge University Press
The Edinburgh Building, Cambridge CB2 8RU, UK

Published in the United States of America by Cambridge University Press, New York

www.cambridge.org
Information on this title: www.cambridge.org/9780521104579

First published 1982
This digitally printed version 2009

A catalogue record for this publication is available from the British Library

Library of Congress Catalogue Card Number: 81–18072

ISBN 978-0-521-23833-5 hardback
ISBN 978-0-521-10457-9 paperback

Contents

Illustrations and Tables

Photographs

Figures

Tables

Note on Transcription of Somali Words

In transcribing Somali words, I have adopted the official Somali orthography which has been in use in the Somali Republic since 1972. This orthography uses Latin characters with minor adjustments designed to accommodate Somali phonetic sounds. There are, however, three consonants which do not conform to the new system of Somali spelling: the aspirate 'h', the palatal 'd' and the 'ayn'.

In the new Somali orthography, the letters 'x', 'dh' and 'c' are used respectively to render these consonants. In this book, by contrast, I retain the conventional symbols used to denote them. Thus I adopt:

ḥ instead of x
ḍ instead of dh
ʻ instead of c

This measure is taken to meet the needs of the English reader who is unacquainted with the official Somali orthography or with Somali phonetic sounds. Where any of the three consonants appear in a Somali author's name or book title, however, I use the official orthography. Bibliographic entries of Arabic names are rendered in Westernized form, while those of Somali ones conform to indigenous designation, i.e. first name comes first.

The glottal stop or Arabic *hamza* is rendered by a closing inverted comma. The cities of Mogadishu, Hargeisa, Merca and Brava retain their conventional spelling.

Preface

This is a study of the use of oratory and oratorical techniques as a tool to obtain political power in a traditional African society. In an attempt to bring forth the causal linkages between oral poetry, politics and power in Somali society, I have chosen to focus on the political oratory of Sayyid Maḥammad 'Abdille Ḥasan, the poet, mystic and warrior leader of the Somali anti-colonial movement at the turn of the century. In selecting the political verse of the Somali leader as a case study, my efforts here aim at several interconnected objectives. One is to investigate the Sayyid's poetic oratory which, aside from its relevance to the politics and strategy of creating a large-scale resistance movement, possesses an intrinsic literary and philosophical interest, and therefore deserves to be studied on its own merits. Another emanates from the need to enquire into the ways and means by which an African resister of imperialism harnessed a remarkable indigenous resource in order to mobilize the public in his favor and against his opponents. Finally, by demonstrating the intimate correlation between the Sayyid's oratorical powers, which he used consciously – and consummately – to achieve political ends, and the progress (or lack of progress) of the Somali resistance struggle, I hope to add a new element to the study of African resistance in general.

More specifically, it is hoped that the elucidation in this book of the Sayyid's use of oral poetry as a weapon to rid his country of alien rule will encourage others to investigate the indigenous weapons of African resisters of imperialism elsewhere. Such efforts may help to enrich – perhaps revolutionize in some cases – our perceptions of the question of European intrusion and African response.

Though the Sayyid and the Somali Dervishes occupy its central stage, this study seeks to illuminate the quality, extent and influence of oral poetry in Somali life and lore. To facilitate the reader's appreciation of my approach and quirks of style, it may be helpful to interject here an autobiographical note. I was born and raised as a pastoralist in the west central part of the Somali peninsula, an area which – with the advent of colonialism and the consequent introduction of European notions of fixed boundaries – was to be split into the Mudug province of the Somali Republic and the disputed Ogaadeen region.

Growing up a herdsman in the vast, scorching plains of Africa's Horn presented challenges and opportunities as well as peculiarities of life which it will not do to go into here. I will just mention one feature of my early life which bears on this book. This is that literacy was unknown in the culture of my youth, except to a few roving holy men (*wadaads*) who boasted a rudimentary knowledge of Arabic and sacred law. These taught the Qur'an and basics of religious sciences, and conducted marriage ceremonies. However, the *wadaads*' literacy, such as it was, had no appreciable impact on the population at large, whose native tongue, Somali, was unwritten and in fact remained so, to all intents and purposes, until 1972. This meant that public and private life was conducted by oral means, a notable medium being oral poetry. Like nearly all of my fellow herdsmen, I aspired to acquire skill in this coveted craft, received informal instruction in the art of verbal composition from established poets, and even myself attempted a few versifications which, I confess, earned their author no notable distinction as an oral poet. Perhaps I quit pastoralism too early – at fifteen I migrated to sedentary culture where I learned to read and write – to witness the blooming of whatever latent talent I may have had in the field.

If the artistic gains of my early association with pastoral poets and reciters remain dubious, the impression they made on me has been quite indelible. In this connection the name of 'Abdille 'Ali Siigo stands out in my memory. He was a venerable elder who almost every evening after the camels had been milked and secured in the kraal would, by the fireside, chant the poetry of Sayyid Maḥammad late into the night before a captivated audience of men, women and children. He was a dramatic chanter who seemed to command even the attention of the camels which sat nearby, lazily chewing their cuds. So the fire crackled, its red flames casting a hazy glow over his silvery beard, giving the elder's expression a pale, ghostly aspect. Outside the kraal fence the winds howled monotonously, pierced by the occasional roar of a hungry lion. Every now and then this would stir the camels from their dreamy drowsing, causing them to stop chewing and prick their ears, alarmed by the danger outside. Meantime, elder 'Abdille chanted ecstatically, seemingly oblivious of everything but his rhymes.

Sayyid Maḥammad's verse – which always has a forceful appeal to a Somali – when dramatized by this elder generated an emotional atmosphere which, needless to say, impressed my adolescent mind. I hope I have succeeded in drawing on something of that experience for the benefit of this book.

The core of the work resulted from a doctoral dissertation submitted to Northwestern University's Graduate School in 1979. The dissertation itself was based on a 12-month research sponsored jointly by the Social Science Research Council and the Graduate School of Northwestern.

It is not possible to thank all the people to whom credit is due for the writing of this book. Naturally, I am grateful to my advisor, Professor John A. Rowe, for his critical advice, moral support and patient interest in the progress of my work; to Carl Petry and Abraham Demoz of Northwestern University who, as members of the examining committee of my doctoral defense, read the dissertation and gave me much critical insight which helped to refine my focus of the subject and to pinpoint the methodological concerns of my research efforts; I also owe a special debt to the staff of Northwestern's Africana Library, in particular to Hans Panofsky, Daniel Britz and Barbara Rivers for their help in tracing obscure materials needed for my work.

In London, I owe a debt of gratitude to the two 'elder statesmen' of Somali studies, B. W. Andrzejewski and I. M. Lewis, who not only gave advice and encouragement during my four months of archival research in England, but read the typescript critically and suggested improvements; I am indebted also to Richard Greenfield of St Anthony's College who gave similar advice.

In the Somali Democratic Republic, I am similarly indebted to numerous individuals for their advice, kindness and encouragement. Among these I must mention Mr. I. M. Abyan, then the Director General of the Ministry of Culture and Higher Education, who helped secure research clearance for me and asked stimulating questions about my work. I must also acknowledge the assistance of Dr Shariif Saalah and Dr Maḥammad Aadan, both at that time high-ranking officers of the Somali Socialist Revolutionary Party, who provided me with the necessary authority to move freely about the country and to ask my informants questions of a sensitive nature without bureaucratic and security impediments. Again in Somalia, I am obliged to acknowledge the help of members of the Somali Academy, especially Aḥmad F. 'Ali Idaajaa, Sheikh Jaama' 'Umar 'Iise, Yaasiin 'Ismaan Keenadiid, 'Abdullahi Ḥ. 'A Suuryaan, Yuusuf Meygaag Samatar, M. Ḥ. Ḥ. Sheeka-Ḥariir, who not only adopted me as an honorary member of the Academy but also shared with me their immense knowledge of my topic.

In addition to scholars, other persons have been especially helpful. 'Ali Samatar Maḥammad, M. K. Salaad, M. M. Yaḥya and my brother, Ismaa'iil, gave me much practical assistance while in the field. Their support helped to facilitate and promote my work in Somalia; as did the moral support of my friend Donald Jones of Evanston, Illinois.

Many thanks are due to my Cambridge editors Dr Robin Derricourt and Ms Elizabeth Wetton, and subeditor Ms Susan Moore, for their editorial assistance. Finally – and most of all – I want to thank my wife, Lydia, who not only typed the manuscript but has been my companion and co-laborer throughout my research efforts.

Introduction

The distinguishing mark of 'real art', Leo Tolstoy wrote in his much debated essay, 'What Is Art?', lies in its 'infectiousness'[1] – a potent property, in Tolstoy's view peculiar to art. This property enables the artist to infect others with his feelings 'compelling [them] to rejoice in another's gladness, to sorrow at another's grief and to mingle souls ... which is the very essence of art'. Whatever their merits in the context of Western literary/artistic traditions, Tolstoy's views of the infectious and invading power of art would probably have been shared by Sayyid Mahammad 'Abdille Ḥasan, who may have expressed a similar sentiment regarding the power of art when he spoke of his poetry as 'issuing forth with the blinding flash of a thunderbolt', or, to vary the metaphor, 'the engulfing darkness of gale winds'.[2] For a poet to attribute an irresistible, almost mystical power to his own creations, as the Sayyid often does, may sound somewhat immodest to a Western audience, but such a claim is permissible in Somali pastoral/literary conventions where the talented poet is viewed with something akin to superstitious awe. Through the power of his poetic orations, the Sayyid, as we shall see, was thought to 'inflict wounds' on his enemies, and indeed those who were attacked by his literary barbs often responded as if they had received physical wounds.

The Sayyid, moreover, took pains to ascribe the power of his verse to the 'strengthening' hand of 'Divine Truth',[3] and to a sense of mission which he claimed to have sustained not only his poetry but his person, enabling him to weather the many dangers which his stormy career exposed him to. The mission – with which he gradually became imbued – was to rid his country of alien Christian rule. Thus he sang with evident conviction: 'I have sought and found the Prophetic guidance / [which appointed me] to tell the unbelieving white invaders: / "This land is not yours."'[4] It must be said at the outset, therefore, that the standard of truth or of excellence by which the Sayyid wished his poetry to be judged was a religious (Islamic) truth, a circumstance which again seems to have the peculiar ring of Tolstoy's controversial proposition that 'In every period of history . . . it is by the standard of [a] religious perception that the feelings transmitted by art have always been appraised.'[5]

Elsewhere in his essay, Tolstoy argued that art is 'one of the indispensable means of communication without which mankind could not exist'[6] – its principal function being to convey the feelings of one man to others. This too would hardly sound strange to Somali ears long accustomed to the use of oral poetry, not only as an important means of communication but also as the principal medium by which Somalis ask the abiding questions: Whence come we? What are we? Whither go we?

In dealing with a historical subject from the standpoint of oratory and rhetoric, this study may be said to have taken an unorthodox approach in historical methodology, for in essence it relies on a branch of literature, notably poetry, as the core of its source materials. What may be unorthodox is not that we seek to utilize literature in order to investigate a historical question – history and literature are known to illuminate each other – but that the type of literature employed for the task should be an oral literature, and an oral verse at that, with its bent to the lyrical and the transient rather than the historical and the permanent. Hence, our reliance on such oral data to explore a historical phenomenon may raise, methodologically, a few eyebrows, in view of the historians' conventional bias in favor of documents and documentary sources for the reconstruction and the interpretation of the past. Yet our recourse to a strong utilization of oral verse in the attempt to chronicle and interpret the history of the Somali anti-colonial movement was not motivated by any flair for whimsical experimentation in historiographical method. Rather, it was born out of necessity.

Those acquainted with the language and culture of the pastoral Somalis will have appreciated the pre-eminent, sometimes sinister, role which poetry plays in Somali life and thought. Whereas in the industrialized West, poetry – and especially what is regarded as serious poetry – seems to be increasingly relegated to a marginal place in society, Somali oral verse is central to Somali life, involved as it is in the intimate workings of people's lives. For reasons which we hope to elucidate in this study, the pastoral Somalis attach great value to their oral verse and cultivate it with an undying interest. Indeed the one feature which unfailingly emerges even from a casual observation of Somali society is the remarkable influence of the poetic word in the Somali cultural and political scene. The Somalis are often described as a 'nation of bards'[7] whose poetic heritage is a living force intimately connected with the vicissitudes of everyday life.

In seeking to account for the unusual hold of the poetic art on the Somalis, some scholars would look to environmental factors for clues. The life of Somali nomads, it is said, is a life of wandering and danger, devoted as it is to eking out a living in a demanding environment. In the great boredom and bleakness of their surroundings, the theory goes, the Somali nomads turn to their poetry, the one thing which does not cost them anything and provides them with drama and entertainment.[8] According to this view, without the twin inspiration of their faith and verse, the Somalis would waste themselves in fury and desperation.[9]

This is a quaint argument, though it may have some merits. Environmental bleakness *per se* hardly makes for poetry or poetic creativity. To interpret the lyric verse of the Somali pastoralists merely as a survival mechanism, a feeble and self-pitying cry designed to mitigate life's cruelties to man, is to miss the significance of the poetic craft in Somali society.

What then makes poetry such a pervasive force in Somali society? To the Somalis the question is not so difficult to answer: poetry is the medium whereby an individual or a group can present a case most persuasively. The pastoral poet is, to borrow a phrase, the public relations man of the clan, and through his craft he exercises a powerful influence in clan affairs. For unlike Western poetry, which appears to be primarily the concern of a group of professionals dealing with, more often than not, an esoteric subject matter intended for the members of what seems an élitist secret society, Somali pastoral verse is a living art affecting almost every aspect of life. Its functions are versatile, concerned not only with matters of art and aesthetics but also with questions of social significance. It illuminates culture, society and history.

In addition to its value as the literary and aesthetic embodiment of the community, Somali poetry is a principal medium of mass communication, playing a role similar to that of the press and television in Western societies. Somali poets, like Western journalists and newspapermen, thus have a great deal to say about politics and the acquisition of political power. Because it is the language and the vehicle of politics, the verse which Somali poets produce is an important source of Somali history, just as the printed and televised word perfoms a similar function in the West.

It is the duty, for example, of the Somali pastoral poet to compose verse on all important clan events and to express and formalize in verse the dominant issues of the age – in short, to record and immortalize in verse the history of his people. And since the poet's talents are employed not only to give expression to a private emotion but also to address vital community concerns, his verse reflects the feelings, thoughts and actions of his age.

While I have not proposed an explicit theory or model of the relation between political power and oral poetry in Somali traditional (non-literate) society, the general approach of this study – with regard, for example, to the kinds of questions raised, the data presented, the narrative constructed and the conclusions drawn – would seem to entail theoretical implications. Insofar as these may be of interest to students of non-literate societies dealing with questions of power and political communication, they may be expressed as follows: 1) In Somali pastoral sanctions, the power and prestige of the poetic craft must possess universal recognition and acceptance in the community; 2) such power and prestige derive from the monopolistic conditions surrounding the composition and utilization of oral poetry; and 3) in the transmission of ideas, the poetic medium must be persuasive, efficient and easy to grasp and memorize.

The widespread community acceptance of the validity and efficacy of the poetic medium in social relations seems to stem from pastoral notions of feud and vendetta, especially the institution of *godob* discussed in chapter 1. Among the various components which comprise the *godob* institution is the concept of speech vendetta – the notion that certain kinds of oratorical forms can be used for slander. To borrow a pastoralist phrase, poetic orations serve the potent task of either 'violating or ennobling the soul' of a person or a group. When poetic formulations are used to wound someone's honor, a case of *godob* has been generated. The resulting grievance, if it is not redressed or offset by a counter poetic formulation, becomes grounds for violent hostility between persons or groups. Indeed poetic slander has been the source of many a lethal inter-clan feud, for an insult or slander in poetry is considered in pastoral sanctions to have the same effect on the victim as a physical assault.

By the same token, the power of poetry can be (and is) used to reconcile two parties who are on the brink of war. Thus, in pastoral ethos, poetry is both the instrument to precipitate and sustain feuds and a principal means to bring feuds under control.

The second point making for the power of poetry in pastoral culture concerns the monopolistic nature of the craft. In pastoral society, as in others, a relatively small number of people are endowed with the talent to compose high-quality verse – artistic genius hardly comes in abundant supply. As a result, the inaccessibility of the art to most members of the population makes it a scarce commodity, the exclusive tool of a favored few. The few, aware of the high demand for their skill and the privileged status which their trade confers on them, use their talents to maximize their social and political influence. Hence, the pastoral bard occupies a prominent place in society. Lord of the desert and the dominant voice of the clan, he is envied by his less endowed kinsmen. It is his coveted task to articulate and register in verse the concerns of the community and the noteworthy deeds of his people.

This brings us to the last and perhaps the most important factor to account for the influence of poetry in pastoral Somali society. Given its regular features of alliterative and metrical structure, Somali pastoral verse is easy to memorize, far more so than prose can be. The significance of this fact is easy to grasp if we bear in mind that in an oral culture where writing is unknown, except to a few roving holy men, the only libraries or reference materials men have are their memories. Thus the events which are truly memorable in clan affairs are committed to verse, first so as to underscore their importance and, secondly, so that they can better be remembered. In this way versification enables the pastoralists not only to transmit information across considerable distances but also to record it for posterity. Hence, Somali pastoral verse functions both as a social communicator and as an archival repository.

Owing to the power of their talents in social relations, Somali poets tend to be political manipulators *par excellence*, using their potent craft to make and unmake politicians and public men. Magicians of words, they have the wherewithal to inform and persuade the public effectively. Consequently, they are respected and feared, the pride of their clans whose panegyrics they sing and the bane of their enemies whom they slander and discredit through the artful marshaling of their sinister rhymes.

Sayyid Maḥammad 'Abdille Ḥasan was, or at least perceived himself to be, one such magician of words. Rooted in the pastoral tradition and gifted in the art of political versification, he sought to utilize his oratorical resource as a political weapon in his protracted campaign against three colonial powers and their Somali collaborators. Our aim in this study is to examine what the Sayyid made of his poetic talent and to assess the nature of the impact (if any) of his political verse on the course of the resistance struggle.

Chapter 1 discusses the environment of the pastoral Somalis and the peculiar factors which predispose the society to the pursuit of oratory and eloquence, and goes on to a discussion of examples of prose oratory. Chapter 2 attempts to put forth a modest analysis of Somali oral poetry with emphasis on poetic oratory, its principles and uses. We provide examples of political poets who strove – with notable success – to leave their imprint on society through the eloquence of their words.

Chapter 3 is a 'straight' history, enunciating the onset of colonialism in the Horn of Africa and tracing the origins and growth of the Somali Dervish resistance movement. In this chapter we present evidence that the early phases of the Dervish resistance constituted an indigenous response of the Ogaadeen Somalis to the imposition of Ethiopian rule in western Somalia, and that the British, who were to bear the brunt of Dervish fighting, became unwittingly enmeshed in what was essentially an Ethio-Somali problem.

Chapter 4 attempts to present an extensive analysis of the Sayyid's verse with a view to relating it to the ebb and flow of Dervish fortunes. The Sayyid is shown to have deliberately put to use the power of 'my mighty tongue' in his long-lasting efforts to capture the hearts and minds of the Somalis for the Dervish cause. The extent of his success is assessed.

The last chapter begins with a critical review of the literature on the Somali Dervishes and proceeds to a discussion of the multifarious personality of the Sayyid – as a political poet striving with 'utmost sincerity' to present the 'truth' of his case to the people, as a Muslim mystic (Sufi), yearning for the quiet and contemplative life, and as a warrior chieftain of a highly militarist organization. The contradictory demands, it is argued, of these 'inner obligations' were responsible for the stormy, at times erratic, behavior that was to mark the later phases of his career.

As well as to historians, this study may be of interest to anthropologists, sociologists and political scientists, and perhaps even more to students of oral literature, communication, oratory and related disciplines with interest in discussions of the organic linkage between language and socio-political power. Students of oral literature may, for example, be interested in the discussion of the composition, transmission and distribution of Somali oral poetry, while the place of the poet, especially his influence in group decision-making, may be of relevance to sociologists, and his powers to inform and persuade the public to studies of communication as well as oratory and rhetoric.

The principal focus of this book is however directed to African historians, in particular those interested in what Professor T. O. Ranger has called African 'primary resistance'[10] to European occupation. The example of the versatility of Somali pastoral poetry and the Sayyid's utilization of it as a weapon in the resistance struggle may shed some light on other manifestations of African resistance to imperialism. The Sayyid's verse, as we shall have occasion to witness, represented a deliberate effort to influence opinion and action through the clever fusion of the aesthetic with the didactic. Aware of the importance of public opinion in an egalitarian society, he used his verse as a forum to inform and persuade the public and to propagate the Dervish cause.

The challenge of winning the support and cooperation of others must have been part of the tasks of every leader of African resistance. In societies with hierarchical institutions where the leader could build on an existing structure of centralized authority, the tasks of persuasion might not have been as formidable or as crucial to the success of the resistance effort. But in segmental societies where egalitarianism or village democracy was the dominant norm, the leader had to rely more on persuasion than on coercion. As the Somali example demonstrates, he had to sell the cause to the people. Propaganda, public relations and other forms of promotional techniques must have been of paramount importance to the progress of the struggle. The promotional effort – if it is to succeed – in turn requires a medium to communicate the leader's ideas to the masses, a medium whose power and prestige the people recognize and respect.

In the Somali case, the medium is shown to be poetic oratory. Professor T. O. Ranger showed the importance of religious media in the Shona-Ndebele revolt of 1896–7,[11] though some of his propositions have since been challenged, unsuccessfully in my view.[12] In the Mau Mau uprising, oaths and oathing are known to have played some role.[13] A comprehensive re-examination of the manner in which these and other anti-colonial movements used indigenous tools to obtain mass participation may provide some insights into the phenomena of African responses to European imperialism.

1

Elements of Somali Pastoral Oratory: Prose

1 THE CULTURAL MILIEU

While a general treatment of the range and categories of Somali oral-literary forms and genres along with their cultural significance and social functions is beyond the scope and intent of this study, a precursory look into a few arbitrarily selected themes of pastoral oratory and rhetoric may prove helpful. Although a formal study of Somali pastoral arts of oratory and skill in public speaking remains to be undertaken, few students of Somali language and culture have failed to observe the importance of artistic speech in Somali pastoral life. The works of such scholars as Richard Burton,[1] M. Maino,[2] Margaret Laurence,[3] B. W. Andrzejewski and I. M. Lewis[4] refer to the Somalis as a 'nation of bards'. Their appraisal is echoed by Somali commentators on numerous occasions, most notably by the late president of the Somali Republic, Dr 'Abdirashiid 'Ali Shermaarke, who spoke of his countrymen's lyric verse as 'one of the two national assets of inestimable value'.[5] The other asset the president had in mind was Islam, and in putting poetry on the same level as Islam, the president paid no small tribute to his country's poetic heritage.

If not also a nation of nomads, the Somalis are a nation in which nomadic pastoralism plays a dominant role in the life of the people. Not only do more than half of the Somali people still continue to pursue pastoralism as the chief mode of economy, but urbanized nomads dominate the modern state.[6] They form the class of people to whom, in another context, I have referred as the 'transitional generation'.[7] These are former nomads who migrated to urban centers within the last thirty years and took over control of government from the departing expatriates in the wake of decolonization. Although bred in the countryside and essentially pastoral in culture, the transitional generation, nevertheless, has a commanding place in the economy and the civil service. And despite the ring of incongruity in the phrase, the long-urbanized Benaadiris – who resent the supremacy of the recently-arrived pastoralists – complain of the 'nation's nomadic bureaucracy'.[8]

The prevalence of pastoralism makes Somalia unique in eastern Africa. While animal husbandry seems to be an important economic pursuit in eastern Africa as a whole, it is in Somalia alone that the majority of the population follows pastoralism. Kenya and Ethiopia, Somalia's neighbors, both have a minority of their populations who practice pastoralism, but it is interesting to note that even here a greater part of that minority is of Somali ethnic origin or of closely related peoples.[9]

The distinguishing features of Somali pastoralism with respect to ecology, mode of living, social institutions and kinship systems have been ably brought out by I. M. Lewis[10] (for northern Somalia) and Enrico Cerulli[11] (for southern Somalia) and it would benefit the interested reader to consult their pioneering works on the subject. I will therefore limit my observations to introductory matters except where a topic of prime relevance to this study (as, for example, the discussion of camels and camel culture) is concerned. With few exceptions, all Somalis belong to one of six kinship groupings which, to adopt I. M. Lewis' term,[12] I will refer to as clan-families. Four of these – the Daarood, Dir, Hawiye and Isaaq – are predominantly nomadic pastoralists, while the other two, the Digil and Raḥanwayn, are largely agriculturalist. These clan-families and their descendant clans are represented graphically on fig. 1, p. 10 and it would be useful to become familiar with them in relation to fig. 2, p. 11, which shows their territorial distribution. In the course of this discussion, we shall have occasion to refer to them, especially to the pastoralist clan-families and their sub-groupings.

The environment of the Somalis is both demanding and dangerous and, except in a few places, drought and famine, disease and pestilence, predatory beasts, and feud and war are constant threats to the people and their herds. A standard evening prayer after the flocks and herds are securely placed in the homestead kraal says, 'O God, save us from whatever creeps and whatever gallops, and whatever springs up and whatever roars. O God, make us the grain that escapes unharmed between the mortar and pestle.'[13]

Yet this land of seeming danger and desolation is a promised land to the Somalis, and their folklore is replete with passionate yearnings to possess it. 'I speak the truth', said one of their poets in a curse-attack on Haile Selassie of Ethiopia, whose empire he felt was encroaching on the pastoralists' traditional pasturefields:

> I speak the truth: this land is our land
> Hodayo, Wardeer and the plains of Dahare[14]

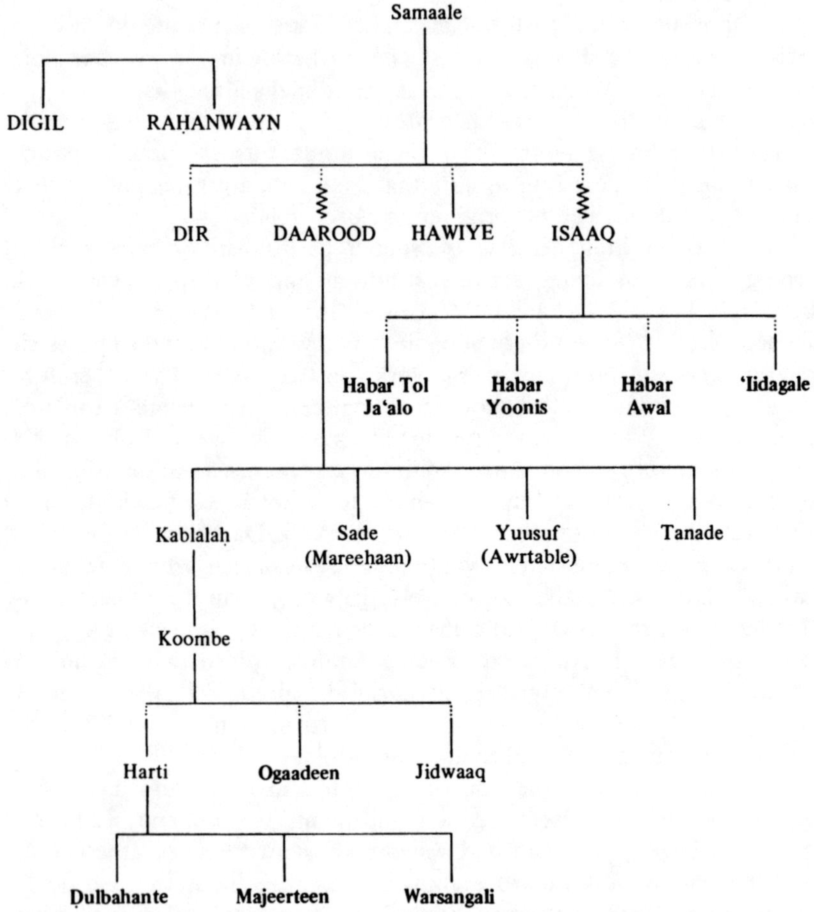

Figure 1. Somali clan genealogy. The two agricultural clans of Digil and Raḥanwayn are on one side, and on the other, the predominantly pastoral Samaale clan-families: Dir, Daarood, Isaaq and Hawiye. According to tradition, the word 'Somali' (properly, 'Soomaali') is a derivative of 'Sammaale', name of the mythical founder – ancestor of the pastoralist clan-families, and etymologically comes from 'Soo maal', 'go and milk', thus stressing the pastoral ethic in the culture. For alternative possible sources of the word 'Somali', see I. M. Lewis, *A Pastoral Democracy*, pp. 11–13.

Bold type indicates numerically powerful clans and sub-clans who figure significantly in the events discussed in this book. A dotted line indicates omission of genealogical steps deemed unnecessary for this chart; wavy lines indicate maternal kinship. Parentheses indicate a variant name.

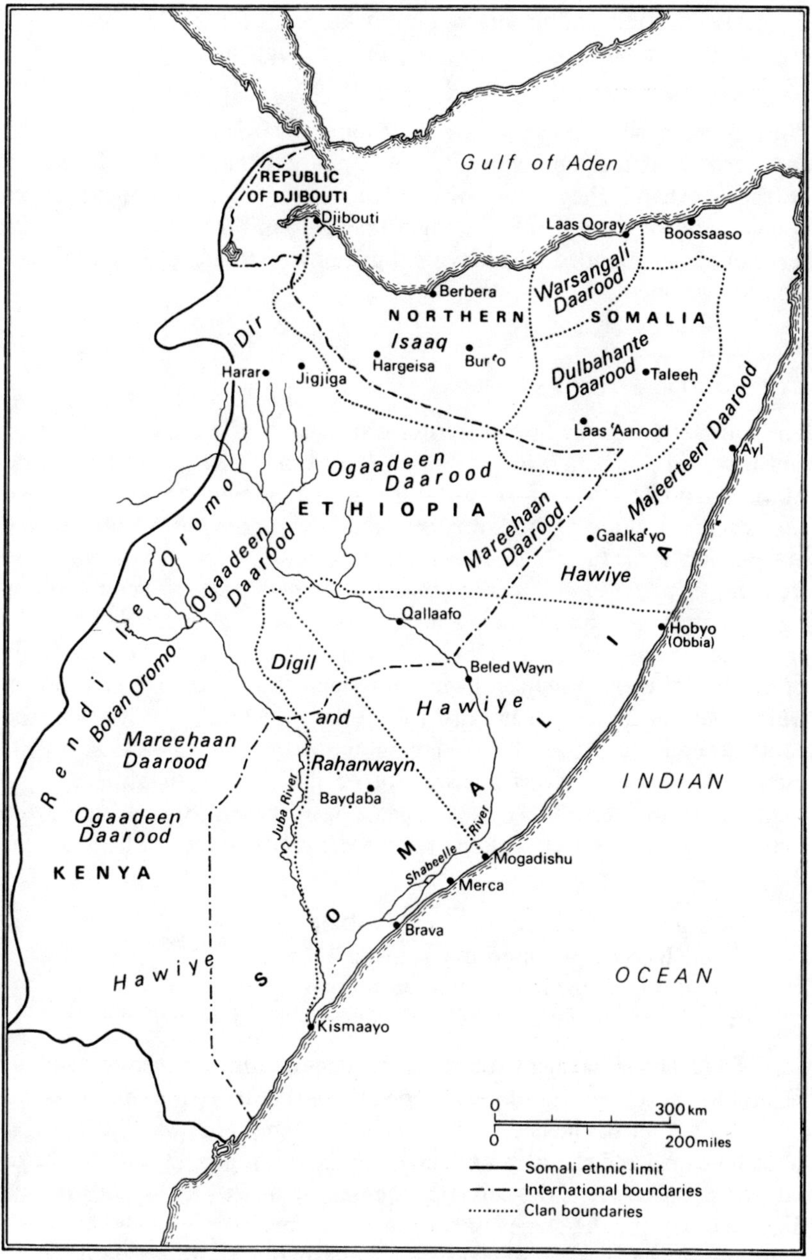

Figure 2. Distribution of major Somali clans and contiguous peoples.

And Ḥananley, beautiful pastures on the other side of the river.[15]
Also the hills of Harodigeet and Daalooki vales[16]
And the plains overlooking the corral of Jigjiga . . .
These the confines of my land are.[17]

Thus, Somalis show an ambivalent attitude towards their environment; and nowhere is that ambivalence more apparent than in their folklore: on the one hand, they speak of the land as having a 'Prophetic curse upon it' and on the other, as being a 'blessed land teeming with mystic herds of camel attended by benevolent genies who lavish gifts of stock on the impoverished'.[18]

2 THE CAMEL: MOTHER OF MEN

The foundation of the Somali pastoralists' material culture is the camel and it would not be a wrong analogy to say that what cattle are to the Masai[19] and the Nuer,[20] camels are to the Somali pastoralists. The survival and welfare of the Somalis in their demanding environment, the independence of their character, the range of their activity and the frequent occurrence of their wars are in large measure accounted for by the camel. As the following pages will show, the camel is both the source of life and the cause of losing it, and its husbandry is the honorable profession of men. Whereas sheep and goats, and to some degree cattle, which play no mean role in pastoral life, are the charge of women, the camels exercise both the labor and imagination of men. As the pastoralists put it, 'Men and camels thrive on each other' ('Waa isku baḥaan').

Maḥammad 'Abdille Ḥasan, whose political oratory occupies the central stage in this study, categorized the relative values of livestock in the following manner:

He who has goats has a garment full of corn;
A milch cow is a temporary vanity;
A he-camel is the muscle that sustains life;
A she-camel – whoever may have her – is the mother of men.[21]

The image of the garment full of corn suggests impermanency and unreliability, as the raising of corn depends on the undependable seasonal rains. So is that of the cattle, described as a temporary vanity. Thus, it is the he-camel and she-camel which compete for importance in the life of the nomad. The one is described as the muscle (*halbowle*) which sustains life, the other, the she-camel, as the mother of men.

At the outset, it may be said that the Somalis show no mystical or ritual attachment to their camels of the sort associated with other Eastern

African pastoralists. Their interest in the camel and their love of it is entirely pragmatic and if they cherish it, it is because this generous beast does not fail them. To begin with, the camel is the only domestic animal which does not require a large quantity of the one resource which is so scarce in the Somali climate: water. In the hottest, driest period, the camel needs to be watered once every 20–25 days. In the rainy season, given a fresh supply of green pasturage, the camel need not be watered at all. Come rain or drought, the camel's generosity to man is crucial to his survival. The she-camel's milk is delicious, refreshing and thirst-quenching;[22] her meat is tasty and tender like veal; her skin is utilized as draperies for the nomadic hut which shelters the Somalis from the elements. The burden-bearing he-camel is the main transport vehicle and carries the children, the aged, the sick and the nomads' belongings for hundreds of miles every year. (It may be of interest to note, though, that Somalis do not ride their camels under ordinary circumstances.) In an uncommonly dry season, the last drops of water in the land are extracted from the stomach of the camel. This is done through a process called 'uusmiirad' in which the stomach is hung from a tree after being pricked open with a thorn at various places. Liquid filters through these openings and is collected by wooden buckets.

Although Somali camels consist of several species, they are all one-humped dromedaries, but in the absence of a scientific study of them, it is difficult to catalogue the various local breeds with accuracy. The Somalis themselves distinguish several varieties of camel which include the Geel-'Ad or white camels of the plains and the Goodir,[23] in the mountain regions. The Goodir are characterized by short, thin fur which is barely visible on the skin. Finally, there are the Boor-'Ad or white dust camels of the Haud and the Dagoodi of southwestern Somalia. The most noticeable difference is between the Dagoodi and the plains camels, with the Dagoodi taller, darker but less hardy than the Geel-'Ad. The Dagoodi, found in the well-watered region between the Shabeelle and Juba rivers, is highly priced and is proverbial for its milk-producing capacities, but requires more frequent watering and is therefore less widespread. 'Ayyuun camels, on the other hand, are the camels of the maritime plains. They are shorter, leaner and tend to be of a more temperamental disposition than the interior camels.

It will be seen from these notes that the differences Somalis note among their camels refer to color, height, temperament and milk-giving capacity. Thus they are differences having more to do with the effect of climate than with species variation. There exist of course several species of Somali camel which, as yet, have not been adequately studied.

At the age of four or five, camels start breeding. Under ideal conditions, a calf is born every other year, the period of pregnancy being a year and some days. The new-born camel is, in Somali eyes, a magnificent sight, with its white silky hair and its lanky, if clumsy, limbs. Within hours of its birth, it is able to stand on its feet, but is unable to walk for some days. If the camel-camp is moved before the babies have learned to walk, men or even boys carry them on their shoulders with the mother following.[24]

With negligible supplements of grain and tea, milk and meat constitute the pastoralist's diet. Camel milk is thinner and lower in butter content than either cow or goat milk, but is known to be high in nutritional value.[25] Camels are milked twice (morning and evening) in the dry season, and three times (morning, noon and evening) in the wet. It takes three persons to milk a camel which has a baby.[26] Milking is done as follows: the baby camel, kept separate along with other calves during grazing, is brought to the mother. The fibrous soft band (*maray*), wrapped around the four nipples to prevent the baby from sucking the mother during grazing, is removed. Then the baby is allowed to stimulate (*godol*) the mother into letting down the milk by sucking at the nipples. Unless they are *igar* (milch-camels without babies), Somali camels need to be stimulated by their calves to give milk. When the milch-camel releases the milk, a sign indicated by tautening and enlargement of the nipples, the baby is kept off by one person, usually a young boy. Then two men, one on each side, rapidly milk with both hands into a large wooden bucket (*toobke*). The bowl is held directly under the udder atop an uplifted knee which, with one foot resting on the other leg and the thigh, forms a triangular shape. It is a delicate balance which the baby, eager to suck, will easily upset unless it is kept off. With some camels speed in milking is essential, as the flow of milk will stop in perhaps five minutes. (The baby camels are fed on left-over milk instinctively reserved by a nursing camel for her baby.) Milch-camels whose babies have died are either trained to give milk without filial stimulation or are induced to respond to the stimulation of an alien baby (*sidig*). *Igar* is a milch-camel trained to respond by a gentle patting on the nipples. *Sidig* is effected in one of two ways: one is to put the skin of the dead baby on the back of another baby of roughly equal size (*maqaarsaar*). This induces the mother of the dead baby to accept the new one as her own. However, if this method fails, recourse is had to an operation called 'tolliin' (literally, 'sewing'). The camel is hobbled down side by side with the alien calf. A sharp splinter (*tuurin*) of about five inches is driven across the nostrils to smother her temporarily. The pain and suffocation produce delirium in the mother and induce her to accept the nursing by the alien calf. The concept of *tolliin* in Somali represents an image of subjugation and servitude and figures prominently in Somali verse as such. Witness, for

Milking a camel. This is an *igar* milch-camel, as there is neither a baby nor a second milker to be seen.

example, 'Ali Jaama' Haabiil's poem in which the poet ridicules the Ḍulbahante for their 'unquestioning submission' to Sayyid Maḥammad's autocratic ways: 'Let him cant and bluster / for he holds the tyranny of the piercing *tuurin* splinter over them.'[27]

A good milch-camel, at the height of lactation, produces about two gallons a day in the wet season, a gallon in the dry. Environment dictates that for the better part of the year, flocks (sheep and goats)[28] and herds (camels) should be grazed separately. Camels can range long distances, as much as a hundred miles within a fortnight, in their search for forage; but the flocks must be watered every few days and therefore cannot wander as far afield from permanent watering places. Thus, in the dry season, the nomadic hamlet – consisting of women, children, married men and their household effects, the burden he-camels, a few milch-camels, and the flocks – grazes as a unit, keeping a radius of thirty miles from a water hole.

The rest of the camels are placed in the care of unmarried males ranging in age from about eight to twenty-five. Their task is demanding and their life scarcely enviable. In their search for sufficient forage, the camels move far and frequently, which means the young men have to build makeshift kraals from thorn bushes every few days, if not every day. At night the camels have to be put in the kraal to secure them from plundering humans and from animal predators such as lions and hyenas. The young men have to make the long march with the camels to a water-point at least once every month, often over forbidding terrain and in a debilitating climate.[29] Moreover, they have to keep on the look-out for the marauding bands of looters who are often on the loose. Thus, the wilderness and the camels are a training ground for the youths and it is here that the values of courage, endurance and self-reliance are inculcated in them.

The number of nomadic hamlets or camel camps which move together range from one lone household to thirty or forty hamlets, depending on conditions of weather and relations obtaining among the clans. On the whole, the largest concentration of kinsmen occurs on two occasions: when members of two or more clans hostile to each other are forced, for whatever reason, to graze in the same locality or to frequent the same

A portable pastoralist house. The ladies are wearing the traditional *tobe* costume.

water holes, or when, at the height of the drought, the concentration of water in a few reliable wells brings together many pastoralists. Here kinsmen band together to invest in joint ventures such as digging a well, sharing the scarce camel milk among various households, protecting water or grazing rights. But as I. M. Lewis has, in my opinion, admirably demonstrated, the Somali pastoralists do not maintain absolute ties to localities, and lineages do not correspond to territorial attachment but derive their validity from agnatic relationships (*tol*). Although clans are identified with certain territories in a general way, land and water are possessed or dispossessed by a contractual principle (*ḥeer*) – a code of customary rules which regulates the behavior of lineages towards one another – and, if that fails, by force of arms. With minor qualifications, I. M. Lewis accurately assessed Somali pastoralist thought and practice

Table 1 *Camel names*

Geel (pl., Geelal)	A popular collective term for camel
Goodir, Geel-'Ad, Boor-'Ad, 'Ayyuun, Maydal, Humbi and Dagoodi	Collective camel nouns but unlike the first group, these refer to camels of particular territories or of particular colors. Thus, 'Geel-'Ad' refers to western plains camels, 'Boor-'Ad' to Haud camels, ''Ayyuun' to maritime camels, etc.
Deeble and Ḥiito	Camel names used only in poetry
Tulud	A general term for a single camel
Hal	A she-camel
Qaalin	A she-camel of two to three years
Abeer and Baatir	A choice she-camel which is ready to bear a calf at any time
Ayro, Geyḍo, Seenyo, Mayḍo, Idiin, Idil, Wayroḥo and Wayd	Names which describe dual concepts: as proper nouns, they refer to a particular she-camel, but as abstract nouns, they stand for a herd of camels and are often used in poetry in praise of the camel
Awr and Rati	Popular he-camel names
Koron	A gelded he-camel raised for burden-bearing
Gool	A gelded he-camel raised for meat
Baarqab	A strong stallion for servicing she-camels
Ubad	Baby camels
Niríg	A baby she-camel
Nírig	A baby he-camel
Horwayne and Ḥerris	Camels under the charge of unmarried men as opposed to the milch-camels kept by the nomadic hamlet
Irman	A general term for camels in lactation
Ramag	Newly delivered milch-camels whose milk is a special delicacy reserved for honored guests and men of station
Igar	A milch-camel whose baby is dead

with respect to territory when he wrote: 'In conformity with this shifting system of movement and lack of absolute ties to locality, lineages are not based primarily on land-holding, and possession of land has no mystical or ritual value. Political ascendency is not conferred by or symbolized in mystical ties to the earth but derives from superior fighting potential.'[30]

Like the Nuer for their cattle,[31] the Somalis have a multiplicity of names for their camels, and my preliminary investigation has turned up several dozen names referring to various species, states and developmental stages of camel. Proper names are descriptive and are given in accordance with color, height, beauty, origin, and so on. I sketch graphically in table 1 a few camel names to show something of their variety and cultural significance. The names proliferate *ad infinitum* and it would not be rash to conjecture that under careful collation a thesaurus of some size could be compiled on them.

In their songs, as in their serious verse, Somalis address camels and I have sought in vain for a major Somali poet of this century or the last whose work does not in some way address this ubiquitous beast. There is a special category of songs for watering camels, a special category for herding them, another for milking them, another for driving them and yet another for rustling them. When at night camels are secured in the kraals, and campfires are lit, the poetry, banter and bluster carried on endlessly are for the most part about camels: who raided what camels

Watering the herds.

and when, the herds of lineage X being superior to those of lineage Y, the merits of lineage A's daughters over those of B because they bring more camels in bride wealth.

The love of and preoccupation with camels is not only the result of their great economic importance, but also of their links with social relationships: a man's station in society is measured by the size of his herd; he pays in camels for a wife or wives; physical damages and homicides as well as redress for slander are calculated on a standard of measurement based on camels. Thus, blood compensation for a man is a hundred camels; that for a woman is fifty. (It will be remembered that in 1975 the government tried to remove the discrepancy and equalize compensation for homicide of men and women, and thus provoked a religious uprising in which ten sheikhs were summarily executed.) Camels are slaughtered for sacrificial purposes so as to impress Allah or the founding ancestors in a special way.

Camels are the cause and compensation of the loss of life and limb which so often is the outcome of quarrels over them: the sanctity of property is rather tenuous in Somali notions of ownership. It seems to reside, although a pastoralist would deny this when confronted with it, in the ability to usurp it or defend it against usurpation, and the Somali saying, 'Camels are in the kraal of him who has power'[32] seems to lend support to the fluidity of ownership in pastoral sanctions. Thus, in the free-for-all attitude towards them, Somalis show no marked compunction against seizing camels on sight, and no small proportion of the wars and feuds Somali pastoralists conduct on each other and their neighbors, such as the 'Afar and the Oromo, are provoked and sustained by the desire to possess camels. It is a mark of honor to have taken part in a successful camel raid, and poets celebrate such raids in their verse. Thus, the aged Mareeḥaan poet reminisced:[33]

I remember the day I rode the heavy-sinewed horse
And I made the plan of the battle entirely mine
And in the dark I made out the beauty of *Idil*[34]
And at a sign from me the boys surged forward rushing the herds.
Oh! fine-nippled beast! how she galloped before us.
Then we brought her to a well-watered valley where the he-camel serviced her.
Oh, how I planned skilful schemes! but now have I not become weak?
Lord, of thee I implore the holy water of heaven.[35]

Another pastoralist poet exulted:

Peace worsens the condition of my homestead;

I live by Allah's bounty and by raiding camels
And my happiness is the place where the dust of war rises![36]

Next to the defeat of the British force under commander Richard Corfield (which was occasioned by Dervish seizure of herds belonging to British-protected lineages), the most memorable episodes in the opinion of many pastoralists concerning the twenty-year struggle against British colonialism relate to camel raiding. Prominent among such raids are the Daboolane camels (30,000 head) seized by Dervishes from the Habar Yoonis Isaaq in 1909, the Miinanle camels (50,000 head) captured from the Dervishes around 1911 by the Majeerteen, and the Hagoogane camels (60,000 head) seized from the defeated Dervishes by British-protected lineages in 1921.[37]

Camel culture pervades contemporary society and the influence of camel vocabulary and concepts on modern life appears to be extensive. In literature, writers draw their images and inspiration from pastoral figures denoting relations between man and camel. Thus, the lover in the modern drama says that owing to unrequited love, he is stricken with *ḍukaan*,[38] the disease which camels in drought suffer from. Similarly, the singer of popular song likens the tender sentiment he feels towards his lady to what a camel feels towards her suckling baby: 'I groan in agony of love', he sings, 'like a camel whose baby is unjustly sequestered away from her'.[39] For her part, the woman poet admonishes her suitor to give her 'fine pastures, and pat her gently on the udder so she'd give milk'. The jealous husband, in his bitter sarcasm and ridicule, points out to his wayward wife, that it is only the 'camel which enjoys being milked by two men at the same time, and that not in all seasons, but solely when she is in full lactation. Anything else of the feminine gender shared by two men is soon debased',[40] he moralizes.

When they gained their independence and the two former territories of British and Italian Somalilands joined to form the Somali Republic in 1960, the Somalis found it fitting to adopt a camel name ('Maandeeq') to stand as a symbolic name for their newly-acquired freedom. 'Maandeeq' means a milch-camel which satisfies the mind through the generosity of its milk. The well-known northern Somali poet and patriot, 'Abdillaahi Tima-'Ade, composed a poem which he called 'Maandeeq' to celebrate the advent of independence, and the term became popular in press and radio in the heady, euphoric days of the early sixties.

In social as well as in business vocabulary, the camel stalks the city. The conversationalist says, 'I groaned for your point',[41] when meaning to acknowledge a strong impression of something said, the term 'groan' (*guuḥ*) being the sound that a camel makes when coming to water or joining her young. A person speaks of 'sahan' when making a preliminary investigation of a question or subject, the word 'sahan' (scout) being the one pastoralists use in locating new pastures for the herds. Government transport (*gaadiid*), the term used to describe the fleet of government vehicles for personnel transport, is the word the pastoralists employ to refer to their burden-bearing camels. 'Laylis', traditionally used to denote the breaking of a burden-bearing young he-camel, is nowadays used to signify exercises in a school workbook. The term 'warfin' (express mail delivery) derives from the same root as 'waraf' (slingshot), the old weapon used to pelt the destructive birds which peck on camels' humps. Similarly, the scholar acknowledges a debt every time he uses the term 'raadraa'' (to trace something), which is used to denote the word 'research'. The word is employed by the nomads when tracking lost animals or when tracing stock thieves. The Marxists too have a debt to the nomads in appropriating 'hugaanka', a pastoralist term for leading a camel by rope, as the modern term for their bureau of ideology (Hugaanka Ideologiyada).

The camel nomenclature surveyed here represents a fragment of a fragment, collected as it was in an amateur way by one whose interest in the subject was only indirect and who, in any case, lacked the linguistic tools which the tackling of such a subject requires. It is hoped that it serves, however, as ample demonstration of the extent to which the pastoral values and habits continue to influence the acts and thoughts of modern Somalis even if they no longer pursue pastoralism.

3 THE ROLE OF THE PONY IN CAMEL RAIDING

It may be helpful to follow up the discussion of the camel with a few remarks on the Somali pony before concluding this section. Until recently, the destinies of the horse and the camel were interlocked. The pastoral Somalis say the horse and the camel thrive on each other ('Waa isku baḥaan'). The observation signifies the importance Somalis attach to the horse as an instrument in camel raiding or defending camels against raid. The Somali horses are swift ponies which are thought to have descended from the Arabian variety and to have reached the Somali cost with the introduction of Islam.[42]

Somalis recognize two breeds of their ponies, the so-called 'Galbeed' from western Somalia and the 'Bari' or eastern pony. Although the eastern pony is slightly smaller (thirteen to fourteen hands in height at the shoulder) than the Galbeed, it is preferred to its western counterpart. It is stronger and hardier than the Galbeed on account of its adaptation to the less well-watered regions of eastern Somalia. Red, grey or beige in color, the Somali pony is furnished with hard hoofs and a sturdy form which make it a useful animal in a demanding environment. It can survive, indeed thrive, on poor grazing and a modest supply of water – it requires watering every other day if grass is dry and it is on active duty.

In times of water scarcity when the herds are away in the Haud, the Somalis give their horses a mixture of water and milk, usually two parts of milk to one part of water. At a guess, the daily ration for one pony is the milk of two good milch-camels mixed with a quart of water.

The Somalis show great kindness to their horses, rearing and caring for them with marked meticulousness. A man talks to his mount, sings to it in familiar language and will crawl on stones under a thorn bush to extract for it a bite of something to eat. The horse, like the camel, has been the object of the Somali poets' serious verse. In this matter, Sayyid Maḥammad and his predecessor and kinsman, Raage Ugaas, won a lasting reputation for their brilliant, descriptive praise verse on the horse.[43]

The pastoral Somalis seldom ride their horses for sport, reserving the energies and services of their beloved beasts for the gravest of moments when dear life hangs on a sudden flight or pursuit. Before delivering a raid, the pastoralists will lead their horses for miles, only mounting when the object of their enterprise is in sight. The strategy is to keep the pony rested and in fit condition right up to the time of the action. Then they go into action with lightning speed, rounding up the herds and bolting away with them before the owners of the looted stock have time to launch a counter-offensive.

The Ḍulbahante (from whom the dreaded cavalry of Sayyid Maḥammad's Dervish movement came) are reputed to be the best pastoralist horsemen. In a subsequent section on the childhood life of Sayyid Maḥammad, I hope to show that the legendary numbers of the Ḍulbahante ponies are explicable in environmental terms. The climate of the Nugaal, a region which constitutes the heartlands of the Ḍulbahante, is highly suited for breeding and rearing ponies. In addition to the Ḍulbahante, there were numerous Somali clans in whose economy and way of life the pony played a significant role. These include several lineages of the Isaaq, the Ogaadeen and Warsangali Daarood and the 'Umar Maḥamuud sub-lineage of the Majeerteen clan-family.

The Somali pony has, in recent years, fallen on bad times. Where in the late nineteenth century and early twentieth, a small lineage of roughly a hundred fighting men could boast a hundred or so beasts per household, one now sees a few solitary herds in northern Somalia. Some of these in the Nugaal are even no longer domestic. The reason for the astonishing reduction of Somali ponies is not hard to divine. With the establishment of centralized authority, beginning first with colonial administrations and subsequently the national government, feuds and stock theft have been brought virtually to an end. The end of feuds meant in turn the end of the usefulness of the pony. Thus, while there is some pastoral interest in the pony for prestige purposes, it has clearly lost, and probably will not regain, its luster and appeal for the pastoral Somalis.

4 FORMAL SPEECHES AND THE *GODOB* INSTITUTION OF CUMULATIVE GRIEVANCES

> The Somalis are . . . no mean orators; and to be a man of distinction in a tribe you must have a reputation not only as a fighter and a man of many possessions, but also as a convincing spokesman. The Somali orator is extremely prolix and very histrionic; but, despite this, he is undoubtedly impressive. He possesses the first qualification of the public speaker, namely, self-confidence; and he has the utmost scorn for any rival. The consequence is that, whenever a British officer gives an audience to the leaders of a tribe to discuss any political question, he is faced by the prospect of a feast of oratory, which often lasts for a whole day. The most famous spokesman of the tribe will be the first to hold forth. Careless of repetitions and buoyed up with a sense of his own importance, he will state his tribe's case with an unceasing flow of words and gestures. This speech may extend to half an hour. The man whose reputation is only second to that of the first spokesman will then intervene. Convinced that the tribe's case is being mangled, he will himself proceed to harangue the luckless British officer in almost precisely the same terms. And so it will go on until every member of the tribal deputation has delivered his oration. It may be that the British officer will be impressed by all this rhetoric; but his decision, based on the true facts of the case, will probably have been made before all the purple patches will have fallen on deaf ears. This is the tragedy of the Somali School of Rhetoric.[44]

It may also have been the tragedy of the British colonial enterprise in northern Somalia. While grudgingly acknowledging the possible merits of Somali pastoral oratory, Douglas Jardine's words would seem to betray the familiar touch of colonial condescension, Victorian smugness and complacent ignorance – the sort of attitude which hardly boded well for Anglo-Somali relations. What seemed mere 'histrionic[s]' and 'careless repetitions' to him may, to the pastoralists, have been a carefully constructed form of oratory, each phrase or expression of which was designed to support some aspect of an argument or convey a subtle shade of meaning. Had British colonial officials, to speculate a moment, given due consideration to the 'histrionic' preachings of the roving holy man whom they splendidly came to dub the 'Mad Mullah', they might have spared themselves – and Somaliland – twenty years of a costly war. But more of this later.

In their speech as in their stock, the Somalis show a marked preoccupation, and as a Somali elder put it, in disparagement of his people's tendency to volubility, 'We Somalis just talk, talk, talk, whether or not we have something to talk about.' Despite the elder's scorn of pastoral verbosity, it can be said that the spoken word is the center of pastoralist life and lore. Language, written or oral, plays a dominant part in the life of any community and, to borrow one writer's phrase, tends to become 'the soul of the nation'.[45] In this the Somali pastoralists cannot lay claim to uniqueness or particularity. But they do seem to belong to those societies in which speech is cultivated as an art, and a man's position in his group depends, to a considerable extent, on his powers of oration. To be able to convince others by the powers of one's diction and flow of words is an asset which many Somalis aspire to and not a few possess.

This emphasis on oratory and persuasion rooted in pastoral egalitarianism seems to be a dominant feature in Somali society. To begin with, the Somali pastoral system is characterized by a marked absence of central authority and a corresponding lack of inherited offices or a hierarchy of chiefs to run it. All claim to be equal and show nothing but scorn and disdain for what, in Western metaphor, may be termed 'duly instituted authority'. But where all are equal, anarchy is not far to seek, and that, at least at a superficial level of observation, is what seems to characterize the relations between Somali clans. On a closer look, however, it becomes fairly clear that some men in fact do wield greater power and influence in society than others and that a high proportion of these men usually have what Somalis call the 'gift of speech' (*hibo hadal*) – 'gift of the gab' might be a more familiar description of the point but would convey a derogatory, and therefore misleading, impression.

The importance of oratory in political control in traditional society has been duly, if belatedly, noted by contemporary Africanists, and in this respect Maurice Bloch's urgent appeal to 'open up discussion'[46] on this 'neglected area' stands out as an eloquent example; as does Asmarom Legesse's notable demonstration of the role of oratory in conflict resolution among the Somali-related Boran Oromo.[47] Somalis think much about improving their speaking abilities and they tend to show a passionate preoccupation with 'fine expression'. A number of points can be raised in respect to the prevalence of oratory among the Somalis: the first is that speech is the vehicle of politics in so highly a segmented society as the Somalis', and he who would lead others must persuade rather than coerce. In a non-literate society where the privilege of written communication is either limited to a tiny fraction of the population or wholly non-existent, it is only natural that the spoken word should serve both as a medium for communication and as a means for persuasion. Secondly, the Somali language tends to lend itself, as one scholar put it, to 'dramatic expression'.[48] Although, with the exception of a few coastal areas, Somali was an unwritten language until 1972, it is a highly developed language with a rich oral literature. The images are lively, the expression is vivid and one scholar speaks of its 'poetic style',[49] while another likens the Somalis to the ancient 'bards of Greece'.[50]

There is yet another view which attributes Somali over-emphasis on poetic oration to their harsh environment. With a country – the theory goes – barren of almost all materials needed for painting, sculpture and pottery-making, discouraged by Islam from making graven images, too unsettled to accumulate artifacts, it is only natural that the Somali pastoralists should turn to the only medium which would cost them nothing, namely, verbal expression.[51] According to this view, poetry compensates the Somalis for the 'bleakness of their usual life', and the dangers of drought, disease and hunger can be banished momentarily by the recitation of mellowed lines.

Whatever the merits of these arguments, it is doubtful that any hypothesis attempting to account for the Somalis' passionate love and cultivation of artistic oration which does not take stock of what the Somalis call 'godob' is likely to lead anywhere. For want of a better phrase, I render 'godob' as the institution of 'cumulative grievances'. In a negative sense, 'godob' can also be translated as 'reciprocal vendetta'. This notion is at the heart of clannish feuding and of the pastoral obsession with stylized speech. In pastoral ethos, a man assaulted physically or verbally has a claim of *godob* on his offender, a sort of debt of wrongs which has the characteristics of a debt in goods. The offender, like a debtor in commodities, owes so much in *godob* injuries to the victim (creditor).

Godob injuries resulting from a character slander vary from the simple offense (*gaf*) which can be rectified by a mere apology, slander (*qadaf*), amendable only by the payment of compensation (*ḥaal*), to the mortal offense (*ihaano*) which often leads to blood vengeance.[52] In the institution of *godob*, the victim need not seek redress immediately, as he is often barred by inauspicious circumstances from doing so, but may bide his time indefinitely, so that the resolution of a case of *godob* may not be effected for generations nor by the participants of the offense, but by the offspring of the participants. Moreover, in the ethos of *godob*, fifty or even a hundred years may pass before the descendants of a murdered man may move to settle up accounts with their foes by killing one or several of his descendants or nearest kin. Similarly, if a clan loses property or blood to another, retribution need not be effected in the present generation, but it is bound to be executed, for a debt of *godob* is one of those unforgettable and unforgivable social transactions which must receive compensation sooner or later.

Somalis recognize two types of *godob*: a *godob* resulting from physical injury or usurpation of property, and *godob* which results from verbal assault. Both are equally damaging in their consequences and the one can be converted into the other. To avoid confusion, I distinguish the two aspects of *godob* by referring to the one as speech vendetta and the other as blood vendetta.

The pastoral Somalis, egalitarian and lacking an impartial authority to compose differences, readily resort to violence. Battles are fought to safeguard honor, to redress past wrongs, to seize property or defend it against seizure, to protect pasture and water rights, or simply to release pent-up tensions. Where resources are meager and competition for them is high, as it is among the pastoralists, conflicts are frequent and pursued to virulent ends. Moreover, in the absence of an impartial arbiter, the ultimate instrument for conflict resolution is force.

Force is exercised not only in action but also in words. Words are formalized into rhetorical expressions, coined into proverbs or composed into poetic utterances with the intention of discrediting a rival or enhancing one's position and prestige. They are used to fan up hostility or, conversely, to reconcile warring factions, to flatter a powerful enemy and thus deter him from executing an injurious act against one's person and property, and to show self-effacement so as to gain pity (an important feature in clan relationships).

In such a setting where the word is truly powerful and a vendetta in speech can (and does) easily lead to vendetta in blood with disastrous consequences, it should scarcely be difficult to appreciate the role of the orator, the raconteur and the poet as individuals who use their potent crafts for political and social influence. The methods these individuals exercise to maximize their 'power of the tongue' will be treated shortly; for the moment, we should illustrate the relation between feud and formalized speech by quoting Ma'alim 'Abdullahi Ḥ. Rabaḥ of the Maḥammad Subeer Ogaadeen on the subject. What he says of poetry applies to other forms of rhetorical utterance:

> Poetry brings evil and dishonor as well as fame and respect. For instance, a clan attacked in poetry, if they cannot find among them a poet to redress their honor, would resort to fighting . . . camels and men are inseparable ('Waa isku baḥaan'). Camels are looted

> and men killed because of *gabay* (poetry). The more camels a man has, the more men at his disposal, the greater his resources and ability. The more camels a clan owns, the greater their resources. Camels bring men together. If a clan loots camels and kills men from another clan, the injured clan may bide their time and not rise in immediate revenge. But if the victorious clan attempt, as they often do, to immortalize their victory in verse, then the looted clan feels humiliated and would immediately seek to remedy their honor and avenge their wrongs. The looted clan's poet(s) versifies laments, listing their grievances and urging their fellow kinsmen not to eat or drink until they have remedied their honor. Thus, revenge follows revenge and feud, feud.[53]

Theft and raiding of camels are a pastoralist pastime; a man may be a camel thief and would admit to, in fact boast of, being one. But let that fact be stated in a formalized oratorical or poetic medium and a *godob*, a ground for renewed hostility, has been committed.

5 ORATORY AND FORMAL ASSEMBLIES

We have said that the pre-eminence of the spoken word has its roots in an essentially democratic society in which men who wield influence do so mainly through their powers of persuasion rather than coercion. Formalized oration was stated to be important not only in the day-to-day interaction between individuals, families and groups but also in the acquisition and exercise of socio-political control. In Somali pastoral sanctions, to formalize words is to invest them with power – a formidable, almost mystical power – which can be and often is exercised for good or ill. This may be the place to go further into the question of speech formalization. We may begin by asking, at what point does a given utterance become a formalized speech act? How are words used to ennoble or injure someone's honor? The answer requires an analysis, however brief, of Somali notions of rhetoric, oratory and speechmaking.

To employ a simplistic schema for purposes of clarity, the pastoral Somalis distinguish between two types of speech – each of which has a set of principles and rules governing its expression – through which formalization may occur. The one is poetic speech, a form of oratory artistically refined and articulated in the medium of a classical prosodic formulation. Such a speech gains the power of formalization from an intense interplay of poetic rhythm, metrical structure and syllabic arrangement. The formalization of speech through the artful use of poetic devices will be explored shortly in the chapter on Somali pastoral prosodic systems. For the moment, we should turn to an examination of the manner and principles by which speech is formalized through the use of prose oration.

A prose oration acquires the solemn characteristics of a formal speech when, to use a pastoral metaphor, it is delivered as a 'tree speech' (*hadal geed*), often to attend to a matter of collective interest such as politics or litigation. The significance of trees in Somali life and lore has found ample expression in the words of the oral poet who reminded his kin that 'On the Ban-'Awl plain there is a tree for poverty to shelter under.'[54] The gatherings of Somali herdsmen are almost invariably held under the shade of a tree. So important is the refreshing shade of a tree in the barrenness of the land, that the term 'tree' (*geed*) has come to assume a synonymous meaning with 'assembly' (*shir*). Thus, Somalis speak of four trees to refer to four types of assemblage which serve as the source and sustenance of oratorical formulation. Presented in order of decreasing importance, they are graphically shown in table 2.

Table 2 *Somali assemblies*

Type of assembly	English rendition	Characteristics
Geedka Ḥeerka iyo Ḥukunka	The Tree of Justice and Jurisprudence	This is the tree of the so-called 'ḥeerbeegti' or men of law, who arbitrate in matters of dispute.
Geedka Ḥaqqa iyo Ḥukunka	The Tree of Truth and Justice	This is the tree of the Sheikh, and it relates to situations in which religious sanctions are the basis of law and conflict resolution as distinct from secular sanctions (*ḥeer*).
Geedka Hindisaha iyo Haloonsiga	The Tree of Bluster and Bravado	So named because it is the tree of young men where they brag about the superiority of their respective clans, their camels, houses, the beauty and merit of their girls, the valor of their men, etc.
Geedka Qaansada iyo Quraarta	The Tree of the Bow and Chisel	This is the tree of industry. All objects and crafts necessary for living in the country are manufactured under this tree. Things produced here include: military tools (bows, spears, daggers, darts), knives, horse and camel saddles – in short, all manner of household and personal implements.

There is no fixed time for the convening of a meeting nor any special person or group with ascribed authority to call one. *Shirs* are held on an *ad hoc* basis as the need for them arises. The Somali word for assembly oration is 'hadalka shirka', a compound noun from 'shir' (assembly or congregation) and 'hadal' (talk). An assembly meeting is distinguished from informal chitchat (*sheeko*). The difference is both one of size and of substance. Whereas the formal assembly is a solemn proceeding with substantial representation of the members of a lineage or lineages, the *sheeko* participants scarcely exceed the male members of several households and the meeting does not have in view a particular question to resolve or a particular goal to attain. No decisions are reached in a *sheeko* meeting and the banter and bluster which go on endlessly are inconsequential, except in cases where some inadvertent orator or poet slanders by a calumnious pronouncement the character of an individual or a group, and thus generates a case of *godob* (cumulative grievance). In the latter situation the meeting suddenly turns into a *shir* and sets about to amend the resultant wrongs, or failing that, breaks down in disarray, leaving the outstanding grievance to be settled by a subsequent *shir*, or alternately by precipitating blood vendetta or destruction of property.

The typical *shir* convenes under the shade of a tree, usually one of a variety of the acacias which so uniquely thrive in Somali climate. There is, to my recollection, no particular arrangement as to seating, although choice positions are reserved for elders and clan notables. Privileged seating is determined in relation to coolness of shelter and nearness to speaker. In theory, all adult males are fully entitled to participate in the deliberations of the assembly, and to give their opinions on any matter of interest to the group, but in practice three types of men dominate the meeting: the orator (*'odkar*), the poet (*gabayaa*) and the expert-in-tradition (*ḥeerbeegti*). Two additional individuals hold ceremonial offices: the chairman (*guddoomiye*) and the wordbearer (*doodqaad*, literally 'argumentbearer'), both appointed by popular consensus because of their skill and mastery in officiating at public functions.

The chairman opens up the discussion by saying, 'The assembly is in order' ('Shir guddoonsan'), upon which the speaker begins and the wordbearer responds to him antiphonally. Thus, when the speaker says, 'Hear me, kinsmen' ('Tolow halla i maqlo'), the wordbearer responds, 'So it is' ('Waa sida, waa kow'). The wordbearer repeats this phrase whenever the speaker completes a statement or makes a pause throughout the speech, so that a Somali oral delivery sounds much like dialogue, a question and answer. The wordbearer is a conduit between speaker and audience and his repetition of stock phrases is a confirmation that speaker and audience are communicating on the same wavelength. After the speaker completes his delivery, he usually gives the floor to a poet, who covers the same ground in poetic oration. Orator and poet between them present a case, facing a corresponding number of opponents. Sometimes, however, a speaker may be talented both as a poet and an orator, and thus combine the functions of both. Whatever the number of speakers on one side, they are leveled against an opposite set of speakers, equal both in number and talent.

The deliberations of a formal assembly are clearly dominated by two parties, namely, those who argue the case, the so-called ''odkar-gabayaa' (orator, poet), and those who decide upon it on the basis of the argument presented to them, the so-called 'ḥeerbeegti' (experts in tradition). The poet and orator act the role of the lawyer while the *ḥeerbeegti* combines the functions of the jury and the judge in modern society. A case debated by a poet or an orator and deliberated on by a competent *ḥeerbeegti* truly becomes a battle of wits and of words. Not only is knowledge of history, customs and traditions essential, but also the ability to articulate them into a coherent whole is equally, if not more, indispensable. For although they do not concede it in so many words, Somalis tend to emphasize style over substance in resolving litigation, so that the skill with which a case is presented seems to carry greater weight than its actual merits.

It would be in order at this point to look briefly into the attributes and the criteria by which the poet and orator on the one hand, and the *ḥeerbeegti* on the other, are judged qualified to perform their roles. First, the oratorical class: the Somali term for orator, as we have seen, is ' 'odkar' from ''od' (voice) and 'kar' (able). Thus, a literal translation from the Somali would give us 'voice able' or 'capable of speech', as if to say those not endowed with oratorical talents are incapable of speech.

In respect to their mastery of speech and oratorical skill, Somalis differentiate '*odkar* into four ranks as illustrated in table 3. Their powers of oration, and hence their importance in society, come in this order, with the *afmaal* leading the field, followed by *aftahan* and *afmiishaar*. Whereas *afmaal* and *aftahan* use their assets to good effect, notably for reconciliation, *afmiishaar* is 'the man of universal scandal and provocation, trafficking in malice and insidious rumors and inciting clans to feud'.[55] But if he is hated and despised, *afmiishaar* is also feared, and individuals and groups seek his goodwill, but failing that, his neutrality. Some would even go to the length of bribing an *afmiishaar* either to flatter their lineage or to attack rival lineages and enemies. 'An *afmiishaar*', says one elder, 'who is also a poet is the most vicious character in our society. He has powerful instruments for persuasion but always uses them to create mayhem.'[56]

Table 3 *Somali orator ranks*

Type of orator	Rank	Characteristics
Afmaal	First	'Af' (mouth) and 'maal' (wealth) – he whose mouth is wealth. He is an individual of towering prestige who has the reputation of never having lost a case in which he has argued. (This is in fact not wholly accurate for I have been in a *shir* where an *afmaal* lost an argument to another *afmaal*.)
Aftahan	Second	'Af' (mouth) and 'tahan' (generous) – he whose mouth is generous. Although his position is not as widely acclaimed as that of the *afmaal*, he too occupies a commanding position in oratorical contests.
Afmiishaar	Third	'Af' (mouth) and 'miishaar' (saw) – he whose mouth is a saw. *Afmiishaar*, as we shall see, is important in a negative sense. This class of orators seems to have emerged with the development of mass, nationalist politics and impersonal political organization.
Afgaroo'	Fourth and lowest	'Af' (mouth) and 'garoo'' (deformed) – so named because he lacks oratorical prowess and public speaking skills and is therefore an object of scorn.

The migration of a great mass of Somalis in the last forty years from pastoralism to city life and the weakening of ethnic and family ties attendant upon wholesale urbanization seem to have given *afmiishaars* great opportunities to create mayhem. Freed from collective kinship accountability and protected by powerful patrons, *afmiishaars* found the impersonal society of the city a fertile field in which to exercise their dark rhymes and to ruin reputations with impunity. Patronized by politicians and powerful men, they began to derive status, influence and economic privilege from their gift of the gab, and nowhere was this more obvious than in their intimate attachment to the powerful in the politics of pre- and post-independence Somalia.[57] Their powers to assassinate character – thereby ruining careers – and their unprincipled readiness to sell their talents to the highest bidder made *afmiishaars* a despised but keenly sought-after class of hangers-on, enlisted by contending political parties which saw the great political mileage to be had from the services of *afmiishaars* as propagandists and public relations men.

Afgaroo', on the other hand, is the pathetic case, the man of universal contempt. Derisively he is often referred to as 'he who cannot defend his camel' ('Hashiisa ma ḍa'sade'). The contemptuous aphorism makes the telling point that, given the importance of camels in the Somali pastoral economy, a man who cannot defend his camel with words – as with arms – has, in pastoral eyes, lost his right to live in the desert.

Three infinitives describe the criteria by which Somalis judge the performance of a speaker: to know (*inuu yaqaan*), to remember (*inuu ḥusuusto*), and to convince (*innu qan'iyo*). To know the corpus of customary law, traditions and case precedents, to remember the argument of his opponent(s) so that he can rebut it point by point and to persuade his hearers of the validity of his own argument – these are indispensable qualifications. As one elder put it:

> Somalis of my generation cherished two things more than any others in social relationships: the ability to persuade and the ability to remember. The gift of memory helped a man in an assembly of elders to refer back to the reservoir (*balli*) of the past and draw examples from it. The gift of speech helped him to mesh in examples in a persuasive manner, in a manner acceptable to the ear. All Somalis of old have coveted the gift of speech and many pòssessed it.[58]

The pastoralist indeed seems to have extraordinary powers of retention. B. W. Andrzejewski and I. M. Lewis have pointed out that it is not unusual for a pastoralist to 'commit to memory' a poem of 150 lines after hearing it chanted only once.[59] The pastoralist, who is aware of his superiority to his urbanized countrymen in this respect, tends to ridicule literate people for being too dependent on written symbols as aids for remembering.[60] They maintain, perhaps not without justice, that writing has a dulling effect on the mind; hence, the contempt they shower on those who rely on the pen in place of their 'natural faculties' (*maskaḥdooda*). Maḥammad Ḥ. Ḥuseen Sheeka-Ḥariir, or Man of Beautiful Story, a recent *émigré* from the countryside who is well known for his oratorical prowess reflected nomadic sentiment in large measure when he said:

> Men of old used to tell me that the Somalis who have the gift of speech are the pastoralists. It is a well-known fact that pastoralists live on animal products. And animal products heighten the sensitivity of the brain and enhance reception of the mind. The animals, especially camels and goats, feed on plants of innumerable kinds. These plants contain *braakiin* (natural salts?). Our children grow on the milk and flesh of mineral-rich animals. The ones who do not excel in speech and intelligence are town children who eat food without milk or meat. Food that lacks milk and meat destroys the

> intelligence . . . the so-called educated people who acquire book knowledge collect all they learn in books according to written symbols. When such people are called upon to give a public speech, they resort to their written symbols. Without these they can hardly open their mouths. To register our contempt for such a person, we say: 'He who looks at a paper never becomes a memorizer' ('Ḥaashi ḍowr ḥaafid ma noqdo').[61]

If the pastoral Somalis prize the arts and skills of effective speaking, it is because effective speaking is necessary to persuade the men who play a crucial role in their judicial system, the so-called 'ḥeerbeegti' or panel of judges. While a thorough exposition of the place of *ḥeerbeegti* in Somali pastoral jurisprudence is outside this book's concern, it is necessary to look briefly into this institution in order to appreciate the gripping power of oratorical argumentation among the pastoralists. 'Ḥeerbeegti' (*ḥeer* 'customary law', *beegti* 'to know') is a collective term referring to a body, of legal experts who mediate in individual, intra-clan and inter-clan disputes and have therefore risen to positions of prominence and prestige in the land. Their chief power and influence seem to derive from two sources: their knowledge of customary law and legal precedents on the one hand, and, on the other, their ability to persuade litigants as to the soundness of their decisions. Hence, the *ḥeerbeegti* are both orators and learned men. Their task is arduous, requiring, as it does, both time and training. There is no formal training a man must undergo in order to become a qualified *ḥeerbeegti*; one simply learns gradually the techniques of mediation and through time comes to impress on others one's talents as an impartial arbitrator. The time it takes to develop these talents is long, and as a result most *ḥeerbeegti* are elderly men well into the last third of their lives.

The typical *ḥeerbeegti* is an amicable but grave elder. He sits in a meditative pose. His speech is slow and deliberate; his bearing is grave and attentive and the occasional stroking of the beard lends a measure of importance to his person. While the argument is in progress, he assumes the pose of a neutral character, showing no sign of sympathy or feeling toward any party. Ideally, he should neither take a bribe nor be partial, and in the words of one elder:

> Two things are out of character with the *ḥeerbeegti*: to take a bribe and to be partial. The *ḥeerbeegti* suspected to have taken a bribe finds himself disgraced and falls into the status of 'he whose daughter would not be married because of his bad name' ('gabaḍaa guurwaa').[62]

The typical gathering of litigation begins with the *guddoomiye* (chairman) opening the discussion by the words 'Assembly is in order'. Then a member of the *ḥeerbeegti* takes the floor and directs a question to the parties in dispute: 'Who has an interest or claim?' ('Yaa dan leh?') Then he who has a complaint responds 'I have an interest.' 'Against whom do you have an interest?' ('Yaad dan u leedahay?') 'I have an interest with X belonging to clan Y.' The *ḥeerbeegti* then asks him, 'Do you speak for yourself or does another speak for you?' ('Maadaa doodin, ma nin bad idman?') It is unusual for an individual who has a complaint to speak for himself unless he also happens to be an orator. Usually he gives the name of his advocate (*qareen*) who stands up to identify himself to the audience.

The *ḥeerbeegti* then proceeds with the second line of questioning which consists of the complainer being called upon to define the nature of his complaint. In doing this, the *ḥeerbeegti* narrates a range of damages within which all complaints are expected to fall. Thus, he would ask, 'Is it wife or wives? ('Ma ḥilaa?') 'Is it stock?' ('Ma ḥoolaa?') 'Is it blood?' ('Ma ḥinjirbaa?') 'Is it slander?' ('Ma qadaf baa?') 'Is it an abuse of the protected?' ('Ma magan baa?') 'Is it a matter of household damage?' ('Ma mooraa?') Each of these has a fixed legal code defining it.

When the nature of the case has been decided upon, the complainer or his spokesman is given the opportunity to expound upon it. An argument usually consists of four parts. The first part is introduction (*arar*), a combination of boast and partial exposition of thesis. It contains poetic rhetorical expressions or a series of pithy remarks, wisecracks and bravado, all designed to grab the attention of the hearer and to set credentials of the speaker. The second part is *afeef*, a sort of advance refutation in which the speaker forestalls an anticipated attack on his argument, and builds up defenses around the weaker areas of his argument by mentioning the weakness himself. The aim is to undermine an opponent even before he has an opportunity to present his argument. The third part is *baaniso*, the corpus of precedents, conventions, case histories, supporting material, etc. It is here that the speaker runs riot, as it were, attempting to say everything that can conceivably be said. Volubility is a Somali commodity and a characteristic proverb on speechmaking says, 'If a man with more talk than you speaks before you, he leaves nothing behind for you to speak on; if he is to speak after you, he keeps you in dreadful trepidation.' The phrase 'more talk than you' is revealing for it points to the emphasis Somalis place on verbosity and to the ethos of speaking whereby a man aims to simply 'out-talk' his opponent.

Somalis admire men like the Ogaadeen chieftain, Goojow 'Ade, who went to the tree of the rival Jidwaaq Daarood and offered to speak on

'114 points' (the significance of the number 114 is religious as the Qur'an has 114 Sūras or chapters) as an introduction to his argument and another 114 points as the corroborative material, all of which were to be stated from memory.[63] Legend has it that Goojow's intention was to deceive the Jidwaaq into believing his protestations of negotiated peace while, in actuality, he was using the forum to await the arrival of his raiding party. He kept the Jidwaaq spellbound for two days. When he reached the hundredth corroborative point, he managed to talk the Jidwaaq assembly into sleeping. Finally, one exasperated Jidwaaq wondered aloud: 'Is this Tree being employed to coax into stupor a man whose hour of death is nigh or is it being employed to await a man who is not here?' The tree turned out to have served both ends; eventually the raiding Ogaadeen arrived and put the unsuspecting Jidwaaq to the sword.

It would be wrong, however, to imply that verbosity is both the means and the end in pastoralist argumentation. In the first place, the pastoralist orator faces the same challenge which every speaker faces, namely, the challenge of holding the attention of his hearers. The pastoralist audience is equipped with the ultimate weapon in the assembly: that of shouting down, in a most unceremonious manner, a bad speaker. In the second place, it is in the *baaniso* stage that the speaker introduces his argument in force. The aim is to mesh in the main points of his argument with the tail end of the *baaniso*, weaving it in florid language, so that it becomes quite difficult for the opponent to realize at what point he has entered into 'the case proper'. The pastoralists say a good speaker 'steals on his opponent'. In the hands of a skilful orator, the merits of the case are difficult to separate from the merits of established wisdom.

Baaniso is followed by the fourth and final part in which the speaker thanks the elders and notables for allowing him to speak. It ends with a pithy, humorous remark designed to provoke laughter and amazement. As a rule, every speaker or set of speakers is given an opportunity for rebuttal and it is after the last rebuttal that the *ḥeerbeegti* begin their deliberations. It may also be added in passing that a poetic orator is expected to cover all the four stages of the speech in verse.

The decisions of the *ḥeerbeegti* are binding, deriving their authority and power from the general conviction and consensus that their judgement would be impartial. But if the decisions of the *ḥeerbeegti* are binding, they are hardly ever clear-cut. The spirit of compromise dominates their proceedings, and their rulings reflect compromise rather than verdicts of guilt and innocence. Total defeat for one party is, moreover, avoided for fear that the resultant humiliation may unleash a new outburst of *godob*. It may also be pointed out that some disputes defy solution by *ḥeerbeegti*, in which case the *shir* breaks down in disarray and recourse is had to force for the rectification of grievances. But even here disputants return to the *ḥeerbeegti* to compose differences after energies are exhausted in fighting.

6 ORATORY AND CONFLICT RESOLUTION: THE DAAQATO–BEERATO FEUD OF 1962–3[64]

With the above remarks as a general introduction, it may be helpful at this point to describe briefly the juro-political proceedings of a specific *shir*, so as to bring out something of the dynamics and verbal tug-of-war attendant upon such *shirs*. To do this, we will take the Browsed-Maize case of 1962–3, so named because members of the Daaqato clan, a pastoral people, and the agricultural Beerato clan fought over a grazed maize field. The Daaqato inhabit the lower reaches of the Leopard River (Shabeelle) northeast of the town of Qallaafo (see fig. 2, p. 11), while the Beerato cultivate the rich alluvial plains to the south of the town. Driven by famine and by a feud with another clan, the Daaqato moved their herds of cattle and camels to the south into rangelands which they regarded as their traditional pasture haunts but which at the time were being farmed by members of the Beerato. In an evening browse, the herds of the Daaqato accidentally (the Beerato would say deliberately) wandered into a Beerato maize field and damaged the crop. A nocturnal skirmish ensued in which a Daaqato man and two Beerato men were killed.

The disturbance spilled into the town, which was inhabited by both groups, and the succeeding three months saw the outbreak of inter-clan violence, not on the scale of a pitched battle as in olden days but sporadic clashes which nevertheless were disruptive enough to bring the normal life of the town almost to a standstill. Daaqato and Beerato young toughs, armed with modern rifles, roamed the streets in broad daylight and engaged in periodic shoot-outs and assassination of each other's prominent clan leaders. In keeping with the style of Somali pastoral feuds, each clan sought to deprive the other of elders and able men.

The Ethiopians, who constituted the sole central authority in the region, did not bother to intervene. They had little reason to do so since their contact with the Somali population was limited mainly to two occasions, notably when it was time to exact *gibir* or tribute and when they needed to round up livestock to replenish their own provisions. Understandably, neither of these activities – which were grounds for much unrest among the Somali population – served to enhance Ethiopian popularity. Thus the Ethiopian army, garrisoned in a massive fortification on a hill overlooking the town, watched with studied indifference as members of the two clans kept up their internecine bouts. Regarded by the Somalis as an occupying army and preoccupied with the defense of their fort against the periodic midnight raids of Somali nationalist guerrillas, the Ethiopians had little incentive to maintain law and order. On the contrary, they seem to have welcomed a development which might have favored their position by the likely mutual killing of rebellious subjects whom they regarded, and were regarded by, as common enemies.

The fighting continued for three months with neither side gaining a decisive edge over the other, a situation which encouraged the Beerato to hold a war dance called 'jaarile' one evening in which they celebrated with much oratorical banter their success in killing a prominent Daqaato notable. Gloating with uncommonly sarcastic language over the fall of their victim, they sang:

Yesterday at noontime
  We faced the Daaqato in battle
And slew the valiant among them,
  Spreading their flesh in broad daylight
For the vultures to feast upon;
  And this has been heard all over the land.[65]

The loss of their elder, immortalized in a taunt song, proved too much for the Daaqato. Hitherto, only a minor Daqaato lineage had been directly involved in the feud but, with the death of their elder and the singing of the taunt song, the event took a clan-wide significance. A week later the Daaqato arrived with a force of 200 and encamped on the outskirts of the town, determined as they put it, to teach this 'worthless scum of saucy slaves' a lesson they would never forget. The derisive adjectives were meant for the peasant Beerato who in former times occupied a subservient position *vis-à-vis* the aristocratic Daaqato, but who in recent years had succeeded in freeing themselves from pastoral domination. Indeed some thirty years before, a similar feud erupted between the two clans, in which the Daaqato inflicted a resounding defeat on the Beerato, forcing them to sue for a humiliating peace. This truce was ignominiously remembered as the 'Shoe-Eater Peace' ('Kaba-'Un') because the Daaqato compelled the Beerato peace delegation to hold shoes in their mouths as a symbol of their submission. In Somali pastoral ethic, to force a man to hold shoes in his mouth is the worst possible insult that can be inflicted.

It was against this background that the Daaqato came out in force to 'give the Beerato a lesson in good behavior'. And few doubted the Daaqato meant to carry out their threat, least of all the outarmed and outnumbered Beerato who stood no chance against the superior power of their foes. Faced with an unfavorable situation, the Beerato wisely refrained from coming out to meet their adversaries in battle and withdrew from the town to form defensive positions along their village some three miles south of town.

Upon learning of the Beerato refusal to come out for a fight, the Daaqato warriors, fully armed and thirsting for blood, began to move in on the Beerato village and there was fear of a general slaughter. Then something unexpected happened: six Daaqato elders rushed out of a hut on the outskirts of town and, running spiritedly, overtook their marauding kinsmen and wheeled around dramatically to face the main body of attackers. With outstretched arms, the elders made an impassioned plea to the young men to call off the action.

While they had no binding authority on the warriors, the six elders belonged to a circle of 'able men' who governed the clan and has a power approaching veto over such a weighty matter as the declaration and execution of war. Their advice therefore could not be lightly dismissed, nor their opposition easily overridden. To circumvent this problem, the warriors claimed to have the endorsement of other members of the clan leadership, especially 'the bush elders' who, they maintained, not only authorized the campaign but actually helped to organize it. (This was the first reference to the 'bush elders' as a united faction within the clan's leadership and their role in the feud will become obvious later on in the discussion.) To this, the six elders countered that the matter of war was too grave and too vitally concerned with the welfare of the clan to be decided by the bush elders alone – a group, they pointed out, which constituted less than half the entire leadership. Therefore, to the dismay of the young men – who were greatly excited for action – the elders demanded that the matter be settled in a clan-wide palaver where the issues of war and peace would be debated before the whole clan. In the mean time, the six elders warned them sternly of the dire consequences of taking unauthorized action. The excited warriors might have defied the elders – they were certainly reluctant to disband – had not one of them, a dark middle-aged man with a bald head that glistened in the sun and a pair of squinting, hawkish eyes, stepped forward and, waving a rifle aloft, advised his fellow warriors to comply with the order of the elders pending the proposed tribal palaver. To judge from the immediate withdrawal of the men, he seems to have been their *amaan-duule* or war leader.[66]

The next morning the Daaqato began to congregate under the shade of a pair of enormous *ḥadduun* trees on the edge of the rocky road leading eastward to the town of Mustaḥiil. This road, built by the Italians during Mussolini's occupation of the Horn of Africa had not seen much repair since the time of the Fascists, and therefore was not usable by motorized vehicles. As the Ethiopians ventured into the Somali countryside only in convoys of trucks and armed vehicles, the Daaqato did not run undue risks in congregating so near the main Ethiopian garrison. Moreover, for reasons mentioned above, there was not much fear of Ethiopian intervention. Just the same, the Daaqato took the precautionary measure of placing guards on a nearby hill to keep an eye on the Ethiopians.

The selection of the *ḥadduun* trees as the place of meeting seems to have stemmed from a pragmatic consideration: located on a hillside near a small valley criss-crossed by a system of irrigation canals and rows of harvest-ready maize fields, it was an ideal place to congregate. That they were not the rightful owners of the corn-fields – which they appropriated for the moment as war booty – does not seem to have exercised the Daaqato conscience.

Although most of the participants came from neighboring homesteads, it took the Daaqato the whole morning to assemble: men – young and old and in parties of tens and twenties – kept arriving, until by noon the assembly had grown into a colorful crowd of warriors, venerable elders, notables and representatives of different *mag*-paying units.[67]

By noon the Daaqato began to address themselves to serious business and in the first few hours the assembly was a scene of verbal anarchy: men huddled confusedly in groups or milled about carelessly in disorderly clusters, exchanging harangues and mutual insults. It appeared that each man of substance in a crowd of 200 or so wished to say his 'piece' at once and spontaneously without regard to other haranguers. This resulted in a bedlam of bubbling voices.

The confused and confusing state of the *shir* was rooted in what appeared to be a serious division in the ranks of the clan's leadership, the so-called 'able men' who were evidently deadlocked over the issue of war and peace. The dilemma became painfully acute when the thirty 'able men' present in the assembly returned from a morning private caucus in which they apparently failed completely to agree on a consensus course. It was the realization by the general assembly of this failure that triggered the commotion.

To judge by the charge of 'influence-pending' (*musuq-maasuq*) leveled against them, the peace elders seem to have taken advantage of the chaotic situation by lobbying and successfully splitting the warrior ranks. The extent of their success became evident when fifteen of the most venerable elders banded together and, moving toward the tree trunk, admonished all to silence – a motion that met with surprisingly easy compliance. One of the elders, a towering man named Qamaan Ḍeere (Qamaan the Tall), formerly a fierce warrior chieftain but now mellowed with age and urbanization, stepped forward and, with upheld hand, indicated his wish to speak. A hush descended on the crowd. 'Hear me, kinsmen,' he began, in a deliberately slow voice which seemed to emphasize the word 'kinsmen'. He was a man of strikingly winsome physique with large sloping shoulders and an enormous beard which seemed to vibrate animatedly whenever he delivered a serious oration or was crossed in the debates of the council-of-elders. He was therefore nicknamed 'Shivering Beard'. 'Hear me, kinsmen,' said he:

> There is a time to make war, a time to make peace and a time to decide whether to make war or peace. Whether I am for war or peace, I am reluctant to say but I am not reluctant to say that I am for Daaqato. Daaqato are my flesh and blood and in them I have my being. A man without kin is like a camel without corral – lost and gone astray. She is bound to be devoured by the hyenas.
>
> Having seen the contention which arose among us over a matter which agitates so many and some so passionately, pitting us one against another, the young against the old, kinsman against kinsman and brother against brother – I believe we are unprepared for war or peace but perhaps we are prepared to decide. This perhaps is the time to decide whether it will be war or peace.[68]

Then, lowering the outstretched arm, he tilted his face to the left, then to the right, slowly and gravely scanning the 200 pairs of expectant eyes and thundered with a shiver of the enormous beard, 'Do Daaqato agree this is the time to decide?' Nods and whispers of approval flowed from the crowd and the gravity and silence which now characterized the *shir* made a striking contrast with the bubbling chaos of moments before. Savoring the effect of his oratory on the men, Shivering Beard continued effusively, 'Alḥamdullilah. Praise be to Allah. Then let us proceed in the way of our forefathers and in the custom of our people by appointing the wise and sagacious among us to counsel the Daaqato in reaching a sound decision.'

The elder's suggestion to 'proceed in the way of our forefathers' was a direct appeal to traditional sanctions which, in a case like the present, called for the appointment of a body of *ad hoc* officers to guide the assembly to a solution. These included a chairman (*guddoomiye*), a wordbearer (*doodqaad*, literally 'argumentbearer') and a council of elderly arbitrators (*guddi odayaal*). In addition, there was to be the inevitable body of lawyer orators (*'odkareyaal*) to be appointed by the disputing parties.

The selection of the largely ceremonial offices of chairman and wordbearer was a mere formality. Shivering Beard offered to nominate two individuals whom he commended for their 'reputed' skill in performing such tasks. The assembly seems to have agreed with him, since the two men were merely asked to stand up – so they could be seen by everyone –

and accepted by popular consent. The selection of the vitally important committee of arbitrators was, however, another matter. For reasons which I shall refer to shortly, the clan's elders – of whom thirty 'able men' were in attendance – failed to form an arbitrating panel to mediate the dispute. As a result, soon after the chairman and wordbearer were appointed, the respective leaders of the peace and war factions commenced to appeal directly to the whole assembly. To boost its case, each side presented several men of 'weight' as speakers, and an investigation of each of their speeches would entail an unmanageable (and unnecessary) excursion into inconsequential details. I shall therefore limit my comments to the speeches of the two main orators.

As soon as the chairman perceived the contenders' wish to address the whole assembly directly, he called the meeting to order with the words, 'The assembly is in order' ('Shir gudoonsan'). The wordbearer moved close to the chairman and in a clear voice reiterated the chair's words, whereupon a rustic elder named Shire Gaab (Shire the Short) stood up to enter the argument for the pro-war faction. He was a 'bushman' and his language sparkled with country idiom and witticisms. He began with the inevitable 'Hear me, kinsmen' and with words which 'dripped with blood' he carried the assembly to the height of belligerent passion:[69]

> 'If my worthy cousin [a reference to Shivering Beard] is proud to be Daaqato, so am I. If Daaqato are his flesh and blood, so are they mine. But I ask you: What is the source of our pride? Why are we all proud to be Daaqato? [pause] I will tell you why I am. Because Daaqato are Allah's great and beneficent gift to me. For Allah said in his holy word, "And we have made thee into distinct nations and clans so that you may know one from another." The profound wisdom of this verse reveals that Allah intended mankind to be organized into nations and clans and that the idea of the clan is built into the very essence of mankind, foreordained by Divine Wisdom as part of the universal order. So if I am proud to be Daaqato, it is because being Daaqato is being part of a people mandated to clanship by divine order.
>
> 'But can we really point to ourselves with pride after what has happened these past weeks, after slaves have slain the young and wise of Daaqato in wanton jest? Think, my cousins, think of the Beerato slaves dancing over the dead of noble Daaqato. Think of our noble blood shed by the bullets of slaves, and our flesh cut up by crude spears. Think of the Daaqato dead picked on by vultures! Pride? Honor? What pride? What honor? Daaqato have

been humbled by slaves. The slayers of Daaqato remain unpunished and the dead of Daaqato continue to lie in their lonely graves unavenged. Remember the poet's words: "If you die, there is a time when /To die is better than to live."'[70]

'Aye, to die is better', several in the audience cried.

'Alas,[71] kinsmen.' Shire Gaab shook his head disconsolately. 'I am old and feeble but if I had any mettle left in me, if I had youth I'd fly over these canals and maize fields into yonder village' (pointing at the Beerato encampment) 'to strike the blow that at once would avenge the dead, remove the stain of shame from my kin and teach impudent slaves to know their place. Even as I stand, feeble though my feet are, I'd fain hobble along, trusting to my walking cane to ferry me over . . . to that odious encampment . . . Is there anyone who'd embark on an honorable course? Anyone accused into sleeplessness by the aggrieved shades of the unavenged dead?[72]

Upon these words a loud commotion broke out from the audience. 'Kinsmen! Kinsmen! To the odious encampment . . . to remove the stain of shame.' Several dozen men, obviously in a state of frenzy, rushed about in dazed circles, fingering excitedly the triggers of their weapons.

Shire Gaab:	Alas, kinsmen!
Wordbearer:	Alas, alas!
Shire Gaab:	Shame, kinsmen!
Wordbearer:	Shame, shame!
Shire Gaab:	Who will marry our daughters?
Wordbearer:	Who will marry our daughters?
Audience:	Nobody, till the shame is removed.
Shire Gaab:	Then arms, kinsmen . . . Remove the shame . . . Let no Beerato live.
Audience:	Aye, let no Beerato live.

Again a convulsive commotion erupted, with men running to and fro hysterically. Some dashed off toward the 'odious encampment' of the Beerato, determined to take matters into their own hands and had to be restrained physically. Others writhed about on the ground, overcome by affected or real delirium. At length, the frantic efforts of the chairman together with the helping hands of the elders, succeeded in quieting down the excited men, restoring a semblance of order.

Each key part or phrase in Shire Gaab's oration was repeated antiphonally by the wordbearer, producing the sort of weird litany of war-talk which incited the orderly assembly into an unruly mob of screaming warriors. Satisfied with his performance, Shire Gaab ended self-effacingly with the words, 'I have nothing more to say, kinsmen.' It was clearly a formidable job awaiting the pro-peace orator if he was ever to cool off this mass of inflamed passions.

The pro-peace orator was none other than Shivering Beard who apparently favored peace all along, though nothing in his opening statement revealed his true sentiments. He stood up, his ponderous beard quaking over the hushed audience, showing his exceeding agitation. 'Hear me, kinsmen,' he began, his voice barely audible, prompting the wordbearer to repeat after him:

> I too am proud to be Daaqato, but for a different reason than my worthy opponent's. My esteemed cousin has wisely cited the words of Allah but, I fear, unwisely misapplied them. May he be forgiven the sin of misapplication. It is true that Allah has made mankind into nations and clans but not in order for them to make war on each other but to make peace, not in order for them to spill blood but to prevent the spilling of blood, not in order for them to hate and despise one another but to love one another. Did my worthy opponent mean to use the Holy Qur'an to incite Muslims to kill fellow Muslims? May Allah forgive him. Does anyone here really believe that it is the will of Allah for Muslims to kill Muslims? [pause]

He succeeded in extracting reluctant headshakes from the audience, even from members of the war faction who had to agree that it was contrary to the will of Allah for Muslims to kill Muslims. Sensing that his argument was producing some effect, Shivering Beard bellowed thunderously, 'Do you agree that Beerato are Muslims?' The wordbearer repeated this after him.

'Yes,' someone said, 'but they killed our men.'

'We killed their men, too,' was his measured response.

Having seized the assembly's attention, Shivering Beard made a stirring counter-attack neatly demolishing his 'worthy opponent's' argument point by point and expounding on the virtues of peace and brotherhood. He then introduced an element of nationalism and national consciousness which he used to put the opposition on the defensive:

> Permit me to return to the text ... 'And We have made thee into nations and clans'. We see very clearly two principles enshrined here: the principle of the nation first and that of the clan second, and only second. I am not surprised that my worthy opponent stopped short of a balanced exposition of the text since such a just

> effort would endanger his argument. But for myself . . . I take pride in being Daaqato but I take even greater pride in being Somali. As we, individually, are nothing without Daaqato, Daaqato are nothing without the larger brotherhood of all Somalis. And this includes the Beerato. If in the past, we and Beerato fought each other, we have done so out of ignorance. Today we are no longer ignorant. We know who our real enemy is.

He made this last remark, striving under the enormous beard, pointing a trembling hand in the direction of the Ethiopian garrison. He continued:

> My esteemed cousin quotes the poet: 'There is a time when /To die is better than to live.' He may be right. In the tricky circumstances of life, indeed there may be times when death is the honorable thing to embrace. But death by a brother? How base, kinsmen! In a moment of strained passions, the Beerato fell on us as we fell on them. And this was a fair fight. The Beerato have not oppressed us; they've not raided our herds nor burned our homesteads. You know who did all these things; I need not tell you.

He paused and the enormous beard shifted again towards the town. A wizened old man who earlier seemed sympathetic to the war faction, said suddenly, 'Wallaahi waa runtii – by God, the man speaks the truth. Who burned our homesteads? Why, the Ḥabash.'[73] A stir of voices followed attesting that the Beerato were not the enemy but still reluctant, unlike that lone reckless voice, to declare the Ḥabash the real enemy. After all, many of the men lived in the town with families and business interests to worry about and were therefore reluctant to declare openly that the fortress authority on the hill was an enemy of the people.

Shivering Beard heaved up again, squirming cumulatively to the weight of his words and delivered himself of a last-ditch appeal:

> Brothers and cousins! I stand here before you, grateful that Daaqato have heeded my feeble words. I speak the truth and Daaqato will not forsake the truth and brotherhood of all Somalis. Daaqato are a wise and valiant people who love kindly thoughts and kindly deeds. O Kinsmen, let it not be said that the valiant Daaqato – the young and old and wise – have this day congregated, deliberated the matter of *fitna* (mischief) and peace and chose *fitna* over peace, *fitna* against fellow Muslims.

Shivering Beard made a dramatic pause, his impressive bearing hovering royally over the mesmerized men. The shrivelled-up old man spoke again: 'The man has given wise counsel and we would be fools to ignore it.' A tremendous stir in the audience: 'Aye, aye, we would be fools to ignore him.' Many voices and gestures of support rang out from all directions – so many that one would think them contrived were they not so natural and spontaneous. In that moment of terrific euphoria, Shivering Beard undertook a calculated gamble by making a bid for an assembly-wide consensus. 'Then,' said he, 'I trust Daaqato are with me for peace.'

'We are for peace,' the capricious crowd boomed.

'Alḥamdullilah!' said he, then called on a *wadaad* (man of God) to solemnize the 'decision' of the assembly with a prayer. But before the *wadaad* was able to invoke the blessing, Shivering Beard's opponent interjected angrily: 'Shame, kinsmen! ... A turn to answer.' This was followed by an exchange which proceeded thus:

Audience: By God, he speaks the truth. The valiant Shire Gaab must be heard.

Shivering Beard: Peace, kinsmen. Nothing to answer. Daaqato are united for peace.

Audience: By God, he speaks the truth. The orator has hit the matter. Nothing to refute. Daaqato are united for peace.

Shire Gaab: By the essence of man, kinsmen! It is our custom for a man to respond.

Audience: To think of it again ... the valiant Shire Gaab ... he must be heard.

Shivering Beard: Allah be praised. Daaqato are united. Can anyone refute Daaqato?

Audience: Nay, none can refute Daaqato.

Shire Gaab: By the essence of man, I seek to refute him, not Daaqato.

Shivering Beard: Peace ... Dear bonds of kinship ... Daaqato have made up their minds for peace. Call a *wadaad* to bless.

Audience: Aye, aye! Call a *wadaad*. No shoulder-shoving. Daaqato are united for peace.

The thunderous shout of the latter phrase so drowned out the diehards who still stood by Shire Gaab that it now became obvious that the tables were turned. Shivering Beard now acquired complete control (at least momentarily) of the men. No one appreciated this fact more than Shire Gaab, who began to wag his head disconsolately, his face darkening with ominous signs of impending defeat and the certain loss of face attendant upon such defeat. In that awkward moment of unease and embarrassment, Shivering Beard took the stand effusively:

Hear me, kinsmen. My Esteemed Cousin – Shire Gaab – he is my

> superior. He possesses the gift of speech, so gifted that when he speaks the birds descend to hear, smitten by the power of his oration.

Shivering Beard wheeled, walking up to his vanquished opponent, and said with a measure of self-deprecating humility: 'Cousin, I'd not have you as a foe. You and I – we are bonded together by unbreakable bonds of kinship.' Shivering Beard extended a hand of friendship which Shire Gaab, not wishing to be discourteous, shook and replied somewhat icily, 'I am satisfied.'

Shivering Beard called on the *wadaad* to proceed with the formalization of the assembly's 'decision' with a prayer. He then made a closing statement in which he thanked the elders and notables for the privilege of addressing them, commended the assembly for making a sound decision and advised that a peace delegation be appointed who would 'reason together' with the wise of the Beerato to calculate the losses suffered by each side during the feud. 'If they owe us blood', he was certain they would be ready to make the 'necessary restitution. And if we owe them blood, we will do likewise.'

And so it was that a peace delegation was appointed to discuss terms of blood compensation and other outstanding matters with the Beerato. The manner and processes by which compensations for homicides and other jural transactions of Somali pastoral life are conducted have received ample elucidation from the able work of I. M. Lewis.[74] Therefore, a discussion of these here is neither necessary nor relevant. What needs to be pointed out is that the Daaqato peace delegation found the elders of Beerato – who feared worse things – genially disposed to accommodate Daaqato grievances and the two clans reached a bilateral settlement which resulted in the payment of 500 heads of Beerato cattle and a substantial quantity of grain to the Daaqato. There were rumors that the Beerato made this settlement in order to buy peace.

7 ANALYSIS

To analyze the Daaqato tribal proceedings, a convenient point of departure may be the obvious point, notably, that what began as a bloody inter-clan feud ended as intra-clan political squabbling – a squabbling in which one Daaqato faction was pitted against another and in which the principals used words rather than arms in deciding the issue. After inconclusive skirmishes, the Daaqato – whose pride was stung by their lack of success – came out in force to reassert their traditional supremacy over the Beerato. To achieve this objective, they were prepared to use arms – to teach 'this worthless scum of saucy slaves' a lesson. But when the moment of action came, the belligerent purposes of the clan were thwarted by a serious division in the ranks of their leadership, whose consensus was necessary to conduct the feud. Faced with a frustrating division, the clan resorted to a structural mechanism – namely, the *shir* institution – to compose their differences. In accordance with Somali pastoral norms, the Daaqato sought to regulate their deliberations through *ad hoc* officers. As mentioned above, they succeeded in selecting the largely ceremonious officers of chairman and wordbearer, but failed to agree on the selection of the all-important panel of arbitrating elder/judges. To appreciate the implications of this failure, we need to examine briefly the functions of each of these officers.

As enforcers of orderly deliberations, the holders of the offices of chairman and wordbearer perform important functions but as far as authority is concerned, their role is strictly ceremonial, devoid of any effective weight (jural, moral or otherwise) to influence events. The function of the chairman is to call on speakers in the order of their desire to speak, often indicated by a raised arm or some other bodily gesture, to curb windy or inconsiderate talkers – of whom there are many in pastoral *shirs* – in short, to oversee an orderly execution of business.

The function of the wordbearer, on the other hand, is to repeat loudly and clearly key parts of an argument after each orator so that everyone present has an opportunity to hear and understand what is being said. For this reason, the wordbearer is always a man with the gift of the précis-maker, able to distill the essential components of an argument and to present it in a clear, singsong voice which makes the presentation at once entertaining and appealingly persuasive. It is also his responsibility to summarize, if the judges so desire, the main point(s) of an argument.

Structural constraints – such as the Somali pastoral sense of fair play, the ignominy of being disqualified in the middle of a discussion – encourage the chairman and wordbearer to observe the strict neutrality of their offices. Additionally, a lawyer/orator enjoys the prerogative to declare either of these officers unacceptable on grounds of prejudice to the case. In such a situation, the assembly is obliged to defer to the objection of the lawyer/orator by removing the objectionable officer and appointing another in his place. Indeed this prerogative, designed to discourage the chairman and wordbearer from misusing the nominal authority of their offices, is susceptible to abuse by amoral lawyer/orators who endlessly hold off consideration of their weak cases by accusing the chairman and/or wordbearer of bias, thus forcing the assembly through a frustrating cycle of endless appointments. These obstructionist tactics, similar to the filibustering method in parliamentary debates of Western democracies, may hang the proceedings of an assembly for hours or even days. But a corrective to unscrupulous filibustering exists in pastoral *shirs*, notably in the moral authority of elders to override excessive obstructionism by lawyer/orators.

The question of who appoints these officers and by what criteria may deserve a passing comment. While there are no structured criteria by which aspirants to these offices are judged, they are nevertheless expected to meet certain qualifications. The position of wordbearer, for example, requires the holder to possess an extraordinary memory to restate, without the help of writing, the principal features of a speech and to distinguish between subtle shades of meaning. Nearly always in the prime of life, he is witty, zestfully energetic and tends to possess an artistic style of delivery which entertains the audience even while informing it. The wordbearer in the case at hand certainly demonstrated these qualities, and without his entertaining presence the Daaqato proceeding would manifestly have remained a dreary affair.

The chairman, on the other hand, is a respected elder whose commanding presence adds a strong measure of seriousness and an aura of awesome formality to the *shir*. When the Daaqato assembly was treated to the fiery orations of Shire Gaab and Shivering Beard, the chairman seems to have been the only person to retain his coolheaded composure and control in a mob of screaming hysterics.

There is no formal training which an individual undergoes to acquire these skills. Through the process of trial and error, individuals come to acquire a universal reputation as talented performers of their respective roles. In respect to the matter of appointment to serve in a given *shir*, here again one is struck by the absence of formal structure: officers are spontaneously selected with no guiding or structured procedure to follow.

In principle, any mature male adult enjoys the right to appoint someone, and the assembly would be obliged to abide by his choice, provided the appointee has proven abilities to do the job competently. In practice, however, such nominating is done by the elders who, by virtue of their age and experience, are deferred to by the younger men. We have seen how, in the present case, Shivering Beard made the appointments of chairman and wordbearer shortly after his opening speech. No one questioned his 'right' to appoint, nor the wisdom of his choice.

This brings us to a further consideration of the role of the *ḥeerbeegti* council of judges which did not play much of a role in the Daaqato proceedings for reasons which I will look into briefly now. As we have noted, the *ḥeerbeegti* are an arbitrating panel of judges who mediate in inter-clan disputes and who enjoy a universal reputation as renderers of wise and impartial judgement. There was, however, no place for the services of a *ḥeerbeegti* panel in the Daaqato case since it involved a political rather than a legal issue. The decision to go to war or sue for peace was a political decision and it concerned the members of an immediate lineage who function as a corporate unit (e.g., in the payment and reception of blood-money).[75] Instead of a *ḥeerbeegti* council, the appropriate pastoral organ to dispose of political cases such as this one is a committee of elders (*guddi odayaal*) whose decisions are binding on the members of their immediate lineage. The difficulty here stemmed from the inability of the elders to arrive at a unified decision.

The reasons for this 'scandalous' (as one of them put it) failure emanated from a seemingly unbridgeable gap within the clan leadership. Of the thirty *nimankarmeed* (able men) elders present in the *shir*, thirteen were for war and these tended to be 'bush' elders or traditionalists – men who led a predominantly nomadic style of life. Thoroughgoing pastoralists, the bush elders were shaped by a view of life dominated by the clan and clannish values. As rural herdsmen, they lived in and for the clan, and to make it worth living for, they sought to preserve its integrity. This meant, among other things, taking arms against their traditional antagonists whom they regarded as a 'worthless scum of saucy slaves'. According to the young warriors (when they were confronted by the town elders) the bush elders aided and abetted the clan-wide action against the Beerato, apparently without the knowledge of, or consultation with, the town elders. Shire Gaab expressed their sentiments when he spoke about the 'wounded honor' of the clan which required 'urgent binding'. In their view, the way to bind the clan's wounds was to restore, by means of a feud, its ancient supremacy over the despised Beerato. To them honor meant tribal supremacy.

The seventeen elders who vigorously opposed the feud, on the other hand, had other ideas about honor and ways to make the clan honorable. Modestly urbanized townsmen, they belonged to that fluid class of Somalis whom I have referred to as the 'transitional' generation. While equally committed to the welfare of the clan and just as anxious to observe its self-preserving imperatives, they were also committed to supra-clan values and ideals inspired by the new conditions of their recently acquired sedentarized lifestyle. Unlike their pastoral cousins who ranged freely far and wide with their herds, the town elders lived in an urban setting with all its crosscurrents of supra-tribal ideas and influences. The town of Qallaafo was, in particular, uniquely situated to foster detribalizing influences. As the center of an important grain-producing region, it brought together merchants and grain dealers from all over the Somali peninsula, Ethiopia and even from Yaman across the Red Sea. Its estimated population of 40,000 originated from a mosaic of ethnic stocks including Arabs, Harris, Oromo, Amhara and of course, a multiplicity of Somali clans.

Furthermore, as traders and real estate owners, the town elders were subject to the pressures of a monetarized economy; politically, they felt more acutely the weight of the Ethiopian administration and the monthly requirement to appear physically before the Ethiopian district commissioner (in order to reaffirm political allegiance) was an irritating reminder of their subjection to an authority which they regarded as alien and oppressive. These factors, then, worked to foster in them a sense of pan-Somali consciousness and a corresponding anti-Ethiopian sentiment, inducing them to a commitment to Somali nationalism and national consciousness which overrode their commitment to traditional notions of clan honor and clan supremacy espoused by the bush elders. Indeed, rumors abounded that the hut – from which the town elders emerged on the morning of their face-off with the young warriors – was being used as a local command post by the Somali nationalist guerrillas who constituted a shadow government in the region, often exerting pressure from behind the scenes. If true, these rumors would explain the town elders' determined opposition to their youngsters' campaign against the Beerato.

Therefore, the division of the elders – and hence their inability to advise the clan on a consensus course of action – stemmed from deeper divisions of conflicting values: urban v. rural, tribalist v. nationalist and merchant v. herdsman. This resulted in a tribal crisis of inaction, generating ominous signs of the *shir's* imminent breakdown, whence the principal contenders, fearing a clan-wide fiasco, commenced to take their cases directly to the people.

Though they made a striking contrast, the chosen spokesmen of the hostile factions bore some resemblance to each other. Each was a *ninkarmeed* (able man) in the eyes of the clan, combining qualities of demonstrated leadership with the gift of the gab. While both were illiterate for all practical purposes, they shared the paradox of being minor theologians who could hold their ground in the treacherous waters of Qur'anic interpretation. But here the similarities end: Shivering Beard was also nicknamed 'the Tall' (Ḍeere) and his opponent, 'the Short' (Gaab), and the epithets betokened their contrasting physique which tended to accentuate their attitudinal contrast. Shire Gaab was a nomad – a bush-man in whose world tradition reigned supreme – and Shivering Beard, an urban *émigré* in whose world tradition clashed with innovation.

To examine the content of their speeches is to re-emphasize their commitment to differing values. Shire Gaab's argument rested on two pillars of authority: the pillar of divine injunction and that of tribal precedence. The idea of the clan, he maintained, was 'built into the very essence of mankind by order of Divine Wisdom'. Thus Shire Gaab took a mystical view of the clan and do support this lofty claim, he appealed to the ultimate authority of the Qur'an, whence he cited verse 13 of Sūra XLIX, that famous verse whose interpretation has occasioned abiding controversies as old as the Muslim community itself.[76] The verse speaks of God making mankind into 'nations' (*shu'ūb*) and 'clans' or 'tribes' (*qabā'il*), seemingly not only taking for granted but affirming the sanctity of national and ethnic diversity. Shire Gaab ingeniously seized on the implicit foreordination of separate nations and clans in the text as a manifest proof of God's intention for men to live in, and belong to, separate clans. From this he deduced the argument that his pride and commitment to his Daaqato clan, as distinct from other clans, enjoyed a divine mandate.

Shire Gaab's second point proceeds from his first. Since the clan – mandated by Divine Wisdom – represented, as he put it, 'God's greatest gift to mankind', it is the chief responsibility of each man to preserve the integrity of this precious gift. The Daaqato, he argued, were in danger of losing their birthright – the mandate to clanship – because they proved poor stewards in the matter of preserving the clan's welfare. To strengthen his case, the orator appealed to the force of tribal precedence, exclaiming, 'Alas! There was a time when slaves knew their place.' The point is doubly important: on the one hand, it is designed to contrast unfavorably the Daaqato's notable lack of success against the Beerato in the present conflict with the clan's former supremacy over these antagonists – a time when 'slaves knew their place'. On the other hand, it is calculated to stamp the stigma of slavery on the Beerato, thereby denying them the privilege of clanship and hence, of respect. This line of reasoning was important to his argument since it enabled him to pre-empt his opponent's anticipated rebuttal that the divine precept of 'clanship' equally extended to the Beerato because they, too, were a clan.

Thus Shire Gaab wove theology into tradition to present a powerfully reasoned argument for war. In the end though, he abandoned reason for emotion. 'Shame,' he cried with an affected air of wounded pride. 'Who will marry our daughters?' This belabored rhapsodizing was designed to inflame the pastoralists' well-known weakness for vanity with an exaggerated sense of injured honor, a stratagem that succeeded in bringing the young unreflecting warriors to the height of martial delirium.

The pastoralists say: 'When someone who is a better speaker is to speak after you, he keeps you in a state of nervous trepidation.' Shire Gaab had a painfully good reason to be in a state of nervous trepidation when Shivering Beard commenced to demolish his argument. Wisely avoiding the arcane theology of ethnic separateness, the latter appealed to a higher moral precept of Islam: the precept that all the families of mankind are to live in peace and brotherhood and the corresponding injunction against the shedding of Muslim blood. 'Did my worthy opponent,' he declaimed rhetorically, 'mean to use the Holy Qur'an to incite Muslims to kill Muslims?' He followed this with a rhetorical pause accompanied by the strategic flourish, 'May Allah forgive us.' The strategy which Shivering Beard succeeded in utilizing was to induce in the men the nervous feeling that they were being led, unwittingly, into committing one of Islam's worst sins: the sin of Qur'anic misapplication. The uneasy feeling that they might have committed such a grave error shocked the excited men into a sober, attentive mood and neutralized Shire Gaab's argument.

It was one thing to neutralize an opponent but quite another to win over the assembly to support his view. He needed a rallying cause around which to organize a consensus. Conveniently, he found that cause in the specter of a common enemy personified by the Ethiopian garrison. In so doing, with consummate skill he played upon the general grievances – real or perceived – harbored by Ogaadeen Somalis against the presence and activities of the Ethiopian military in that region.

The effect was electrifying: the fickle assembly which seemed wholly decided for his opponent half an hour ago, appeared now to be solidly on his side, crying with the shrivelled-up old man, 'By God, the man speaks the truth.' But the battle was not won yet. Shire Gaab was by customary law entitled to rebut the rebuttal and Shivering Beard had good reason to wonder whether the capricious support of the inconstant assembly which he now had would survive another flourish of purple patches by Shire Gaab. Such a consideration may have led him to make the next strategic but wholly unorthodox – and therefore, risky – move. Instead of giving the floor to his opponent as required by conventional practice, he submitted the matter, as it were, to a vote of confidence. 'I trust Daaqato are with me for peace,' he declared and perhaps was no less surprised than his opponent when the assembly thundered back, 'We are with you for peace.' Shivering Beard thus carried the day by the unethical tactic of denying his opponent equal time. When later asked about the unorthodox methods of his victory, he responded calmly that he could 'not allow the milk to spill', a pastoral equivalent of the American cliché, 'There is nothing that succeeds like success.'

Meanwhile the exasperated Shire Gaab insisted on his right for equal time, demanding 'a turn to answer, kinsmen', and was confronted with a *fait accompli* by his opponent's ingenious contention that the clan was 'united for peace', and therefore there was 'nothing to answer'. By this line of defence, Shivering Beard contrived to identify his views and sentiments with those of the assembly, so that to challenge them was tantamount to challenging the combined wisdom of the clan. The measure of his success was demonstrated by the din of rude clamor which drowned out Shire Gaab's logical contention that he wished to refute Shivering Beard, not the clan. But by this time logic had given way to emotion and reasoned discourse to the ruckus of the 'rabble', tempting one to evoke the incongruous analogy from George Orwell's *Animal Farm*, where the outcome of the pigs' debate was determined by the bleating of the sheep.[77]

Faced with a frustrating defeat, Shire Gaab could only plead, 'By the essence of man, kinsmen!'[78] – a rustic phrase which literally refers to human male genitalia but is metaphorically a term of oath to swear by, setting man, as possessor of this unique procreative organ, apart and above other beings. In the pastoral view, a man's procreative organ defines his ultimate essence and entitles him to special rights such as the right to speak unhindered and the right to participate equally. It is this right which Shire Gaab invokes vainly in his moment of utter frustration and bewilderment, a rueful admission that he was outwitted, not outspoken.

For his part, Shivering Beard won by changing the rules in the middle of the game, thereby proving himself a flouter of tradition when it stood in his way, even as he appealed to the 'way of our forefathers' when it was in his interest to do so. That he managed to have it both ways demonstrated his personal resourcefulness and innovation as much as the remarkable flexibility and dynamism of pastoral *shirs* to accommodate change and innovation without compromising their principal features as institutions. Though he carried the day, Shivering Beard was anxious to make up with his defeated adversary whom he graciously praised as 'my superior', a prudent gesture which betokened the pastoral principle of magnanimity in victory and, as such, put a touch of grace in an otherwise fraudulent, if effective, performance. Shire Gaab, too, knew when the essence of man (individual right) had to bow to the essence of the clan (collective right) by accepting the clan's decision for peace despite the dubious means by which it reached this decision.

The verbal duelling of the two orators and its impact on the Daaqato proceedings demonstrates both the egalitarian character of Somali pastoralism and the importance of the spoken word in mediating disputes. In a sense, the two phenomena are interconnected: where egalitarian institutions are the dominant norm, as among the pastoral Somalis, power and influence are exercised by persuasion rather than coercion. To a remarkable extent, the privilege of governing depends on the ability to persuade effectively. Given the absence of writing and other media of communication, the spoken word tends to become the sole instrument of persuasion. When the Daaqato leadership failed to arbitrate their devastating conflict, its component factions turned to the spoken word as the arbiter of ultimate resort. Where leadership failed, words succeeded.

Not only did words play an important role in putting an end to the Daaqato–Beerato feud, they played an equally important part in provoking it. As stated above, the inter-clan squabble remained a series of sporadic skirmishes until that fateful night of the Beerato war dance when the clan incautiously boasted of 'slaying the valiant of Daaqato / Spreading their flesh for vultures to feast on'. With the composition and publicizing of the taunt song, the Daaqato felt insulted in some mystical way – in Shire Gaab's words, the clan's 'honor' was 'mortally wounded'. The context of its composition and the prevailing hostilities turned the taunt song into an injurious insult, deliberately premeditated by one clan against another. In accordance with pastoral sanctions, the Daaqato felt that the only adequate response to a formal insult was a formal feud, an interesting example of how, in pastoral ethic, verbal assaults result in physical assaults. Fortunately for both clans, the cooler heads (or hotter words?) of the town elders prevailed.

2

Elements of Somali Pastoral Oratory: Poetry

> The country teems with 'poets' ... every man has his recognized position in literature as accurately defined as though he had been reviewed in a century of magazines – the fine ear of this people causing them to take the greatest pleasure in harmonious sounds and poetical expressions, whereas a false quantity or prosaic phrase excites their violent indignation ... Every chief in the country must have a panegyric to be sung by his clan, and the great patronize light literature by keeping a poet.[1]

So wrote Richard Burton in the 1850s from the Somali coast of Zeyla' in an attempt to share with his countrymen what he thought to be a 'strange' phenomenon, namely, that an unwritten language 'should so abound in poetry and eloquence'.[2] Burton's expression of surprise at finding the unlettered Somalis in possession of developed literature reflects a widespread, if complacent, assumption, especially in the West, that equates literature and literary perfection with writing. Yet contemporary students of literature would tell us that the 'connection' between writing and literature is 'actually accidental', and belongs 'only to a secondary phase in the history of literature'.[3]

Burton, however, correctly noted the prominent place occupied by poetry among the pastoral Somalis and his observation has been steadily echoed by many students of Somali culture and language. The Somalis think of their verse as more than just an artistic enterprise whose sole aim is to enlarge the imagination and to inspire men towards the lyrical and the beautiful. When they talk of poetry, Somalis have in mind something which embodies the totality of their culture and to which they attach the highest measure of importance. In the words of one elder, 'Poetry is the central integrating principle without which harmonious relationships in society would be unthinkable.'[4] Despite the ring of hyperbole in the elder's estimation, oral verse indeed seems to embrace a wide range of cultural and material activities in pastoral life.

To begin with, poetry is not the craft of an esoteric group of beauty-minded men whose role in society is at best marginal. On the contrary, his craft places the Somali poet in the mainstream of society and his energies and imagination are constantly drawn upon for social purposes: his kinsmen expect a Somali poet to defend their rights in clan disputes, to defend their honor and prestige against the attacks of rival poets, to immortalize their fame and to act on the whole as a spokesman for them.

His forum is the tribal assembly and it is here that he engages in poetic contest with rival poets representing opponent clans. Alternatively, the poet employs his artistic talents to present his own private individual feelings and emotions before his kinsmen with a view to winning sympathy for whatever cause he undertakes to advance. Thus, while the cultivation of beauty and high thought, the perfection of language and imagination and other virtues associated with art are the tasks of a Somali poet, his paramount responsibility is utilitarian: to inform, persuade or convince a body of kinsmen of the merits of whatever tasks he seeks to undertake.

Poetry has the force of ritual among the Somalis and it is resorted to in the formalization and execution of almost every public act of importance: a man explains his behavior towards others in poetic oration; marriages are contracted and terminated through the use of verse; verse is chanted to fight wars and perpetuate feuds as well as to put an end to wars and feuds; and blame and praise are spread most rapidly through this medium. In short, poetry for the pastoral Somalis is a principal vehicle of political power.

We have stated that not all words are equally effective in influencing public decisions and that rhetorical discourse gains in power in proportion to its formalization. Against this background, the hold of the poetic craft on the Somalis becomes obvious when it is understood that poetry represents for them the ultimate formalization. Somewhere in the interplay of lyrical beauty and fusion of thought with expression, poetic oration turns into a force of the most potent sort which as one Somali put it, 'strikes with irresistible force'.[5] In fact, in talking with Somalis about the effect of verse on them, one does not get a logical explanation of what it is in poetry that appeals to them or moves them. The following rather sophomoric retort by Sheikh 'Aaqib 'Abdullahi Jaama', himself a poet, is a standard response: 'The appeal of poetry,' he said, 'lies in the fact that it is poetry'![6]

1 MESSAGE

With negligible exceptions, Somali verse is an 'oral' art and is part of a significant body of unwritten literature which includes prose stories, proverbs and folk-tales which the Somalis cultivate with an undying interest. It is often performed or rather chanted by the poet himself or by a memorizer. The interest of the audience in the recitation is keen, as there are many self-styled critics and poet-aspirants who make it their job not only to judge the merits of a given work, but also to learn the techniques of the reciter. Such attention and vigilance is made necessary in the absence of written aids or references. Hence, those aspiring to become poets, which includes nearly everybody, must be alert to the only chance they have of hearing the poem. Ideally, the hearer aims to memorize the work but failing that, to get a sufficient grasp of its ideas, rhythm and sound patterns. In this way, the performing forum is a sort of training ground for budding poets.

The bulk of Somali poetry is 'committed' in the sense that it is composed and chanted in relation to a specific occasion for the purpose of achieving a specific end. A Somali traditional poem has a story to tell, often an argument to advance. As a rule, the occasion which prompts a poet to compose verse is socially significant: for example, reconciling two hostile clans which are on the brink of war through a poetic appeal. (We shall see later how this is done.) Although a poet may also compose to give expression to a private inspiration, emotion or passion, his ultimate concern as a poet is to influence the opinions of others towards a certain vital issue. In this connection, B. W. Andrzejewski and I. M. Lewis are not wide of the mark when they observed that were a work 'like Shelley's "Ode to the West Wind" translated into Somali alliterative verse and chanted to a Somali audience, they would wait till the end and then would inevitably ask, "In what circumstances did the poet first recite the poem and what was his purpose?"'[7]

In the scheme of Somali versifying, therefore, it will be understood that the doctrine of 'art for art's sake' has no place. But to say that every poem contains a specific message which a hearer seeks to find is not to say that such a message can be abstracted with ease. While the central meaning is direct in some poems, in others it is hidden or, as the Somalis put it, 'closed' (*qafilan*) and requires considerable intelligence on the part of the hearer to decipher.

Whether a poet obscures the point of his poem or makes it plain depends on the circumstances and conditions obtaining at the time of composition. 'Ali Ḍuuḥ, the Ḍulbahante poet, for example, in his declarative petition, 'On Account of Fourteen Points', pleads plainly with the Ogaadeen to return his looted camels:

On account of fourteen points return the camels to me:
From the Gabaysane season (a plentiful year) when I was a mere lad
Until today when I am old, wearing silvery hair

There never occurred between you and us a matter for vendetta;
Know this – and so return the camels to me.
The man of many years brings forth wise advice;
Youths and fools understand not the so obvious point – pray, return the camels to me.
Listen, you did not find the camels astray;
A predator-thief brought them to you
And such rapine works all of us into death – pray, return the camels.[8]

He proceeds in plain language to state fourteen points showing why the usurped herds should be returned. Another poet, Ḥuseen Ḍiqle, clothes his poem in mysterious language and sings of the rapacious caprice of 'Lion Justice' when in truth he was not thinking of lions at all but of his people's plight under a tyrant chief.

The centrality of the 'message' or the immediate point explains, at least partially, why Somali verse is thesis-oriented and the ease with which it becomes a debater's tool; the element of the argumentative and rhetorical bulks large in Somali verse. It would be a mistake, however, to assume that a Somali poem is in bondage to its 'story', that its *raison d'être* is the 'message', and nothing else. Somalis see their verse in two senses: the immediate and the transcendental. While a poem commends itself for its sense of the immediate and the relevant, it derives its enduring validity from another quarter: from the fact of its permanency and its comforting qualities in an impermanent and uncomfortable environment. A good poem, once its immediate point is appreciated, passes into a secondary phase whereby it acquires a new lease on life. It becomes a part of the people's spiritual heritage. It is memorized and chanted for pleasure; raconteurs quote it to entertain and disputants apply it to new situations similar to the original ones, and in so doing, score not a few points. Thus, the Somali Government recently rehabilitated – after a long banishment allegedly for 'clannish' sentiment – Salaan 'Arrabay's lines:

If you die, there is a time when to die
Is better than to live,
A time when life and prosperity
Are forbidden to an honorable man.

The original context of the poem centered around an inter-clan squabble and the poet's purpose was to instigate the humiliated party to seek blood vengeance against their affronters, to accept death rather than lead shameful lives. At the time of writing, the poem is being re-applied for nationalistic purposes. It is used to encourage men to die for the defense of the country. In this way, poems receive new meaning and vitality by being applied to new situations long after the original events which gave rise to them have faded into oblivion.

2 ALLITERATION

Next to didacticism, the most regular feature in Somali verse is alliteration (*hikaad*). With the exception of limited, quite recent innovations, all Somali oral verse uses the technique of alliteration. The type of alliteration utilized by Somali prosody is that of initial sounds (the so-called initial or head rhyme). This feature of alliteration figures so prominently and with such regularity that it can be identified with relative ease even by a person who is unfamiliar with the language. The lines in the majority of Somali poems consist of two hemistichs, every one of which must include at least one selected consonant or vowel designed to produce a noticeable sound (artistic) effect. Thus, in the Sayyid's poem, 'The Double-dealer', ('Musuqmaasuq') alliterating in the letter '**m**' we have:

*M*usuqmaasuq Soomaali waa *m*eheradeediiye
Hadba *m*idab horlay kuula iman *m*aalin iyo layle
*M*alahmalahda iyo baanahaa *m*owdku ka adeegay
Dissembling is the Somalis' inveterate habit,
They come to you every day and night with a new color.
Oh! Death to duplicity and bluster.

All vowels are regarded as alliterative (*hikaadsan*) with one another; to illustrate a poem using an alliterative vowel structure, we may take an abstract from 'Ismaa' iil Mire, the Dervish poet-warrior, in his poem, 'My Lad', in which he sought to provoke a feud between two lineages of the Ḍulbahante clan:

Wiilyahow *i*lmaa igaga timid *a*ragtidaadiiye!
Qalbigaa *i* oogsaday markaad tiri *a*deerow e!
*A*btirsiinyo reer 'Ali haddii *E*ebe kugu raa'shay
*A*niguna an odayoobayoon *a*nafadii daayey,
*A*shahaado mooyee haddaan *e*ebo ridi waaye.
*A*llaa igu og inaan aabbahaa 'idi *u* aarayne!
My Lad, the sight of you brings tears to my eyes!
It caused my aching heart to throb the moment you called me 'Uncle!'
In kinship, if Allah affiliated you with the weakling 'Ali people,
And I am old and too enfeebled to pursue the intrigue of revenge and vendetta,

Reduced in my frail being to hold on to the Creed of Faith,
Since I am unable to hurl the avenging spear.
By Allah, no one will avenge your father's cowardly murder.

(It may be of interest to add that the poet succeeded in instigating the two lineages into a feud which claimed over twenty lives but also succeeded in bringing about another consequence which he did not intend – imprisonment by the British Government who blamed him as an agent-provocateur among the clans.)

In the case of poems with short lines undivided by a caesura, the beginning of every line includes a designated word which alliterates with a word in the next line. Thus, it may be said that the alliterative relationship between two consecutive lines of a poem with short lines is similar to that between two parts of a line in a poem of long lines with hemistichal divisions. To illustrate this, we take a *geerar* (war song), a genre characterized by short lines. Though the system of spelling adopted by the author for the rendition of the Somali is archaic and inadequate, the English version is lucid and lively.

Ma sidi *g*eloga,	Like the bustard,
o *g*uluf mel ku daremei	Who has seen an enemy somewhere
yah *g*am'i wai haben.	I cannot sleep at night.
Sidi arka iyo *g*osha	Like the lion and lioness
o *g*abnihi laga layei	Whose young have been slain
*g*urḥan ma igu bote.	I would make much clamor.
Sidi *g*odir irman,	Like a *goodir*, when with milk
o elmihi ka *g*halen	Whose young have been slaughtered
*g*arti mau ulule.	I would groan for justice.[9]

3 POETIC ELOQUENCE

The language of Somali verse shows a strong prejudice towards beauty. Vividness, clarity and precision of thought are prized but they are regulated by the rigid rules of alliteration. The choice of words depends as much on their sound as on their meaning. Currently, there is some debate in Somali poetic circles as to the restricting, and hence, debilitating effects which devotion to alliteration imposes on Somali verse. Something of the difficulty faced by the Somali poet, unaided by written tools, can be appreciated when it is realized that a poem of a hundred lines, a length by no means uncommon, demands two hundred words of similar sounds to begin its two hundred hemistichs. A poet, therefore, in his eternal search for alliterative sounds is tempted to go on an endless journey of word-hunting. (This point was also brought out by Andrzejewski and Lewis.) In an attempt to restock his ever-dwindling vocabulary stock, he reanimates archaic words, rehabilitates outmoded ones and may even invent new ones so that the resulting work from such a tedious enterprise is in danger of breaking down under the combined weight of archaisms and obscurities.

Word-borrowing is also resorted to and sometimes foreign words take up key alliterative positions in a poetic line with a curious, if entertaining, outcome. Thus we are amused, even as we sympathize with him, when Salaan 'Arrabay, aiming to alliterate in '**l**', boasted:

> *L*a'da ḥarafka laankiyo ba'daan *l*ooyar ku ahaaye
> *L*agjar Ferenji niman baa akhriya *l*aawis iyo been e
> In the alliterative sound of '**l**' I have been an expert,
> But it is the habit of some men to indulge in lies and white man's lecture.

Here 'looyar', 'lagjar' and 'laawis' are Somali corruptions of the English 'lawyer', 'lecture' and 'lies' respectively. Alliteration, needless to say, constitutes the shibboleth of the weak poet, and a favorite subject of conversation among Somalis is the untalented poet who gets carried away by alliteration into an uncharted terrain of 'reverberative acoustics' which have no relation to the subject of his poem. Thus, Maḥammad K. Salad, poet and literary critic, complained of a certain poet:

> who trying to alliterate in '**t**' took off at *T*aleeḥ [the Dervish capital in northern Somalia] and then went soaring towards *T*anzania and from Tanzania to the *T*hames via *T*anarive. Then sensing the wrath of his outraged audience catching up with him, he took a mighty desperate leap to *T*oronto, but unable to find a respite from his angry pursuers, he soared again, this time in the direction of the Far East where he kept hopping about between *T*hailand, *T*aiwan and *T*okyo. His hapless audience eventually traced him to Tokyo only to find that he had taken precipitous flight to *T*imbuktu via *T*angier![10]

Despite its pitfalls to the untalented and the unwary, alliteration poses no insurmountable dilemma to the capable poet. On the contrary, Somalis say it gives him an opportunity to rise above the rabble of upstarts. His language is rich in vocabulary and his mind is fecund, his memory is keen, his knowledge of environment is thorough and his expression is eloquent. While the incompetent poet gropes for words, the master has no difficulty in finding not only the right word for the right thought but also the right sound. The elders say when Maḥammad 'A. Ḥasan, a man acclaimed by the pastoralists to be a master, spoke: 'Few men will venture to speak for fear that the Sayyid will disgrace them by the power of his eloquence. When the Sayyid spoke, even the birds were riveted to the ground.'[11]

The pastoralists also overcome alliterative ambiguities through the teaching of the elders. In almost every audience there are men whose knowledge of language and literature is above the average. These men serve as critics and interpreters and no stigma is attached to the practice of the young and the unimaginative turning to the help of 'connoisseurs' in understanding difficult passages. The services of the interpreter, moreover, are indispensable in the sense that a poetic recitation holds a collective interest for all. For the poet employs his talents in matters of public interest and his material and inspiration are often drawn from communal experience.

4 METER

All pastoral verse is intoned: this means that every Somali poem has a melody or tune to which it is chanted. The musicality of pastoral verse is obvious enough and derives from its consistent feature of regularity, the poetic rhythm. Although the syllables in a poetic line are so arranged as to produce similar rhythms, or in some cases an identical rhythm, to the preceding or succeeding line, it is by no means easy to identify what it is in syllabic arrangement that produces the rhythm. The significant differences of opinion among contemporary students of Somali poetic scansion rules as well as the modest progress made even after numerous years of earnest research, testify to the complexity of the subject.

In considering the feature of regularity which makes an expression poetic, Somalis emphasize, in addition to alliteration, the concept of *miizaan*. 'Miizaan' literally means 'balance', and a line is considered poetry when the units making it up are not only alliterative with each other but also balance one another. Thus in Sayyid Maḥammad's triplet:

> Eeb-bow *g*ar-ka ha-daan qab-sa-day *g*aaḥ-she na-ba-dii-ye
> Eeb-bow *g*am-maan i-yo wa-ḥaan *g*i-ni 'as ḍii-baa-yey
> Eeb-bow ga-row ka-ga ma he-lin *g*oo-la-shaan wa-da-ye,
> Lord, however much I'd plead with them, the infidels refuse to honor the peace,
> Lord, they do not reward me with praises for my gift: the red stallions and precious mares which I lavished upon them,
> Lord, the choice camels which I sent them do not earn me their esteem,

a Somali pastoralist would readily identify the words 'garka' and 'gaaḥshe' to be alliterative in the first line, 'gammaan' and 'gini' in the second, 'garow' and 'goolashaan' in the third line, and note that the whole triplet alliterates in the letter '**g**'. He would also recognize that the lines have rhythmic regularity and as such would be balanced. But he would not be able to state exactly what it is that produces this regularity, this balance. For the pastoralist is more of an aesthete than an analyst. In composing or evaluating a poem, he does not attempt to analyze it or break it into component parts or elements so as to examine their relation to each other and to the whole. Instead, he perceives in the fusion of thought and sound whether a given poem is meaningful and beautiful or whether it is distasteful and meaningless. Thus, while criticism is rough and remorseless in the rigorous standards of versification, the criticism we have in mind is not the type that discriminates or judges by taking apart but one which perceives through internalization. In this connection, John Johnson puts the point well when he writes:

> One may consider scansion rules to be a set of linguistic constraints which are superimposed on top of the already existing linguistic constraints which make up the grammar of the language. Constraint further constrained ... For years we have asked Somali poets and reciters to explain to us the rules of prosody. But that is like asking someone to describe the rules of grammar of [his/her] language.[12]

If, however, we return to examine the lines again, we would notice several particulars which do give us some leads as to the element of regularity in them. We would, for example, notice that not only are the lines divided into parts of unequal length by a caesura but that each second part or off-verse contains six syllables of which two have long vowels: *gaaḥ* and *dii* in line 1; *ḍii* and *baa* in line 2; and *goo* and *shaan* in line 3; while the on-verses each contain three long-voweled syllables: *ee*, *bow*, *daan* in line 1; *ee*, *bow*, *maan* in line 2; *ee*, *bow*, *row* in line 3.

Having noticed these features, we begin to suspect that there is in fact a relationship between *miizaan* (metrical rhythm) and the alternation of long and short syllables and their various arrangements. Our suspicion is borne out by the findings of 'Abdillaahi D. Guuleed, an indigenous student of Somali oral poetry who maintains that Somali poetic scansions are governed by what he calls a law of 'fixed (syllabic) proportionality'.[13]

Guuleed is one of numerous scholars (prominent among whom are Maḥammad Ḥ. Ḍama', John Johnson and Francesco Antinucci) who used the new opportunities provided by the adoption of an official national orthography for the Somali language in 1972 to collect and study extensive amounts of Somali oral poetry with a view to identifying and analyzing their scansion patterns. A discussion of their varied findings along with the consequent – and at times conflicting – theories concerning Somali scansion rules would be too involved to relate here.[14] It should be noted, though, that while preliminary findings by these scholars have already yielded fruitful results which enable us to know a great deal that was hitherto unknown about the structure and internal mechanisms of Somali prosodic systems, a coherent explanation of how these systems scan remains to be formulated. However, the useful start already made in the field by Guuleed, Johnson and others, encourages us to look forward to the promising discovery of an exciting system of scansion rules for Somali prosodic arts which may well have significant implications for the study of oral literature.

5 COMPOSITION, TRANSMISSION AND DISSEMINATION

The interest of the audience in a recited poem is related to questions of composition, transmission and dissemination. These are vitally important questions providing useful insights into the functions of the poetic craft in Somali society as well as bearing on the very nature of oral poetry in general. The manner and circumstances in which oral poetry is composed and transmitted have for long generated, as live subjects often do, lively debates and controversies among folklorists, anthropologists, oral-literature experts and students of related disciplines. It may therefore seem inadequate to lump them together in a small section. The rationale for doing this stems from the fact that this is not a study of oral poetry – or even of Somali oral poetry *per se* – but an examination of certain uses of oral poetry which relate to questions of power and influence in Somali society. Nevertheless, it is hoped that a discussion of Somali oral composition and distribution, however brief, will shed some light on current debates in studies of oral poetry.

The first principle to underscore in Somali oral poetic composition is that the Somalis have a keenly developed sense of individual authorship and creativity so that a poem, once composed, becomes the property of its composer. It is regarded as a matter of great dishonor in Somali pastoral ethic – in effect, a theft liable to punitive sanctions – for anyone to claim falsely the authorship of a poem or to utilize it without giving credit to its creator. In matters of composition and publication, Somalis recognize what may be called, for want of a better term, an unwritten copyright law, no less strict than those observed in literate societies. Culturally, the principle of individual composition and ownership is enshrined in such proverbs as 'A message is a debt' ('Fariini waa qaan'), emphasizing the grave responsibility on the shoulders of those entrusted to transmit a poetic message, or 'he who claims what he hath not labored for is a fraud' ('Wuḥuusan shaqaysan sheegte waa shaqaab'). To illustrate this principle of unwritten copyright laws in matters of artistic production, it would be worth relating a rather memorable incident in 1963 which occurred in my home town of Qallaafo in the Ogaadeen. In Qallaafo, as in most Somali towns, a pervasive social pastime is the consumption of *qaat* or *chaat* (*Catha edulis*), a mild narcotic in which many Somalis are fond of indulging. I have elsewhere[15] discussed the culture of *qaat* in Somali society, especially its significance for the preservation of the oral traditions in urban settings. Here it will suffice to say that when *qaat*-eaters gather to socialize (or have a 'chewing party', as Somalis put it), they sometimes retain a poet to entertain them.

One afternoon in Qallaafo, a session of 'chewers' (including myself) invited a young poet – the mention of whose name charity forbids – to dazzle the 'high' merrymakers with his gift of the gab. The poet came to live up to the group's high expectation, pouring out 'words of wisdom' in the classical *gabay* genre. This together with the potent qualities of the *qaat* of that day induced in the men and women a predilection – to borrow the local metaphor of the impious – to 'commune with Allah' or simply, in American idiom, to become 'spaced out'.

Somewhere in the middle of the poet's chanting and dramatic gestures, an elder who hitherto sat in a corner by himself and did not say much as he was peacefully and reverently working at his bundle of *qaat*, interjected suddenly and angrily, 'Liar – thou art a liar and a charlatan.' The outburst was so unexpected that the resulting unease and embarrassment took some time to sink in and dispel the jolly mood of the chewers. It was the more breathtaking because such outbursts were so out of character with this grave elder whose only shortcoming was a long-standing habit of *qaat* consumption. He had popping eyes and sunken cheeks, the indelible mark of veteran chewers.

At long last the poet enquired, 'Who?'
'Thou,' the elder responded.
'Why do you insult, uncle?'
'Because thou claimest what thou hast not labored for.'
'I only claimed what is mine.'
'Repeat those lines thou has just chanted.'

The poet repeated and I reproduce some of the text in question along with an imperfect translation:

Allahayow nin ii daran maḥaan daafta hore seeḥshay

Nin i daaqsanaayana maḥaan daafiduu kariyey
Jiḍku nin uuna doonayn maḥaan hadalka deeqsiiye
Ma degdege e ḥaajada maḥaan ugu dulqaad yeeshay
Waji debe'san dayma an dareen gelin dubaaqiisa
Qosol dibabadda ḥaalloon ka iman ḍuunta da'alkeeda ...
Isagoon digniin qabin maḥaan kaga deyaan siiyey!
As the Lord lives, I've many a time lavished hospitality upon mine oppressor;
And I prepared his dish who seeks my downfall;
And I sweet-talked to him who is odious to me.
As haste is not my wont, I treated him with forbearance:
With a soft face and an unassuming look, I'd seduce him into complacent confidence ...
With false laughter and specious flattery, I'd disarm his defenses,
Then suddenly I'd strike the fatal blow while he is all unawares!

When the poet finished re-narrating the verse, the elder retorted, 'Young man, that versicle is another's ... I know not whose but it certainly is not yours. I heard it before thou wert born.' The poet insisted the lines were his and affected an air of wounded honor, intimating that such undeserved and outrageous calumny as was unjustly leveled against him were sufficient cause to 'set up mats' (*gogolḍig*) – that is, sue for libel before a panel of elder/arbiters. The elder dismissed the threat of legal action with a curt, 'Do what thou wilt.' Both of them fell silent and the silence helped the tension and unease to mount, a situation exacerbated by the inability of the rest of us – unversed as we were in the arcane world of the traditions – to intervene on either's behalf. The unbearable silence mercifully came to an end when the injured poet shuffled about and, declaring his intention to pursue the matter to a solution, stormed out of the room, leaving his bundle of *qaat* behind.

The poet's sudden departure occasioned widespread consternation and prompted muted curses from the frustrated *qaat*-eaters who felt their 'momentary high and happiness' was ruined by this 'accursed quarrel'. Their curses were directed not so much at the elder who precipitated the row as at Allah and the Prophet and a number of angels, as such curses when uttered under the influence of *qaat* often are. In the evening a few of us went to 'Abdullaahi Geesay's teashop where the elders and the grave of the town were wont to gather on the verandah overlooking the Shabeelle River, sipping tea in the cool breeze. That evening the notable tea-drinkers included Daqane Malaas and Soofi Ḍeere (both belonging to the Ogaadeen, a clan well known for its purity of language and excellence in verbal arts). As furtively and politely as we could muster, we approached them with the question of establishing for us the authorship of the poem, in particular, whether they had ever heard it before. 'Why, yes,' said one of them (which one, my memory fails me) after a pause of some moments, 'that versicle belongs to Ugaas Nuur.' Further queries established that Ugaas Nuur, the apparent composer, was a wily chieftain noted for his Machiavellian ways – his poem hints as much – who ruled a confederacy of tribes around the middle of the nineteenth century in the north-western region of Boorama.

So the amiable *qaat*-chewer was vindicated; as for the poet, rumor had it that, far from attempting to take legal action, he left town in a hurry rather than linger around to face the laughter and ridicule which were certain to greet him upon discovery of his unsuccessful antics.

The above incident – by no means uncommon in pastoral literary performance and audience response – serves to demonstrate both the pronounced ethic in Somali society of the concept of individual authorship and the occupational hazards of plagiarism. It also illustrates Andrzejewski and Lewis's observation in their brief but perceptive anthology of numerous Somali poets that 'heated disputes sometimes arise between a reciter and his audience concerning the purity of his version'.[16] It further signifies the vital importance of elders (the unlettered literati, if the oxymoron may be excused) in establishing both the authenticity of poems and their rightful composers. Throughout the Somali peninsula there are individuals who enjoy established reputations as literary experts, recognized for their talent to distinguish between the good and the bad, the authentic and inauthentic in poetic arts. It may not be an exaggeration to refer to these individuals as literary critics in the true sense of the word.

The recognition of individual composition presupposes the existence of individual composers. That Somali oral poets compose their poetry before performing it or entrusting someone to perform it for them was first noted – for the outside world, we may add – independently and almost simultaneously by the Italian scholar, Enrico Cerulli,[17] and Andrzejewski and Lewis, and recently re-emphasized by Ruth Finnegan,[18] author of a notable example, in my view, of meticulous scholarship in contemporary studies of oral poetry. To repeat the observations of these scholars would be to belabor the point; what may be helpful here is to cite the testimonies of indigenous poets with respect to matters of composition. The poets whose evidence is cited below represent a cross-section of composers of the *maanso* forms regarded by the Somalis as the quintessence of their classical verse.

Elements of Somali pastoral oratory: poetry

Sayyid Maḥammad:

The insufferable anguish of the night denies me the pleasure of nourishment,
I cannot swallow, the odious edge of anxiety blocks my throat,
Even the freshest of milk is bitterness to me;
And however much I try, I cannot sleep,
Instead I toss fitfully from side to side on account of this consuming wrath.[19]

Raage Ugaas:

When sleepy men closed their doors before the awful darkness of the night,
I arose: there emerged from the depths of my tormented being, a deep groan
Like unto the rumbling thunder of a gloomy rain
Or the jarring sound of a thousand exploding guns
Or the obscene roar of a prowling, hungry lion.
Only Allah knows the acute hurt of my scarred soul.[20]

Salaan 'Arrabay:

Oh Faaraḥ, I had no desire to take again the toils of poetry;
I had abandoned the travail of reciting importunate nonsense,
Although I am skilled in the art of alliteration, be it the letter 'l' or 'b' . . .

Last night I had no sleep for pain and moaning.[21]

'Ilmi Booḍari:

Listen ye men, God's judgement, I say to you
Is ageless, unbending. And I am forever a poet.
When I am weary, and want no friend but peace,
And say to you, 'This night my songs are done',
Your clamorous voices still would force from me
One ballad more to warm the dwindling fire.[22]

The four poets cited above cover a time span of roughly seventy years, from the 1860s to the 1930s, and their artistic talents and poetic craftsmanship – two matters which the Somalis distinguish – range from the somber philosophical observations of masters like Raage Ugaas, to Sayyid Maḥammad's bitter anti-colonial diatribes, to Salaan 'Arrabay's wrenching lament over the frailty which old age visited on his enfeebled body, to 'Ilmi Booḍari's passionate love lyrics. What they have in common is a shared view of the task of poetic composition as a lonely and laborious process, at once humbling and ennobling. It is instructive to note how persistently the themes of 'gloom, darkness and sleeplessness' – a midnight visitation – run through the anguished confessions of these deeply tormented men in their supreme moments of artistic inspiration. Raage, whose extent of 'torment' and 'scarred soul only Allah knows', arose to labor on his lonely job of composition 'before the awful darkness of the night'; the Sayyid cried of the 'insufferable anguish of the night' of poetic composition which 'denies me the pleasure of nourishment', while Salaan 'Arrabay would rather 'abandon the toils and travail' of poetic creation although he is as 'skilled' in it as any man. Yet, afflicted with the passion to compose, he had no choice but to strive on with the reluctant rhymes with 'pain and moaning'. For his part, the 'weary' Booḍari abjures solemnly any desire to versify, wishing 'God's judgement' upon his unrelenting companions whose 'clamorous voices still would force from me / One more ballad to warm the dwindling fire'.

What emerges from the self-pitying confessions of these tortured men is a bitter-sweet testimony of the harsh demands which their coveted calling imposed on them. The pattern is familiar: a reluctant poet is overwhelmed with a consuming passion; he withdraws into himself; spends many sleepless nights, even months, attempting to draft the proper language with which to express his deep feelings. Having at long last attained a text which, if he is lucky and deserving, expresses his 'passion' adequately, he presents his case to the world, laying his heart bare before an assembly of kinsmen – and, if his kinsmen should fail to listen, before Allah, the ultimate arbiter in human affairs.

It may be of interest to note that the particular passions which drove Raage Ugaas, Salaan 'Arrabay and 'Ilmi Booḍari to 'withdraw into themselves' had to do with the pains of frustrated love. In Raage's case, the woman whom he loved dearly, 'Abban 'Ilmi Hagoog, was stolen from him by one Aḥmad U. Wiilwaal; in Salaan 'Arrabay's case, his refusal to meet the extortionate bride wealth demanded from him by the kinsmen of his new bride impeded his nuptial happiness. 'Ilmi Booḍari's predicament stemmed from his inability to marry the girl whom he loved, Hodon 'Abdillaahi, on account of his poverty. She left him for a wealthy man named Maḥammad Shabeel (Maḥammad the Leopard). The Sayyid's 'consuming wrath', on the other hand, was provoked by his unsuccessful struggle to prevent the colonial conquest of his country.

Having stressed the centrality of personal/individual composition prior to performance in Somali oral poetry, it may be helpful to comment on the question of its transmission and dissemination. On this matter too, we should turn to Sayyid Maḥammad, who had much to say about how his poetry should be publicized. In his poem, 'Afbakayle', he addressed his lieutenant and chief poem-memorizer, Ḥuseen Ḍiqle, thus:

> O Ḥuseen, by the will of the Lord, let not your mind vanish,
> May the Lord accept my prayer for you,
> Live for a while yet, for you're a man in whom I trust,
> Yet if you die – I am certain that you'll join the ranks of the Blessed,
> You'll go up, up to be with the disciples of Fragrance,
> Now hark, my son, your task is a little word I'd entrust to you;
> Beloved, you'll not forget my words,
> Listen, then, to the chant of my poetic supplications.

In these most grave terms the Sayyid reminded his disciple of his solemn undertaking to propagate without distortion 'this little word which I'd entrust to you / Beloved, you'll not forget my words' – a charge as heavy as it is reminiscent of Christ's valedictory message to his disciples that 'My words abide in you'.[23] The disciple, Ḥuseen Ḍiqle, was however only too human, even with his prodigious memory and with the help of other equally prodigious memorizers, not to have failed occasionally in publicizing in verbatim fashion the more than 120 poems, some of them several hundred lines long, entrusted to his charge. Perhaps it is the Sayyid's realization of this circumstance that drove him to compose his poetic lament, 'Lose Not My Utterance',[24] excoriating the disciple's 'faulty memory' after he received word that certain of his poems failed to reach their destination accurately.

The Sayyid's preoccupation with the fate of his verse illustrates the principle that memorization is the prime mode of the transmission and distribution of Somali oral poetry. A poet presents his composition before an audience, chanting or reciting it slowly, repeating important lines now and then, so that they can be absorbed by the audience. His admirers, who are many if he is a good poet, learn his poems by heart and not only preserve them but also recite them to other audiences and memorizers who in turn learn them by heart and pass them on to other memorizers. As nomadic society is in constant flux, with people constantly dispersing and regrouping, dissemination occurs at a rapid pace. In this way it is not unusual for a poem to be known in the whole country within a few weeks or even days of its first recital.

But if poetic dissemination takes place rapidly, it may not do so accurately. In the process of transmission, a poem runs the risk of being falsified, either through the faults and imperfections of memory or through deliberate distortion. As we have said, Somali verse is issue-oriented and it is likely that at any time a good Somali poem is publicized, there is someone who has a vested interest in it, someone whose interest it is to preserve, destroy or distort it.

Destruction, however, is not a viable alternative since there is no 'document' to destroy as such. It is, moreover, physically impossible to destroy a poem, in view of the fact that poetry spreads geometrically and a given poem at the time of its recitation is likely to fall on multiple ears, as shown in fig. 3.

Constantly on the move in search of the ever elusive and scarce water and pasture, Somali pastoralists are not attached to fixed territories, so that in movement as well as in settlement they are likely to interpenetrate. This means that kinship cleavages, and hence political allegiance, do not correspond to structural settlement on land. The result is that whenever a poem is recited it is likely to be received by a mixed audience whose members represent divergent interests. Although those individuals or groups whose interests are adversely affected by a particular poem may seek to cover it up, there are always others whose interest is for the poem to spread and they would go to extraordinary lengths to propagate it. The two groups have something of a check-and-balance effect on each other.

If the structural relations of the lineages safeguard a poem against

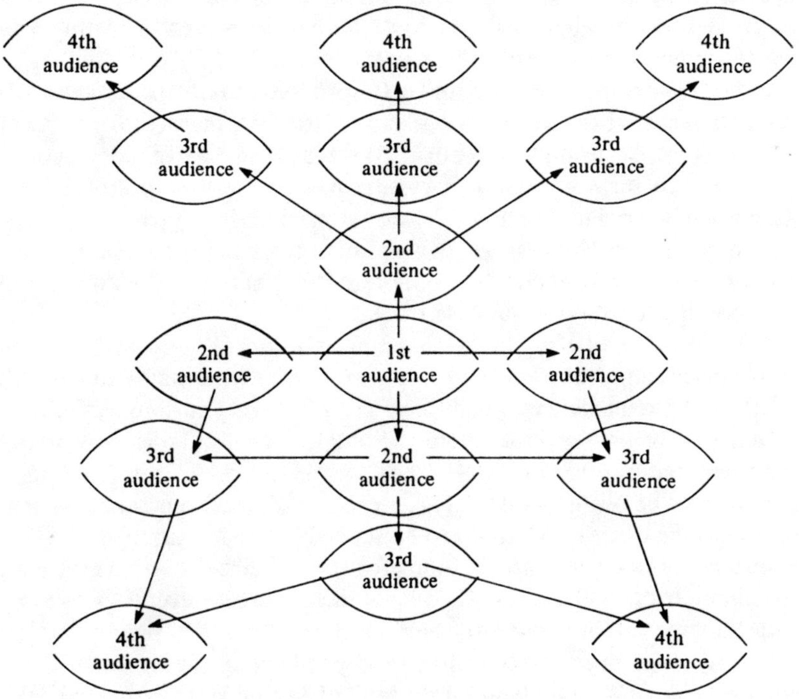

Figure 3. The dissemination of a poem.

destruction, the structural rigidity of the poem itself safeguards it against distortion. As we have seen, the rules of alliteration and meter are formal and inflexible. They impose a strong constraint on the number of alterations which can be made in a given passage: as the addition or deletion of a word or words to a line would affect not only meaning, meter and rhythmic flow of line but also the alliterative arrangement, substantive changes can scarcely be effected without the risk of discovery.

Actually, Somali response to hostile verse is not to distort it or hush it up but rather to compose a counter-verse to stave off completely or at least extenuate its ill effects. The outcome is that the bulk of Somali poetry consists of exchanges: attacks and counter-attacks, petitions, retorts, complaints and counter-complaints, a sort of verbal duelling. As Andrzejewski and Muuse Galaal have pointed out, 'Poetic exchanges are very frequent and are either conducted directly at an assembly with contestants present or consist of a series of polemical poems, recited on different occasions in different places' carried on 'by messengers and travellers who learn them by heart'.[25] Thus, in the decade between 1940 and 1950, the northern Somali town of Hargeisa became renowned as a center of tribal panegyric and home of a polemical series known as 'Nafti-Hafar' (literally, 'self-delusion'), so named because boasting as a theme dominated the series. The poets tried to outdo one another in 'praise of their respective clans' and in the process 'ran riot' (*waa waasheen*) in mere verbal rhetoric which had no relation to the actual merits of their people. According to Yuusuf Meygaag Samatar, a poet and an eyewitness to these contests, representatives of the four pastoral clans (Isaaq, Daarood, Hawiye and Dir) would meet under a group of acacias on the bed of the Herer River, which cuts across the city. There, in the cool breeze under the shade, the contestants 'fought it out', their oratorical bouts lasting for 'days in some sessions'.[26]

The centrality of the 'public' issue gives pastoral verse a dimension of historicity: the narration of a poem includes the narration of the events and circumstances which have given it rise. Thus, apart from its argumentative and artistic interest, Somali verse contains very useful historical material whose significance to the student of Somali studies can scarcely be overestimated. The concern of Somali verse with current issues, on the other hand, tends to militate against its continued survival. Poems are remembered not so much for their intrinsic worth as for their illumination of vital events. It follows then, as these events pass away and the interest attached to them declines, that the poems – unless especially good ones – also decline in importance in the memory of the people. Hence, the time-depth of the bulk of Somali verse is shallow, with few poems extending beyond the middle of the nineteenth century.

But contemporary poems, that is, poems from the beginning of the twentieth century, are remembered remarkably well not only through the traditional methods of transmission but also because many of them have been committed to writing with the introduction of the national script.

The pastoralists have demonstrated remarkable powers of retention and, as we have seen, they are conscious of their superiority over the urbanized in this respect. As noted by Andrzejewski and Lewis, the gifted memorizer, unaided by writing, is capable of learning by heart a repertoire of poems which would not be 'exhausted by several days of unbroken recitation'. The fact that in recitation poems are alliterated, chanted slowly and important lines repeated, of course helps in the process of memorization, but even so, the retentive powers of a memorizer are truly impressive. This is not to say that Somali poem-memorizers and reciters are immune to the vagaries and failures of memory: while their goal is verbatim transmission of the texts entrusted to their care, such texts do in fact suffer corruption on occasion, either through 'faulty' memory or through deliberate distortion. Though the process of textual change resulting from oral transmission is more evident in older poems passed by word of mouth through a vast chain of memorizers over great lengths of time and space, it can be observed even in recently composed poems. Thus, in Sayyid Maḥammad's poem, 'From Time Everlasting' ('Ka Sabaan Ka Sabaan Baan'), composed in 1908 when the Dervishes were settled on the eastern Somali coast near Eyle, we have these minor variations:

> 'And from time everlasting my men have been slaughtered' (*first version*).
>
> 'And from time everlasting my people have been slaughtered' (*second version*).
>
> 'And from time everlasting my community has been slaughtered' (*third version*).

The Somali transmitter does not see a difference in meaning between saying, 'my men', 'my people', and 'my community'. What matters to him is the substance of the poem, and as long as that is not significantly affected, he considers a poem to be transmitted accurately. Even so, oral transmission is surprisingly reliable and a comparison of several versions shows them to be nearly identical. If there is any difference between several versions of a given text, it is hardly ever a difference of meaning. Words might be transposed and new phrases substituted for original ones but the alliterative order and the meaning often remain unaffected.

Elements of Somali pastoral oratory: poetry

The preceding notes will have made it evident that the concept of 'composition in performance' associated with the propounders of the 'Formulaic Theory'[27] does not apply to Somali oral poetry, nor do Romantic/folklorist notions of oral poetry as a 'communal product . . . an instinctive, artless outburst of feeling'[28] which 'naturally' springs to life without prior deliberation. As its practitioners would only too painfully remind us, Somali oral poetry is both individually created and chiefly transmitted through verbatim memorization. Composition and performance seldom, if ever, occur simultaneously and in fact composer and performer are often separate individuals.

6 DIATRIBE, PROVOCATION AND CURSE IN SOMALI CLASSICAL VERSE

Somalis divide their poetry into two general categories: poetry (*maanso*) and song (*hees* or *heello*). *Hees* are modern songs and have their origins roughly in the fourth decade of the twentieth century, while *maanso* is a more traditional form whose roots fade, as do other genres in the literature, into the penumbra of unrecorded time. The numerous forms and genres of Somali verse along with their social context and significance have been treated elsewhere;[29] I therefore wish to limit the remainder of the discussion to three classical genres which are of vital concern to this study: the diatribe, the provocation and the curse.

The diatribe is a class of verse which seeks to undo an enemy by disgracing him (*'aye* or *'eeb*). To slander someone in verse among the Somalis is not merely to heap insult, scorn and abuse over him – although that is a considerable part – it is primarily to execute an act which if undefended would violate his personality and make him less than what he has been. We have seen how in the institution of *godob* (cumulative grievances), a verbal assault is regarded the same in its effects as a physical assault. Poetic diatribe so reduces the status of the victim in the eyes of society that he is compelled to respond in one of three ways: (a) to defend himself in a formalized speech act so as to counteract (*baabi'iyo*) the injurious effects of the attack on him, (b) to accept defeat, or (c) to resort to physical violence which, as we observed, is very often the outcome of poetic attack.

In the exchange of poetic abuse, something more than a code of honor is involved, for when abuse is uttered in verse it becomes institutionalized; that is, it is invested with a new vitality and assumes a life of its own: it is remembered and quoted in all kinds of circumstances and passed from generation to generation to the everlasting humiliation of the victim and his relatives. The story of Hala' Ḍeere, the pastoral archetype for greed, may be worth relating here. Hala' Ḍeere was an Ogaadeen chieftain who sojourned among the Majeerteen Daarood.[30] While a guest at the Majeerteen court of 'Ali Yuusuf, Hala' Ḍeere was attacked in a poetic tirade by a court poet and the event turned into a poetic feud between the Ogaadeen and the Majeerteen. The story concerns the alleged violations of table manners committed by Hala' Ḍeere. Apparently there was a clan etiquette which regulated not only what a guest should eat but how much and when he should eat. Hala' Ḍeere allegedly violated both. He ate too much too crudely. This gave the court poet who was observing him (poets usually watch when dignitaries are eating) an opportunity to charge the unsuspecting guest with avarice and greed. He composed a poem whose better-remembered lines include:

> Greatness is a gift to us from Allah
> And we've even managed to entertain the greedy Hala' Ḍeere for years.

The poem was then publicized, and the Ogaadeen, according to Islaan 'Abdille, felt 'deeply offended'.[31] They responded with a counter-attack, charging the Majeerteen with miserliness and meanness of spirit: the Majeerteen were a beggarly lot, they taunted, who 'whined and whimpered because you gave a piece of meat to a guest lad'. The rancorous exchange continued for thirty years, according to Islaan 'Abdille, during which time no Ogaadeen would be a guest of the Majeerteen nor a Majeerteen of an Ogaadeen.

The poetic feud even spilled over to the Ḍulbahante who, though a separate clan, are genealogically a step nearer to the Majeerteen (see fig. 1, p. 10). Thus, the Ogaadeen made several attempts to lure 'Ali Ḍuuḥ, the Ḍulbahante poet, into a luncheon which they hoped to use for an attack on the Harti clan-family, which includes both the Ḍulbahante and the Majeerteen. But 'Ali Ḍuuḥ 'refused to fall for the trap' and is said to have responded thus to repeated Ogaadeen invitations:

> I'd to Allah come to your invitation sooner than death,
> But I fear, I fear the women and children will say, 'There! The vermin has come!'
> Over my shame, they'll join in triumphant song,
> Yes, at night, in the Ḍaanto dance, they'll sing of me.
> Then my name will become a byword, like Hala' Ḍeere's.
> Since I will not say 'yes' to your pleas
> Why hold on to my garment's hem?
> Behold, it is dark and I must depart.

The poetic exchange continued to gather steam and the relations of the two lineages deteriorated so badly that there was fear that the protracted tension might erupt into 'open hostilities'.[32] Then one Saahid Qamaan, an Ogaadeen, made a joint appeal to both groups to desist from composing and reciting further abusive verse. He admonished his kinsmen thus:

Brothers-in-law we are – and between us
There ought to be Salaams (peace)
And we've been close relations until lately
When malice has taken control,
What is better than goodness and mutual respect among kin?

Although Saahid's appeal was said to have had a 'cooling-off' effect, it is instructive to notice the incident is still well remembered and Hala' Ḍeere, the original protagonist, has come to represent the archetype for greed in Somali pastoral culture.

Poetic diatribe is also an instrument of war and it is hard to imagine a pastoralist feud in which poetry has not played a prominent role. Somalis in fact say three things are inseparable ('Waa isku baḥaan') and thrive on one another: 'camels, poetry and feuds'.

The influence of the poetic diatribe is perhaps illustrated by the time-honored tradition among the pastoralists that an insult in prose can and should be easily forgiven by an offended person upon receiving an apology, while one uttered in verse is mortal and demands immediate response. A person attacked in poetry, if he is unable to compose verse himself, entreats a poet kinsman to redress his honor by composing a poetic answer, an attack in kind. However, if the insulted person fails to acquire the assistance of a poet in his clan, he will resort to violence. Such a situation in fact gives rise to the many feuds prevalent in pastoralist politics.

Provocative verse (*diradire*), on the other hand, has the express purpose of inciting trouble between two individuals or two parties. Where the diatribe seeks to discredit, to humiliate and destroy honor, the provocation incites a person or group to action by appealing to their honor. An excellent example of a provocative poem is 'Ali Ḍuuḥ's 'Lament', analyzed by Andrzejewski and Muuse Galaal.[33] 'Ali Ḍuuḥ, whom we have mentioned several times before, belongs to the Ḍulbahante clan of the Daarood clan-family (see fig. 1, p. 10). His real name was 'Ali Aadan Goroyo. He was a poet of singular stature but one whose talent was blighted by his flair for composing inflamatory verse. He is best known as the starter of a series of polemical poems called the 'Burner' (*guba*), so named because of the inflamatory character of the series.

The *guba* poems have a simple historical background: 'Ali Ḍuuḥ seems to have composed the first acrimonious poem, 'The Ogaadeen Fools', in 1922, shortly after the defeat of the Dervish movement. In the wake of the Dervish collapse, the British-protected Isaaq clans suddenly found themselves in an advantageous military position versus their erstwhile competitors, the Ogaadeen Daarood. In recognition of their steady support of the Protectorate Government, the Isaaq were allowed to retain their firearms and they used their newly-acquired military advantage to raid the Ogaadeen Daarood with impunity, seizing their herds 'by the thousands and reducing them to poverty'.[34] The Isaaq were also putting pressure on the Ḍulbahante Daarood, penetrating deeply into their grazing areas and seizing some of their traditional wells. 'Ali Ḍuuḥ, poet-spokesman of the Ḍulbahante, may have hoped to take Isaaq pressure off his own clan by bringing about through poetic provocation a renewed hostility between the Isaaq and the Ogaadeen. In composing his incisive poem, 'The Ogaadeen Fools', 'Ali Ḍuuḥ intended to arouse the Ogaadeen to vengeful action against the Isaaq who had seized their herds and humiliated them earlier in the year. In doing this, 'Ali Ḍuuḥ took care to appear not as an instigator of trouble but rather as an outraged kinsman who was appealing to fellow kin to redress their honor. 'Ali Duuh lamented:

> Doollo[35] has been taken from the Ogaadeen, the fools;
> If they want to encamp in Dannood and 'Iid, they are forbidden.
> Other men rule their country, and their two regions
> In Daratoole and Faafan, both verdant and fertile,
> And in the region where there is a watering pond, they do not graze any longer;
> They do not feed milking camels on the *maḍeed* bushes, where camels are wont to be reared . . .
> The Ogaadeen cannot settle by the shallow wells to which they used to travel for water;
> By God, from the red earth valley of Warḍeer they do not get second helpings of water.[36]

'From these lines,' said one elder, 'Ali Ḍuuḥ 'soared and kindled a great fire.' The Ogaadeen stomachs were stirred; they could not sleep or eat until a poet from among them rose and restored their honor by 'cooling off' 'Ali Ḍuuḥ's hot tirade. The Ogaadeen poet in question was Qamaan Bulḥan, and his long poetic retort is better remembered for these lines:

> Oh 'Ali, the Everlasting One has driven on the words of your poem,
> The rustling winds of summer and the warm breeze have carried them,
> They have refreshed us, like the fresh grass and the abundant milk of the herds;

But they have entered our flesh and bone, and although words can often bring relief,
Not everyone in this respect is the same, and they have made my kinsmen live in bitterness.
The men whom you have branded with disgrace have been thrown down.
You have touched and opened old sores on the back of a burden camel.
Stop at this point: I shall contend with you and shall state my case.
You always kindle fires by which you are not burnt yourself,
And setting ablaze a heavy log, you know how to incite people against one another;
But maybe the encampment, all in smoke (and flames) will burn the homestead in which you yourself dwell.[37]

The pastoralists say 'Provocative poems follow one another.' Thus: 'A poem that kindles fire followed by one that puts out the fire, pours water over the embers, and admonishes the people not to listen to the instigator of trouble.'[38]

The provocation and diatribe classes of verse are the instrument of the *afmiishaar* poet ('he whose mouth is a saw') as distinct from the *aftahan* poet ('he whose mouth is generous'). Whereas the *aftahan* uses his poetic skill to beneficent purposes, the *afmiishaar* employs his to intimidate, to blackmail – in short, to accumulate ill-gotten power and influence. A self-seeker, he would sing in his sinister rhymes that one clan's men are prone to 'tremble fearfully' before their assailants as their women are prone to 'saunter voluptuously' before their illicit lovers; that another clan's herds are numberless as the sand while its generosity to the weary traveler is meritless as the dew. In a recent satire, an *afmiishaar* poet entertained his avid fans with the bitter poetic anecdote that Maḥammad I. 'Igaal, prime minister of the Somali Republic (1967–9), was about to 'proscribe the drinking of milk' in the Republic and instead to 'introduce the forcible drinking of spirits'.[39] The remark was an ungallant reference to the premier's alleged penchant for indulging in the bottle. How far such poetic slander contributed to 'Igaal's immediate downfall can only be a matter for speculation.

The curse (*kuhaan*) stands apart from the diatribe and the provocation, which derive their significance from the concept of 'cumulative grievances', that pastoral code of honor which does not allow a wrong to pass unavenged. The curse rests on a belief in the possibility of bringing down calamity upon a person or a thing by a mere pronunciation of evil against them.

Somali notions of curse seem to be close to those of the Hebrews of the Old Testament. There certainly do exist some parallels: as for example, the customary practice of the man of God being called upon to utter a malediction on behalf of the community against an enemy. Thus in Numbers, chapters 22 and 23, we read the story of the prophet Baalam who was called upon by the Amalekites to pronounce a curse on the Jews on their way to Palestine. Like that of the Jewish tribes, the environment of the Somali pastoralists teems with modern Baalams, and the services of the man of God are in constant demand 'to do curse' for various causes and convictions. As among the Jews, moreover – and to some extent in Elizabethan England[40] – cursing is a powerful weapon at the disposal of the wronged, the oppressed and the zealous for God. And if the Jews believed the righteous curse of a person 'in authority'[41] to be unfailing in its effect, the Somalis believe the maledictory pronouncement of a poet to be invariably effective. Whereas in other categories of curse the pronouncement of evil must rest on a sense of guilt to be effective, a poet's curse is not thought to be subject to such a constraint. Whether or not it is deserved, a poetic curse is believed to be a powerful force in and of itself. What, however, restrains the poet from a wanton misuse of his malevolent power is the equally strong belief that an undeserved curse may return to the head of him who unleashed it. Thus, when a poet puts his potent arts to use, it must be in the service of what he deems to be a just cause; otherwise he stands in danger of afflicting himself with his own sinister craft.

Somalis distinguish five types of curse which originate from different sources and are applicable under divergent situations. Each of these curses is distinct and has a specific name. The types of curse Somalis recognize are (1) *na'alad*, (2) *inkaar*, (3) *habaar*, (4) *asmo* and (5) *yu'asho*. *Na'alad* is the type of curse God alone is entitled to pronounce and is a common occurrence in Qur'anic passages such as in Sūra LXIII and CIV, in which God imprecates liars, oppressors, evil-doers, unbelievers, and so on.

The second type of curse, *inkaar*, is at the disposal of all living beings, including plants and animals, and is the weapon of the poor, the powerless and afflicted. Thus Somalis are loath to destroy indiscriminately harmless animals such as wild game and plants for fear of contracting a curse and bringing upon themselves the dire consequences of their *inkaar*. Needless to say, *inkaar* is the sort of curse resorted to by those who do not possess material force to protect their person and property, and the fear of contracting an evil curse restrains the powerful from a callous misuse of their power against the weak. This is important for the survival of the weak and the helpless in an environment where there is no central authority to maintain law and order.

Table 4. *Types of Somali curse*

Type	Usable by	Object
Inkaar	All living beings, including plants and animals. This type of curse is a weapon for the weak against the predatory rapine of the powerful	The powerful, the oppressor and those who use their advantages over others to irresponsible ends
Na'alad	God prophets angels	Sinners, unbelievers, liars, trouble-makers in the community of faith
Habaar	Intelligent beings: men, angels, parents and elders	Infidels, disobedient children, oppressors
Asmo	*Wadaads*: Men of God	Rival clans
Yu'asho, Kuhaan (Also known as Guhaan or Haanfiil)	Poets	Blatant offenders, rival clans

Habaar, the third type of curse, is a willed imprecation against persons or things and as such is only employable by an intelligent being who is capable of choice. Hence, the services of *habaar* are limited to human beings and angels. A parent pronounces *habaar* on a disobedient child, an old person on an unmannered youth and the elder on an ungenerous kinsman. Age seems to play a role in *habaar* curse; as a rule, the direction of *habaar* is from the aged to the young and hardly ever the other way around.

Asmo, the fourth type of curse, is the sort employed by a man of God (*wadaad*). A *wadaad* is capable of cursing not only with words but also with a concentrated evil-willing look at an object or a person. Some kinds of *asmo* involve elaborate ritual in their execution. Such is the case, for instance, when a clan employs the services of a *wadaad* for cursing a rival clan. Here the proclamation of *asmo* is accorded a fixed time and a fixed performance. The ceremony is held before a sunset or sunrise (*'ir-guduud*, literally, 'red sky') under a solemn environment: Qur'anic recitations, invocation of maledictory prayers, the making of charms and talismanic devices and synchronizing body movement with injurious incantations.

Where the effectiveness and fulfillment of the *habaar* curse depends on a just and deserved provocation, that of *asmo* depends on mere wish, without any regard to moral justification. Furthermore, *asmo* is a collective enterprise, utilized by a group or a clan against a rival clan: although some priestly clans, like the Shiikhaash Hawiye and the Ḍulbahante Khayr, tend to predominate in the officiation of *asmo* rites, there does not seem to be any correlation between a genealogical unit and the employability of *asmo*. Theoretically, any male who has attained to the state of *wadaadnimo*, for example piety, religious knowledge and a rudimentary understanding of magic, is entitled to perform an *asmo* rite.

The last, though not least in terms of significance to our discussion, is the *yu'asho* curse. This is the poet's curse and rests on the belief among Somalis that the poet has, as it were, a 'hotline' to the Deity and can therefore intervene, through his poetic oration, in natural events. The composer of poetic curse (*kuhaan*) is called 'afkuleeble' ('he whose mouth is a dart'). An *afkuleeble* is at once weird, clairvoyant and prophetic: he is believed to foretell the future, to possess omniscient attributes and to perceive things which are beyond the natural range of mortal men. His malevolent orations are compared to: 'lethal arrows which fly across the Somali desert and come home to the hearts of those who incur his displeasure, causing joy among his friends and consternation among his enemies'.[42]

The verse he composes is collectively called 'kuhaan', roughly translatable as 'evil will'. The individual poem is called 'gabay-awayti' ('stabber'), the notion being that *gabay-awayti*, once hurled at a person or a thing, has the effect of stabbing the object. It tears away the flesh of an enemy as a weapon does.

The distinguishing feature of the stabber-poem is its brevity: a poetic curse is hardly ever more than twenty lines; the typical poetic curse is often a brief, terse statement of half a dozen to a dozen lines. The lines are short and hurried, and have a sense of urgency which peculiarly lends itself to the *geeraar* form. The images are direct and obvious but vivid and hard-hitting. At their best they strike with an incantatory weirdness which lingers on in the memory long after the poem has been forgotten. Something of the evocative quality comes through in the following lines even after an inadequate free verse translation. The poet, a nomad, is cursing a townsman who deceived him of a goat:

O my Lord, who has created me,
Whose humble servant I am,
O thou great multitude of Allah's messengers,
O the Iqraan angels[43]
Detailed to good work among men,
Who art writing my feeble words,
O saint 'Aidrus, blessed be his name[44]
O Maḥamuud, blessed Grandfather –

A man has wronged me,
That he may be stricken with calamity,
That he may be cut off by evil,
That Allah may prevent him from uttering his prayer,
That he may be disfigured,
That all who see him turn away from him –
To this end, all of you say: Amen.

O Man! the death rite
And the confession of faith,[45]
Would that you had missed both,
Vanish and be no more.
Let there remain no light in you.[46]

Somalis apparently choose to remember events and circumstances in which a poetic curse has proved efficacious, while forgetting those situations in which poetic curse proved ineffective, for one searches in vain for an example of a poetic curse that has failed to achieve its objective. It is true that only under very extreme conditions does a poet compose *kuhaan*, for poetic curse, though a recognized power, is frowned upon in pastoral sanctions and its frequent user may therefore bring social ostracism upon himself. Moreover, once let loose, a poetic curse is uncontrollable, and may not only strike down the cursed object but return to the head of him who has uttered it. As one elder put it, 'composing *kuhaan* is like allowing poison to seep into the air and is ultimately dangerous to both curser and cursed'.[47]

Nevertheless, poetic cursing plays a significant part in pastoral poetry and evidence of cursing there is aplenty in the history of the pastoral Somalis. It would be in order to mention some well-remembered episodes of cursing: the Dervish poet-warrior, Ismaa'iil Mire, is said to have cursed the British Native Officer, 'Arab Ḍeere, who he thought was misusing his authority for clannish purposes in 1923. In a poem better remembered for its philosophical content, he concluded:

I saw a man who will not live long to enjoy his wealth,
He is full, satiated, and has grown fat buttocks like a big ram,
His bags are full of loot taken from men of honor and valor.
Watch silently, Muslims, and see how those who prosper lose their souls![48]

Soon after he was cursed, the official, many believe, 'died instantly'. Another poet attempted in a *kuhaan* to 'move famine, drought and pestilence from the region of his clan' to that of a rival clan and is believed to have succeeded in so doing.[49]

Among other historical events, many pastoralists attribute the death of the British Commander, Richard R. Corfield (slain by the Dervishes in 1913), the defeat of the Italians in World War II and the collapse of the Dervish movement itself to the pernicious effects of poetic curse. Colonel Corfield, according to the Somalis, was cursed a month before his death by one Ina Weesa-ḥume. The story goes that the commander, not understanding Somali inter-clan intrigue, listened to the protestation of the Habar Yoonis sublineage against the poet's people, who belonged to a rival lineage. Impatient and without adequate knowledge as to the guilty party in the dispute, Corfield seized the poet's herds and sold them at an auction. The poet pronounced a stabber-poem on him:

When the Sayyid strikes . . . and you pursue him to rescue the herds,
Would that you and your party had perished in the pursuit,
Would that your maxim guns had stopped firing,
Let the men of God hungry for infidel blood hack you to pieces,
As you're partial in judging, let your mouth be cut off,
You've reduced my kinsmen to poverty . . .
Would that you were cut off before the *gu'* rains.[50]

'Then,' say the Somalis, 'Allah accepted his intercession and Corfield was ignominously hacked to pieces.'

As for the Italians, they were cursed by one Muḥummad Du'aale of the northern Somali Isaaq. As members of the Axis alliance in World War II, the Italians attacked the British Somaliland Protectorate in 1940, overrunning the tiny British garrisons in Bur'o, Hargeisa and Berbera. Within six months their conquest of northern Somalia was complete. According to the Somalis, the Italians allowed their troops to plunder the pastoralists at will during the campaigns. It appears that the poet's people around Bur'o suffered untold hardships. So, the pastoralists say, he pronounced a *kuhaan* on them:

We are the seed of the prophet and men ask us to intercede with Allah for them.
Like burned wood, O Italians, may Allah bring fire upon you;
May shells fired by Shelley[51] rain upon you;
May Allah return upon you the affliction you've brought upon us.[52]

If one were to ask them whether it was these few lines or British imperial might that brought about the defeat of the Italians, Somalis would not be fazed by such a question; for they would not see an either–or dichotomy in the episode but a concatenation of material (British might) and spiritual (curse) force. The one is an immediate, apparent cause, the other not so apparent but regarded as the main contributary cause.

We may note in passing that Sayyid Maḥammad was a man who was said to command the powers of all the curses above, in addition to his other poetic talents. Not only did he excel in the art of the rancorous, provocative verse which so much inflames the Somalis, but he was also in a position, both as a poet and as a man of God, to pronounce the maledictory verse which so much overawes them.

7 TECHNIQUES OF PERSUASION IN SOMALI TRADITIONAL VERSE

Somali pastoral verse, especially the *gabay* form, employs the paratactic technique whereby the poem is composed in distinct lines, each of which stands apart, both in meaning and words, from what precedes it or follows it. Theoretically, every line could end in a period. It is not only the physical structure of the line which is thus separated but also the sense of the line. Thus, in a sermonizing poem in which he brags of his piety and Islamic orthodoxy, Sayyid Maḥammad says:

1 Ḥuseen, I have words for you, listen well:
2 Brother, the faith we received, I hold in high esteem,
3 The sayings of our Lord are the words which I love.
4 At the hours of prayer it is my duty to cleanse myself,
5 Each day of the Ramadan fast I must abstain from food,
6 To withhold even a single kid from the alms of obligation would be to transgress my duty.
7 I must forswear all neglect of my faith,
8 All the obligatory tasks I must fulfil;
9 I must eschew any neglect which has endangered my soul,
10 It is my duty to earn some merit for the day of judgement,
11 It is my duty to kill a ram for the Sheikh laden with his books,
12 And in a sheltered spot I should spread my straw mat for him,
13 And he should be regaled with the best meat of the rump and belly.
14 But I should beware the son of Walabe and his like,
15 And if he says 'Give me something', it is my duty to sink my spear in him.
16 Those who come to me with threats, it is my duty to challenge.
17 It is my duty to attack the Hagar lineage, with their cankered testicles;
18 It is my duty to destroy their dwindling herds,
19 And those of them who are impoverished and destitute should be driven to the river,
20 While those who are left behind should be eaten slowly by birds of prey.

21 The fate of the Iidoor peoples is to remain for ever as stupid as donkeys;
22 And since the day of Adam, it is their lot to trot in terror behind the infidels,
23 They are fated to understand nothing and condemned to madness,
24 Their lot is to hate the faith and to despise the Divine Law;
25 Let them bring upon themselves a curse, these children of the devil,
26 It is their fate to bring sorrow to those who turn with zeal to the holy war,
27 Outcast sorcerers are destined never to breathe the sweet airs of heaven,
28 Their lot is to limp feebly along the road to Hell,
29 My portion is to walk in the company of the Sūra of Watiin[53] and the blessing of Divine praise.[54]

In this whole poem there is hardly a single line which does not stand on its own, from the point of view both of syntax and of meaning. There are no connectives between lines, no modifiers, no suspended ideas which depend on a following or a preceding line for the completion of their sense. It is true that in some lines the ideas seem to be connected so that in reading them together we get a fuller meaning of what the poet is saying. Thus, in two groups of sentences (lines 17–20 and 21–26), in each of which the poet is charging a particular lineage with infidelity and perfidy, we would do well to read them as passages and not as individual lines – if we are to get the full point. But the interdependence of one line with another even here is one of context and not of syntactic necessity. Every line seems to stand as a unit idea and either adds to the meaning of what has preceded it or begins a related idea in a new but parallel direction. Somali *gabay* thus seems to utilize the technique of the 'adding'[55] style said to be a characteristic of all oral poetry.

It is not only the lines which are thus disconnected but also the images. Often there occur in a verse of few lines several images which not only do not go well together but actually seem to contradict one another. In the poem we have just quoted, the Sayyid gives himself the image of a pious man of God and of peace (lines 1–10) who has, as it were, renounced the world in his single-minded pursuit of heavenly glory. Then we are given the image of generosity (lines 11–13). The Sayyid is generous and, in the spirit of nomadic hospitality, would slaughter his sheep for the roving Sheikh and the weary traveler. Thus, in the first part of the poem we are lulled into believing that generosity and piety are the qualities which the poet holds in high esteem. We come to line 14 and we suffer a rude awakening: the pious man of peace suddenly turns into a belligerent, abusive robber-warrior who almost seems to declare the 'butchering of men' as his goal in life (lines 17–20). Similarly, the man who at the beginning of the poem boasted of his unfailing generosity ('he should be regaled with the best meat of the rump and belly') now tells us that if a certain guest came to him and entreated, '"Give me something", it is my duty to sink my spear in him . . . it is my duty to attack the Hagar lineage . . . it is my duty to destroy their dwindling herds . . .'

Piety, generosity and peace are claimed as exalted goals, as are bellicosity, warmongering and miserliness. The images do not agree but seem to be lumped together, screaming. But this is no problem for the Somali hearer (not reader) of poetry. What he looks for in a poem is not precise imagery nor a unilinear pattern of thought, but something with which he can personally identify; images which convey to him a reliving of his personal and communal experience.

The phrase 'communal experience' brings us to the heart of an important source of inspiration for Somali poets. While composition is intensely individualistic, pastoral verse finds its appeal by being firmly committed to the moral and spiritual experience of the community, by recapturing images and ideas which most people in a given community would know and appreciate. As one scholar put it, 'Somali poetry establishes truth by arousing in the people a sensation of shared memory.'[56] It prefers the obvious, the known and the communal to the ambiguous, the esoteric and the individualistic. Thus, the images on which a poet concentrates are familiar ones drawn from the experience of everyday life. This explains why the images of 'heat, drought, famine, rain, milk, love, livestock, fatigue, travel, etc.' abound in Somali poetry. So the Sayyid says in a farewell message to a friend:

> Now you depart, and though your way may lead
> Through airless forests thick with *hagar* trees,
> Places steeped in heat, stifling and dry,
> Where breath comes hard, and no fresh breeze can reach –
> Yet may God place a shield of coolest air
> Between your body and the assailant sun.
>
> And in a random scorching flame of wind
> That parches the painful throat, and sears the flesh,
> May God, in His compassion, let you find
> The great-boughed tree that will protect and shade.[57]

In his rhetorical discourse, the Somali poet does not seek to present a narrowly focussed syllogism so as to construct a unified, unilinear argument; instead, he appeals to some agreed-upon truth or experience through the repetition of evocative images. Thus, Salaan 'Arrabay charges a kinsman with ingratitude:

> There was a man who once knew great distress,
> And lost his wealth, his power, his tribe's respect.
> But now, restored to eminence, he forgets
> His former anguish, and my assistance then.
> Ah, friend, your memory is short as any woman's![58]

By referring to the former 'anguish' of the now powerful and eminent man, the poet is pinning his case on a historical fact which others hearing the poem are familiar with, and probably affirm. Similarly, when the poet attacks the man of ingratitude as having as short a 'memory' as 'any woman's,' he utilizes the image of what in the minds of his hearers is an established fact, namely, the inferiority of women to men. His strategy is to hang his case on the merits of established wisdom and thereby mock his opponent by comparing him to a female.

A poet sometimes wins lasting fame by a careful exploitation of the historico-cultural experience. Thus, Muheeya 'Ali, the wife of a well-known Ḍulbahante poet, won renown – some say notoriety – by the composition of a mere quatrain which she uttered at her husband's expense. Somali elders say the lines are remembered and quoted because: they give voice to women's congenital gripe against men, because she had the gall to challenge a poet of 'Ali Ḍuuḥ's stature in verse and because 'Ali Ḍuuḥ felt chagrined enough by her attack to respond in poetic retort.[59]

In a rough translation, Muheeya's quatrain goes something like this:

> Until I pour out his cup of tea in humour 'Ali Aadan will not be;
> He'll not converse with grace but will storm about with rage;
> And he'll rush me like Koofil and Laaran.[60]
> Before he cuts off my head with his sword I'd better heat up the meal!

Although Somalis attribute the fascination which the lines hold for them to 'sheer audacity and rascality on Muheeya's part', their interest seems to me to rest on her witty utilization of familiar experience, especially her portrayal of women as unhappy cooks for men and her use of the image of the stormy, ill-tempered husband. And certainly 'Ali Ḍuuḥ's poetic retort falls short of her material both in the use of imagery

Table 5. *Political poets*

Name of poet	Clan	Approximate period	Notes
Garaad Ḥirsi (Wiil Waal)	Bartire (Daarood)	1800–1850	This poet represents the earliest recorded poet-leader to have used his verse to achieve political ends. He is also one of the few leaders in pastoral Somali history to have ruled over a state whose peoples cut across tribal lines. With his base along the plains of Jigjiga in Eastern Ethiopia, he ruled over a tribal confederacy which encompassed much of the Jidwaaq and Ogaadeen Daarood. He is well-known for his poetic exchanges with his uncle, 'Igaal Ilay (Bad-eyed), in which the ruler attempted, with some success, to legitimize his rule through the use of poetic propaganda.
Aadan Guray	Mareeḥaan (Daarood)	1820–1870	Though not a chieftain himself, Aadan Guray defended his clan against Majeerteen and Hawiye incursions, engaging in bitter poetic dialogue with the poets of the latter clans. He is, however, better known for his self-pitying songs on ageing.
'Ali Jaama' Haabiil	Isaaq	1850?–1919	The northern Somali, 'Ali J. Haabiil, is best known for his poetic duelling with the Dervish leader, Maḥammad 'A. Ḥasan, and the several of his works which survive, show the extent of bitterness some Isaaq lineages felt toward the Dervishes.
Salaan 'Arrabay	Isaaq	1870–1940	Poet spokesman for the Isaaq in the *guba* exchange, discussed above, pp. 76–8.
Raage Ugaas	Ogaadeen (Daarood)	1880–1910	One of the ablest of pastoral poets, Raage Ugaas represents the purely traditional in Somali verse. He is unique in his unwavering devotion to maintaining peace and goodwill among the clans. Although he died young, he is credited with having devised the formulaic phrase, 'Hoyalayey, hoyalayey' with which the singer of the *gabay* form sets the meter for his song. For an example of his verse, see his 'Lament' on the death of his wife and his 'Respect Due to Power', in Andrzejewski and Lewis, *Somali Poetry*, p. 64.
Faaraḥ Nuur	Arab (Isaaq)	1880–1930	Much of the verse of this poet is devoted to the emancipation of his Arab clan from their submission to the powerful 'Iidagalle Isaaq.

			Throughout his active life, he preached the message of revolt and resistance among his outnumbered clansmen.
Ḥuseen Ḍiqle	Ogaadeen (Daarood)	1884?–1923	Ḥuseen Ḍiqle was not only the chief poem-memorizer at the Dervish court but also a recognized singer in his own right. He excelled in the composition of the 'converted' poetry which he used to good effect in his negotiations (1922) with the Aruusa Oromo of Southern Ethiopia for political asylum for the defeated Dervishes. He is best remembered for his poem, 'Lion Justice', a biting satire on the miscarriage of justice at the court of the Aruusa chieftain, Sultan Nuuḥ Maḥammad Daaḍi.
Ismaa'iil Mire	Ḍulbahante	1884–1950	A leading Dervish general, Ismaa'iil Mire is regarded as a poet of great power, second in the Dervish community only to the Sayyid. He used his verse to further the cause of Dervishism and is best known for his battle song, 'The News to Rome', composed after a Dervish force co-led by him annihilated a British expedition in 1913.
'Ali Aadan Goroyo ('Ali Ḍuuḥ)	Ḍulbahante	1890?–1950	'Ali Ḍuuḥ used his verse for various causes, including a long-standing opposition to the Dervish movement. He is a very capable poet but one whose talent is deeply flawed by his flair for the provocative. Among the pastoralists, he has the reputation of being something of an agent-provocateur (*diradire*) and he is best remembered as the starter of a series of polemical poems called *guba*, 'burner', from its virulent character. The series turned into a sort of poetic vendetta involving the Ḍulbahante, Ogaadeen and Isaaq clans, and is alleged to have poisoned relations among these clans for some twenty years (1922–42).
Qamaan Bulḥan	Ogaadeen (Daarood)	1890–1950	A contemporary of 'Ali Ḍuuḥ, this poet was the chief spokesman for the Ogaadeen in the *guba* series.
'Abdillaahi Muuse	Isaaq	1900–	Although 'Abdillaahi Muuse achieved fame as a man of wisdom and piety, he is best known for his poetic lament over his unhappy marriage and the consequent attack on his beautiful but wayward wife is said to have nearly provoked a feud between her outraged kinsmen and the poet's people. Peace was eventually restored by the poet's agreeing to pay full blood compensation to her kin.

and of the flow of language:

> Listen, Muheeya, I gave you milch camels which are pastured by the roadside;
> You've heard Miira and Goglaa[61] are blossoming with wild fruits;
> In truth the mortar sounds[62] from the people you share a name with;
> A woman dismissed with the triple divorce oath[63] is disgraced;
> That her mirror of honor is broken I have witnesses;
> Be restrained from me, O Daughter of 'Ali, lest I cast you out.

His chief counterpoint is twofold: (1) he has provided her with riches (line 1), while her people are destitute with poverty (line 2) though she mistakenly believes otherwise, and (2) making recourse to his ultimate weapon, he threatens her with divorce. 'Ali Ḍuuḥ's retort would not pass muster with a pastoral audience; convention would require him to pursue her line of argument and his refusal to address the points she has raised, namely, her reference to his stormy temperament, her description of men as tyrants exercising ill-gotten authority over women, 'before he cuts off my head . . . ' is tantamount to capitulation.

The preceding discussion is intended to highlight the perimeters of pastoral verse in a somewhat sketchy and arbitrary fashion. It is intended to be neither exhaustive in treatment nor systematic in the choice of topic. Even so, my hope is that it has alerted the reader to something of the range and complexity of Somali oral verse and the pre-eminent role it occupies in the intimate workings of the people's lives. An awareness of this, I hope, should in turn prepare the reader critically for one of the principal tasks of the rest of this study: the attempt to show that the great Somali anti-colonial leader, Sayyid Maḥammad 'Abdille Ḥasan, successfully harnessed the remarkable resources of pastoral verse in his struggle against colonialism at the turn of the century. Before doing this, however, it may be helpful to undertake a brief historical treatment of the Somali resistance movement which the Sayyid led and the conditions which gave this movement the vitality and dynamism it was to assume for two decades.

3

Occupation and Resistance: The Rise of the Somali Dervishes

The last three decades of the nineteenth century were years of fateful events and momentous developments for the Somalis. During this period the Somali peninsula was partitioned by treaty, and by conquest, among Britain, France, Italy and, most gravely in its consequences, Ethiopia.

Behind the imperial partition of Somalia lay varying motives. The principal concern of Britain was to preserve the northern Somali coast as a supplier of meat and other commodities for her Aden garrison which, given the rising importance of the Red Sea to British plans in the East, was considered vital to the defense of British India. The French, having fallen out with the British over Egypt in the 1880s, wanted a coaling station in the Red Sea to facilitate naval communication with their imperial interests in Indochina. They were, moreover, challenging British north–south expansion (the vaunted Cairo–Cape Town sphere of influence) by an east–west expansion. The French hoped to connect the Gulf of Aden with their possessions in equatorial Africa. The attempt to implement these conflicting imperial ambitions was to provoke a major crisis known as the 'Fashoda Incident' between France and Britain when Lord Kitchener's Anglo-Egyptian troops ran into Commandant Marchand's column from the West Coast at Foshoda, Sudan.

Recently united and a fledgling nation themselves, the Italians were new to the game of imperial aggrandizement and were interested in staking out a piece of land on the Red Sea and Indian Ocean coasts wherever they could find one, provided they could do so without incurring the displeasure of either the French or the British. What they, as other Europeans, did not realize then, was that the main threat to their imperial designs was not to be a European power, but a black power on the rise – Menelik II of Ethiopia.

Both the history of the partition of the Horn and the intricate motives behind it as well as the rivalries and dreams of the principal actors have been ably chronicled.[1] It is therefore unnecessary to retell the tale here.

Occupation and resistance: the rise of the Somali Dervishes

It need only be observed that by 1898, the year of the inception of the Somali resistance struggle, the main spheres of the three European powers and Ethiopia were tentatively formulated, though their boundaries were ill-defined, especially those between Britain and Ethiopia on the one hand and Italy and Ethiopia on the other. The Somali peninsula, one of Africa's few homogeneous regions, was divided into mini-lands – into a British Somaliland, a French Somaliland, an Italian Somaliland, an Ethiopian Somaliland, and what came to be known as the Northern Frontier District (NFD) of Kenya. The unrealistic and opportunistic character of the partition of the Somalis was to prompt, decades later, Lord Rennell of Rodd to observe ruefully:

> If we had been interested enough . . . (and if the world had been sensible enough), all the Somalis . . . might have remained under our administration . . . But the world was not sensible enough, and we were not interested enough, and so the only part of Africa which is radically homogeneous has . . . been split into such . . . parts as made Caesar's Gaul the problem and cockpit of Europe for the last two thousand years. And Somaliland will probably become a cockpit of East Africa.[2]

Inland herdsmen, the great mass of Somalis – who, needless to say, were not consulted in the partition of their pasturelands into mini-imperial spheres – did not come into direct contact with the colonial administrations on the coast. They were therefore ill-disposed either to follow the arcane world of imperial treaties or to appreciate the consequences of such treaties for their country. If the northern Somali poet, Faaraḥ Nuur, was their spokesman, those who were immediately affected by the partition saw it in apocalyptic terms. He sang in bemused disbelief of what was happening to his country:

> The British, the Ethiopians, and the Italians are squabbling,
> The country is snatched and divided by whosoever is stronger,
> The country is sold piece by piece without our knowledge,
> And for me, all this is the Teeth of the Last Days![3]

The initial impact of European colonialism on the Somalis was mild compared to that of Menelik's Ethiopia, an inland power whose periodic raids of livestock frequently despoiled the Ogaadeen Somalis. The Dervish resistance movement, it will be argued shortly, was largely a Somali response to these raids. It is indeed a remarkable irony that the fledgling British Somaliland administration blundered into a war with the Somali Dervishes who were primarily formed for self-defense against repeated Ethiopian raids. Before delving into the immediate conditions which provoked the Somali resistance struggle though, it would be helpful to look briefly into the general phenomenon of Northeast African Islamic revivalism of the nineteenth century – of which the Somali Dervishes were a part.

I THE EMERGENCE OF MILITANT BROTHERHOODS

The Somali resistance movement which Sayyid Maḥammad 'Abdille Ḥasan led at the turn of the century against Europeans and Ethiopians had a strong religious motivation. Religion served both as the ideological basis of the movement and the inspiring force in its day-to-day vicissitudes. The religious element is betrayed by the name of the movement, 'Dervish', from the Arabic 'Darwīsh' (sing.), 'Darāwīsh' (pl.), used to denote a Muslim believer who has taken vows of poverty and a life of austerity in the service of his God and community. It is reflected in the profound religiosity of the Sayyid himself and the reformist puritanism of the Saaliḥiya Order which he represented in Somalia. Indeed any account of the Somali resistance that does not take stock of the religious element would be ill placed to explain the rising of the Dervishes and the success and surprising durability of the movement.

The Dervishes were also shaped by the pastoral environment from which they sprang. As we shall have occasion to point out, both Sayyid Maḥammad's consummate use of poetic oratory as a political weapon and the militarist character of his followers had their roots in Somali pastoral tradition.

In the last quarter of the nineteenth century, eastern African Islam experienced a widespread religious re-awakening. During this period, Islam emerged with renewed vitality and fervor among its Somali devotees. Brotherhoods proliferated with religious centers (*Jamā'a*) dotting the Somali hinterlands and the East African coast from Zeyla' to Zanzibar. The annual flow of Somali pilgrims to and from Mecca tripled.[4] The period also saw a renewed immigration into Somalia of Arab sheikhs and *fiqīhs* who built mosques and opened up theological schools and centers of learning where the teaching of the Sharī'a and of sacred law was re-emphasized. The outburst of zealous Islam in East Africa seems to have been part of a wider religious revival in the Muslim world. The recrudescence of militant Islam in Africa and Asia is said to have been the outcome of the increasing subjugation of Muslims and Muslim lands to Euro-Christian rule.[5] In the eyes of the Muslim faithful, this had been a disquieting trend throughout the nineteenth century which finally acquired a painful climax in the last quarter of that century.

In Egypt, ever since Napoleon routed the last of the Mamlūks at the

Battle of the Pyramids in the 1790s, European influence had continued to grow apace. It culminated in Britain's seizure of Egypt in 1884. The French had begun the conquest of North Africa with Algeria in the 1830s and had completed it with the annexation of Tunisia and Morocco in the succeeding years. In Muslim West Africa, too, French colonial expansion was at work, staking out vast dominions in two decades (1880–1900). On the East African coast, the Omani sultans of Zanzibar had been reduced to impotence by half a century of European hegemony. As early as 1844, the British consul's authority on the coast was so overwhelming that the frequent disputants of succession to the throne sought to enlist the aid of the 'power behind the throne'.[6] In the following decades, the power and influence of Europe over Zanzibari affairs continued to increase. In 1886 the ageing Said Barghash was forced to sign a humiliating Anglo-German treaty of delimitation, which, in a highhanded fashion, stripped the sultan of sovereignty over his East Africa dominions, except for a few coastal towns and their immediate hinterlands.[7]

The fortunes of Muslim Asia were hardly better off. Here, the Sultan of the Ottomans, symbol of Muslim sovereignty and the embodiment of its spiritual integrity, had for long been ridiculed as the 'Sick man of Europe' while his rickety empire continued to crumble under the corrosive activities of European diplomats, traders and concession-seekers. Pressed for political reform, forced to borrow loans at extortionate rates, plagued by foreign-inspired sedition and discord from their Christian subjects and threatened with invasion from without, the Ottomans lived from crisis to crisis in the latter quarter of the nineteenth century.[8]

The shock and humiliation of defeat could not but entail a traumatic impact for the Muslim community, a community which entertains a lofty image of itself, as the 'noblest of mankind'[9] and the embodiment of divine expression. Muslim response to the imposition of Christian rule was, however, varied, ranging from a thorough breakdown of the traditional system and the concomitant rise of a secular state on the European model (as in the case of the Ottomans) to the militant retrenchment of puritanical Islam, as illustrated by the Wahhabi state in Arabia.

With respect to African Islam, a widespread response seems to have involved the rise of the 'reformist movement'. The resurgence of revivalist movements in Muslim Africa in reaction to Euro-Christian hegemony was first studied by J. S. Trimingham[10] and recently, quite ably, by B. G. Martin.[11] At the heart of each of these reform movements lay a Sufi brotherhood led by a charismatic figure, a sort of John the Baptist, who called men and women to repentance and sought to restructure society by rededicating it to the worship of its creator and to conformance with his sacred laws. Concomitant with the rise of the charismatic was the popularization of the millennialist doctrine.[12] The Sudanese Mahdia typified this spirit of millennialism, but traits of it can be detected in the reformist movements of the Uwaysiya of Sheikh Uways Maḥammad of East Africa, and the Somali (Saaliḥiya) Dervishes and the Sanusis of Libya. The socio-political dislocations resulting from European intervention were, in the words of B. G. Martin, seen in 'religious colors, as part of an ongoing struggle between Christian intruders and the Islamic polity'.[13] Furthermore, these movements tended to justify the erosion of the Muslim position *vis-à-vis* the Christians on grounds of divine displeasure – Muslims were allowed to suffer under the Christian infidel because they were under divine disfavor brought on by their wickedly sinful ways in wandering away from the 'Straight Path'. The way to regain favor with God was, therefore, to govern society in strict accordance with his laws.

Beginning with the 1880s, the spirit of puritanical Islam made inroads into Somali life. The change from insouciance to militancy in Somali Islam was noted by European explorers and sportsmen in northeast Africa during this period. Their observations, ably summarized by Robert Hess, speak of a climate of spiritual ferment and anticipation among the Somalis.[14] Captain H. Swayne, a British explorer who made seventeen trips through northern Somalia between 1885 and 1893, admonished fellow travelers: 'The mullahs are the traveller's best friends in the Ogaden; they are intelligent, have great social influence, and are particularly useful in giving introductions, passing the traveller from tribe to tribe.'[15] Yet others found that the mullahs, far from being the traveler's friend, could be his worst enemies, too. F. L. James, who traversed the Ogaadeen on a trip to the Shabeelle River, had much occasion to dread the influence of the 'mighty priesthood'.[16] At Faf, deep in the Ogaadeen, he found the Tariiqa settlement 'a cloud which might precede a storm'. His Somali helpers were berated by other Somalis for accompanying '*kaffirs* [infidels] through the land', and were declared 'no better than *kaffirs* themselves'. It may be wondered why Swayne and James, both of whom are fairly circumspect in their observations, acquired such contradictory impressions of the sheikhs' attitudes toward Christian intruders. Part of the answer may come from James' account elsewhere. Significantly, it was in 1885, at the height of the Sudanese Mahdist revolt in the Sudan, that he found this deep antipathy for Europeans among the Somalis. He attributed this to the influence of events in the Sudan: 'They had sent letters to the priests in the Ogadayn, saying word had come from Mecca urging the people to stop us, as the English had lately killed a great many Muslims [Sudanese].'[17] This observation seems to make plain the element of pan-Islamism in Somali opposition to Euro-

Christians: the English had killed fellow Muslims in distant Sudan. Significantly, this news was said to have been transmitted through Mecca, that great center of pan-Islamic sentiment.

But the Somalis had a more cogent reason to be reluctant to welcome Christians in their midst, notably, the threat at home by Abyssinian Christians. The well-armed Ethiopians were at this time expanding from the highlands into the Somali Ogaadeen. Under pressure from famine and other natural disasters and motivated by a desire to share in the partition of the Horn, they descended on the lowlands seeking not only to recoup their losses from the 'vast herds' of the pastoralists but also to impose political hegemony on the Ogaadeen Somalis.[18] There were about twenty Tariiqa settlements of both Qaadiriya and Aḥmadiya provenance in the Somali interior in the 1890s and many of these were feeling the pressure of Ethiopian expansion. The Italian explorer, Vittorio Bottego, spoke in 1893 of the plight of Somali religious communities whose 'belongings had been looted by the Amhara'.[19] By the time of Bottego's visit, the ancient Tariiqa colony at Qulunqul and the tomb of the founding saint of Qaadiriya's northern branch, 'Abd ar-Raḥmān az-Zeyli'i, lay in ruins 'sacked by the Ethiopians'.[20] Under these circumstances, it was understandable that the Somalis shared what a recent student described as 'the fear of many Muslims that their society was threatened' by Christian invaders.[21]

Of the dozen or so orders which either sprang to life or experienced revivalism in Somalia from the 1890s onwards, two were exceptionally important: the Qaadiriya and Aḥmadiya brotherhoods. The Qaadiriya Tariiqa, or path, was founded by the Baghdadi Saint, Sayyid 'Abd al-Qādir Jilani (d. AD 1166); the Aḥmadiya and its militant offshoot, the Saaliḥiya, trace their ancestry to the great Meccan teacher and mystic, Aḥmad b. Idris al-Faasi (1760–1837). Being older and more established, the Qaadiriya Order commanded greater membership among the Somalis but was (and is) less puritanical than Aḥmadiya and Saaliḥiya. Locally, the Qaadiriya brotherhood is split into two powerful branches. In the north, the Zeyli'iya, named after Sheikh 'Abd ar-Raḥmān az-Zeyli'i who died in the Ogaadeen in 1883, is more influential; while in the south, the Uwaysiya, founded by Uways Maḥammad who was murdered in 1909 by members of the rival Saaliḥiya, tends to be dominant.

One of the crucial elements in the emergence of organized Sufism in Somalia was the rise of the *wadaad* (man of religion). The institution of the *wadaad* is, of course, an ancient one in Somali Islam. As spiritual leaders, *wadaads* mediated between man and God. They offered sacrifices, solemnized marriages, taught the Qur'an and offered prayers on behalf of the clan. *Wadaads* provided spiritual comfort where material comfort was not easily to be had. At a more practical level, the settlement of *wadaads*, often called 'Jamā'a' or 'zawiya', was a welcome sanctuary to weary travelers, fugitives from tribal warfare and society's outcasts. The bonds between *wadaads*, moreover, transcended, and sometimes overrode those between kinship ties. This meant that the community of *wadaads* was potentially a tribeless community.

Yet for all its significance, the influence of the *wadaad* in traditional society remained secondary to that of his opposite number: the *warrenleh* (spear-bearer) or secular man. Perhaps because of their environment, the pastoralists seek solutions to social problems in the secular domain, turning to spiritual remedies only where secular ones have failed. And they give expression to this principle in the proverb, 'God and the warrior chieftain ('*atoosh*) are fighting over us, and we are leaning towards '*atoosh*!' Thus it is the warrior, the arbitrator and orator who make important decisions as opposed to the *wadaad*, the *aw*[22] and the sheikh. Traditionally, the latter's influence rested solely on pious example rather than on any authority attached to their office. Thus Richard Burton might not have been wide of the mark when he observed:

> Like the half-crazy fakihs of the northern Sahara, the Somali widad [sic], or priest, is unfitted for the affairs of this world, and the hafiz or Koran-reciter, is almost idiotic.[23]

But that was in 1854 and a radically different situation seems to have prevailed in 1890. During the latter period, not only were *wadaads* 'fitted for the affairs of this world', they had become deeply involved in them. In fact, the years between 1880 and 1920 can be described as the era of the sheikhs in Somali history. The period produced such influential personages as 'Abd ar-Raḥman az-Zeyli'i, Maḥammad Guuleed Rashiid, Sheikh 'Ali Nairobi,[24] Uways Maḥammad, Sheikh Maḥammad ad-Dandarawi, Sheikh Madar of Hargeisa and Maḥmmad 'Abdille Ḥasan. These were men of religion, whose fame and influence rested primarily on religious prestige. They acted as heads of religious brotherhoods and their involvement in secular affairs ranged from indirect influence over clan leaders like Dandarawi and Zeyli'i in the Ogaadeen to acquisition of actual political power like Maḥammad 'Abdille Ḥasan.

In a sense, the emergence of organized Sufism allowed these religious men to exercise autocratic powers unknown to secular men in the fragmented politics of clan organization. The organization of brotherhoods, unlike that of clans, is strictly hierarchical. The authority of the founding sheikh or his representative over the members of the brotherhood is absolute. The members, called 'ikhwan' ('brothers'), are bound to their spiritual director by a mystical blessing (*baraka*) emanating from the prophet. The leading sheikh or sayyid is, moreover, in possession of the apostolic chain (*silsila*) and the commission (*ijaza*) to propagate the tenets of the order. These two qualifications link him up with all the recognized saints of the order and ultimately to God through the prophet. The relationship between sheikh and disciple is one of complete dependence. In the eyes of his followers, a sheikh has the mandate to bind and free on earth.

Several rituals are used to reinforce the dependence of the members on the head. One is the ritual of *dhikr* (also pronounced *zikr*). This term as applied to congregational worship means the 'frequent mention of God' and refers to a regular worship experience in which the participants chant hymns together, repeating stock phrases in a crescendo fashion to the accompaniment of rhythmic body movement. At the highest stage of *dhikr*, a form of ecstatic delirium is produced in the worshippers. B. G. Martin, citing the psychological study of W. S. Haas, observed:

> Hyperventilation, or states of consciousness approaching the threshold of hyperventilation, could be induced by these collective rites. Under these circumstances, the carbon dioxide – oxygen balance in the brain is altered, creating a greater susceptibility to visions or hallucinations.[25]

In a regular Uwaysiya (East African Qaadiriya) *dhikr* a basic formula links up Uways with God in the following manner:

> There is no God but God
> Maḥammad is his apostle
> Sheikh 'Abd al-Qādir is our Succor
> And Uways is the saint of God.[26]

The first and foremost period of indoctrination is the period of joining. Although membership in these associations is voluntary, admission into their fellowship requires rigorous preparation, a period ranging in time from one to ten years to master the esoteric content of their liturgy. During this period, the initiate goes through a series of graduated merit stages from a simple seeker (*murid*) to a full successor (*khalif*) with authorization to preach and to make other *khalīfs*. As with any other rite of passage, the initiate is subjected to psychic manipulation, as his sheikh gradually reveals to him the secret teachings of the order. There is ample opportunity for indoctrination in the process of khalīfization. Loyalty to the sheikh and commitment to the brothers are obvious criteria of an initiate's progress.

The arduous rite of initiation underpinned by the common experience of the *dhikr* produces emotional interdependence between brothers and

A *Dhikr* circle: members of the Qaadiriya Order in southern Somalia.

spiritual head. Owing to the allegiance of his disciples, a sheikh enjoys far greater powers over his followers than a clan elder does over members of the lineage who have no binding allegiance to their nominal sultans. Moreover, membership in a brotherhood transcends, and ideally overrides, kinship ties, giving the Tariiqa possibilities for effective centralized organization which do not exist in the segmental politics of the clan. This is not to imply that the birth of a brotherhood necessarily means the birth of a political movement. There is nothing inherently political about Sufi brotherhoods, oriented as they are to the pursuit of spiritual ends. Yet to the extent that a brotherhood possesses a centralizing tendency, cutting across several tribes and bringing various groups into the fellowship of one body, it represents a radical departure from the decentralizing tendencies of the clan. The large-scale organization which it makes possible can be used as a vehicle for a political movement. In converting the Saaliḥiya brotherhood into a resistance movement, Sayyid Maḥammad skillfully seized upon this organization potential.

2 THE MAKING OF AN AFRICAN RESISTER: SAYYID MAḤAMMAD ʻABDILLE ḤASAN

In assessing his career, Somali chroniclers are inclined to emphasize three things which Sayyid Maḥammad shared with the Prophet: name, age and the propensity to wage *jihād*.[27] Naturally, this assessment, though more or less correct, reflects the benefit of hindsight. There was nothing about Sayyid Maḥammad's parentage, childhood or early life that would be a guide to his career in later life. His nearest claim to distinction in his early life may have been his descent from a long line of roving holy men. The first of these, on whom we have only fragmentary data, is his great-grandfather, Sheikh 'Ismaan of Barḍeere, who seems to have begun the family's tradition of peripatetic education. Leaving his homeland slightly north of Qallaafo along the Shabeelle River valley in what is now the Ogaadeen, he migrated southwards in the early 1800s and eventually settled with the religious community at Barḍeere along the Juba River. Here he developed a reputation as a pious man of great blessing and his tomb in that community is an object of veneration to this day.

From the great-grandfather to Sayyid Maḥammad, the family kept the tradition of wandering in search of religious education. In 1825 the Sayyid's grandfather left his 'home, relatives and possessions', heading north towards the pastoral Ḍulbahante in northeastern Somalia. Among the Ḍulbahante, Ḥasan Nuur set up religious centers and 'devoted himself to the worship of God, away from the affairs of this life'. Yet he was near enough to the 'affairs of this life' to father twelve sons and eleven daughters.[28] The eldest of these was the Sayyid's father, 'Abdille, who was born at 'Usuura, a settlement of *wadaads*, a dozen miles north of Laas 'Aanood in Ḍulbahante country in 1836. 'Abdille followed his father's footsteps and dedicated his life to a religious career, eventually earning the title of 'sheikh'. Yet he too married several Ḍulbahante women from whom he had nearly thirty children.

The eldest son of Sheikh 'Abdille, Sayyid Maḥammad was born in 1856 at the valley of Sa' Madeeq, seven miles north of Buuhoodle water-holes in the northeastern section of what was to become the British Somaliland Protectorate.[29] His mother, Timiro Seed, belonged to the 'Ali Geri sublineage of the Ḍulbahante clan.[30] Maternally descended from the numerically superior Ḍulbahante and paternally from the warrior Ogaadeen, the Sayyid could boast of a well-placed ancestral background, for the combination of these two powerful Daarood clans gave him superior kinship ties which, with some sleight of hand, he could employ to good advantage in his subsequent efforts to present a united Somali front against Euro-Abyssinian invaders. How skillful he proved at this will be assessed in a later chapter. For the moment, it would be worthwhile to make a few observations about the Ḍulbahante, for it was this clan who formed the core of the Sayyid's following and whose strengths and weaknesses Dervishism as a movement could be said to have reflected.

The Ḍulbahante represent the best and worst in Somali pastoralism. With their great herds and haughty, aristocratic demeanor, the Ḍulbahante arouse the envy of their Somali neighbors. They are bounded by the Majeerteen in the east, the Isaaq and Warsangali in the northeast and the Ogaadeen Daarood and Habar Yoonis Isaaq in the west (see map, p. 11). The surrounding clans with whom they engaged in regular bouts of warfare until well into the 1950s shield them off effectively from external influences. Of their neighbors, they interact most with the Habar Tol Ja'alo Isaaq with whom they conduct feuds and exchange wives.

The country of the Ḍulbahante is the prize of pastoral habitat: well-watered and well-pastured, the Nugaal valley provides a welcome sanctuary from the perennial twin scourges of Somali pastoralism, thirst and starvation. In common with other pastoralists, the Ḍulbahante are good herdsmen and warriors. Along with their flocks of sheep and goats, they raise camels and depend on these generous beasts almost entirely for their sustenance. But unlike other pastoralists, the Ḍulbahante are also excellent horsemen. The comparative plenitude of the Nugaal allows the horse to prosper along with the camel, and the Ḍulbahante possessed great herds of both in the nineteenth century. In the best of times, a well-to-do household might boast a hundred beasts of each. If the camel is a sustenance animal, the horse is a war animal, and the one is essential to raid, or defend the other against raiding. Thus camel husbandry and horsemanship form the ideal career of Ḍulbahante men. This was significant for the success of the Dervish movement, since the bulk of the Dervish cavalry was to come from the ranks of the Ḍulbahante.

Until well into the mid-1950s, the Ḍulbahante were untouched by Westernization and seemed to the British 'wild savages', who lived by the law of the jungle. Even by pastoral standards, the Ḍulbahante have a reputation for pride, independence and martial spirit. Freed from the threat of thirst and starvation by a relatively generous environment, and unrestricted by religious scruple, they devote their energies to giving free rein to their passions. One passion they indulged in regularly in the late nineteenth century was inter-clan feuding. According to local tradition, the warring factions, during the worst period of Ḍulbahante civil wars, were accustomed to constructing an impassable fence around the combatants. The idea was to reduce the chances of anyone escaping alive.

Sayyid Maḥammad's early life and experience were shaped among these unique pastoralists. It was an environment in which men had enough to eat and drink, saw themselves as sole masters of their destiny and took fierce pride in their way of life, largely because they had nothing to compare it with. But it was also an unstable, insecure environment in which a man's life might be lost as easily to a wild beast as to a flying spear of clannish vendetta. The idol and hero of Sayyid Maḥammad's adolescence was his maternal grandfather, Seed Magan, a fierce warrior chieftain who played a prominent role in the 'Ali Geri strife of the 1880s, when the Suubaan and Ḥirsi branches of this lineage had one of their customary bouts.

Yet Sayyid Maḥammad's youthful impression did not consist solely of tribal violence and shapeless vendetta. Religion also had an impact on his early making. At eight years, he was committed to the care of an Ogaadeen sheikh who taught him the Qur'an and rudimentaries of the Sharī'a. At eleven, he learned the Qur'an by heart ('hafiz al-Qur'an') and was promoted into the monitorial position of his class. His classmates teased him as a 'sharp mouth' (*afraḥ*) and the epithet may betoken something of the boy's sharp wit and keen intelligence. According to one student of the Dervishes, the young Maḥammad 'showed in himself qualities of leadership . . . he was inclined to leading children in play. He would also aspire to horsemanship. His father noticed these precocious qualities and advised patience and modesty in him.'[31] The Sayyid would have done well to heed his father's advice: impatience and the absence of modesty caused him to lose the day on more than one occasion.

In the following years Maḥammad 'Abdille continued his religious education but, like most boys of his age, he also doubled as a camel-herder. In 1875 his grandfather died, and the event is said to have shaken the young man. After a two-year stint as a Qur'anic teacher of no noteworthy distinction, he returned to the ways of his forebears: to peripatetic learning which took up the next ten years of his life. He traveled widely in search of religious knowledge, visiting such seats of Islamic learning as Mogadishu and Harar. The young seeker apparently suffered severe deprivations in Harar, for the name of that city would rankle with him as a 'God-forsaken-place that would not extend succor to a needy Mussulman'.[32] According to local accounts, he also visited Kenya and Sudan.[33] In Port Sudan, he purportedly met with 'Uthman Diqna, the former Mahdist general whose remarkable operations in eastern Sudan during the Mahdist revolt won him the grudging respect of his British foes. If such a meeting did occur between the two men, the Sayyid might have been inspired by the Sudanese example into notions of his own *jihād* in Somalia.

Maḥammad 'Abdille returned home in 1891 and married an Ogaadeen woman. By local standards at this time, he was well-traveled, well-educated and well-informed about events in the Muslim world. The method of studying he adopted is well illustrated by his Egyptian biographer, 'Abd as-Sabur Marzuq:

> The Sayyid spent nearly ten years of his life travelling in all regions of Somali country. He would not hear of a sheikh in the country who specialized in any field of knowledge, except he would go to study with him. He sat under him as a student and seeker until he absorbed all he had to offer, then he would go to another. In this way, he acquired all that the Somali and Arab sheikhs could give him and the number of these teachers reached seventy-two sheikhs.[34]

In 1894 Maḥammad 'Abdille embarked on another journey, this time towards Mecca to discharge his *Ḥaj* obligations. With him went thirteen fellow pilgrims, most of whom came from his maternal kin, the Ḍulbahante.[35] Two, Adam and Maḥammad Seed, were his uncles. During their one-and-a-half years in Mecca, the pilgrims fell under the influence of Maḥammed Saliḥ, the charismatic mystic and reformer whose new order, the Saaliḥiya, was at this time popular in Arabia and was spreading across the Red Sea into East Africa. The circumstances leading to Sayyid Maḥammad's 'ordination'[36] as Saaliḥiya *khalīf* in Somalia are unclear. According to one version, the Meccan commissioned the Somali on the advice and urging of his Somali companions.[37] Maḥammad 'Abdille, now *al-Ḥāj*, must have seen his new position as Saaliḥiya's sheikh in Somalia as a fulfillment and a vindication of his many years of spiritual seeking.

But if the appointment was a vindication of a life-long service, it was also a toilsome post, entailing physical and psychic hardship. Under Maḥammad Saliḥ, Sayyid Maḥammad underwent a grueling period of initiatory training including an incarceration of sixty days in which he was kept virtually incommunicado. With his elder, he was obliged to spend the time praying, meditating and mastering the esoteric teachings of the order. One informant describes the character of this training in the following words:

> The thirteen sheikhs suggested to Maḥammad Saliḥ the need to commission a Somali in place of the Arab who represented the Saaliḥiya in Somalia. They pleaded with him that in order to make a forceful propagation for the Tariiqa it was necessary to appoint as its head a Somali with the commission to preach. Maḥammad Saliḥ at first did not acquiesce to their entreaty but merely said, 'In shā Allah, goodness shall befall us.' Maḥammad Saliḥ then

> asked the Sayyid to remain with him until Allah had given him direction as to the course of action. Thus the two remained together for many days. Maḥammad Saliḥ took away all the *kutub* (meditative books) from the Sayyid, removed him to a quiet mosque where the Sheikh and Sayyid performed a strict *tassawuf* (mystic rite of various exercises, meditations and pious devotions designed to bring the faithful into perfection and communion with the Deity). The Sayyid was transformed during this period: he was transformed by the spirit of Allah, made to see visions of the prophet and angels. When it was all over, he was a changed man . . . the spirit which went into his head never really left him for the rest of his life.[38]

The Sayyid came out of it 'shaken and overawed' and the experience perhaps accounts for the reputation of the 'mad holy man' he was to acquire for the rest of his life.

There is an account, in my view more apocryphal than true, that the Sayyid and his thirteen companions bound themselves by a secret vow at the foot of the Prophet's tomb to wage holy war on the four nations that had recently divided up their land.[39] Mecca was then as now the hub of the Muslim world. Bringing together literally hundreds of thousands of the Muslim faithful each year, it served as a great meeting house of pan-Islamic leaders and ideas. The Sayyid's new master, Maḥammad Saliḥ, was a Sudanese from Dongola on the Nile, and as the Mahdist war had been concluded a few years earlier, the Sayyid could not have been ignorant of this episode in the Sudan. Be that as it may, there is no reliable evidence that the Sayyid had developed any ideas of *jihād* during his stay in Mecca.

In 1895 the Sayyid returned to Berbera in the 'power of the spirit'. On the way he stopped for some months in Aden, where he is alleged to have had a minor skirmish with an impudent British naval officer.[40] Once in Berbera, the Sayyid became embroiled in a disastrous theological controversy with the religious notables of the city, who belonged to the rival Qaadiriya brotherhood, and in doing so, threw the city into a considerable commotion. Naturally, this earned him the suspicion and hostility of an administration which had just then put plans under way to impose a tenuous pax Britannica on the coast.

For a better understanding of the Sayyid's lack of progress in Berbera, it would be worthwhile to take a brief look at the history of this ancient port since it came under the British in 1884. Berbera served as the principal outlet for trade from northern Somaliland and to a lesser extent from Harar. The decline of Zeyla' both in trade and Islamic learning, owing to competition from Djibouti, the new French Somaliland port, placed

Berbera in a strategic position as the chief entrepôt of northern Somaliland. Yet the city did not gain any appreciable material advantage from its favorable position. This was due mainly to official British neglect of their Somaliland protectorate. To judge by their actions, colonial officials regarded Somaliland as an outpost of the Indian Empire, and had no ambition for Berbera other than for it to be 'Aden's butcher shop'. However, India's singularly lackadaisical attitude to her Somaliland possession was jolted into a rude awakening by the dramatic victory of the Abyssinians at Adowa. The triumph of Menelik II over Italy made Ethiopia the dominant power in the region, and Menelik let it be known to his fellow imperialists that he intended to have a piece of the Somaliland action. He underlined his intentions by allowing Ras Makonnen, the governor of his recent conquest in Hararge province, to send armed bands into the Ogaadeen. These bands, employing plunder and political occupation at the same time, began to cause havoc in an area supposedly well within the British sphere. Menelik's pressure tactics produced the desired effect for they forced Britain to surrender to Ethiopia 'the most fertile grain producing regions in the west of the British Protectorate and important spring and autumn pastures in the south'.[41]

Yet the act of appeasement did not fully satisfy Menelik; the Ethiopian armed columns continued to forage into the truncated British possession and Ras Makonnen continued to talk tough. The dilemma for British officials was, therefore, what to do with what was left of their possession in Somaliland. So long as it was unoccupied, it remained vulnerable to the designs of the victorious Ethiopians. Was it worth spending money on or coming to a confrontation with Menelik? Yet if completely abandoned, would Aden survive the loss of its sole meat supply?

It was this climate of emergency that prompted the appointment of Colonel J. Hayes Sadler as British Consul-General in Somaliland. The aristocratic former consul at Muscat, who was later to be ridiculed as 'Flannel Hat' by the white settlers of Kenya, seemed 'too senior' for Somaliland, but the sensitive nature of events there demanded 'the appointment of a safe officer'.[42] Sadler was responsible to the Foreign Office which, in 1898, took over Somaliland administration from a grateful India Office. His principal tasks were (a) to make Somaliland pay for the cost of its occupation, (b) to effect a semblance of British presence in the principal regions of the protectorate and (c) in doing so, to avoid 'at all costs' coming to a clash with Makonnen.

The energetic Sadler proved more than equal to his arduous duties. As he was determined that his ward should come out of the Indian closet, he expanded and Somalized the administration. He relieved the costly Indian garrison and replaced it with newly recruited *ilaalo* (constabularies) and a small contingent of military police. At a cost less than that of the Indian garrison, he managed to police the caravan routes to a depth of a hundred miles as far as Hargeisa and Sheikh. So as to exercise some control over inland clans, he expanded the system of appointing *'aaqils* (paid elders) who were held responsible for the conduct of their kin inland. The consul also cultivated excellent rapport with the local *'ulema*, such as Sheikh Madar of Hargeisa and Aw Gaas, the chief Islamic magistrate. To finance his reform projects, Sadler imposed a tax for the first time on 'the most valuable export' of the protectorate: livestock destined for Aden. Since Aden no longer 'bore financial responsibility' for the Somali coast, there was no reason for her to receive her meat supply 'duty-free'.[43]

Sadler's efforts produced a healthy economy and a well-run administration. With 1,000 cattle and 80,000 sheep and goats leaving for Aden annually, the volume of trade reached a record number in 1899–1900. After fifteen years of official neglect, it looked as if Somaliland was at long last entering a new era, an era of economic prosperity and orderly administration. Unhappily for the Somalis, the bold initiatives of the consul coincided with the appearance of Sayyid Maḥammad 'Abdille Ḥasan.

The Berbera to which the Sayyid returned was not suitable ground for evangelization. The economy was booming and the religious arts flourishing under the Qaadiriya banner and the majority of those who counted had too much invested in the status quo to be anxious for its disruption. Thus, the proselytizing efforts of the Sayyid either fell on deaf ears or generated a storm of religious controversy in Berbera. Never adept in the art of diplomacy, the Sayyid made loud and virulent attacks on ancient Qaadiriya practices such as the cult of saints and charged Qaadiriya notables with 'moral laxity'. The ascetic Sayyid also inveighed against the 'luxury of the age', singling out for special blame the chewing of *qaat*[44] and the gorging of the fat of sheep's tail. Both these delicacies were regularly indulged in by the Qaadiriya inhabitants of Berbera. More outrageous in the eyes of the Qaadiriya faithful, it would seem, was the Sayyid's claim that his master, Maḥammad Saliḥ, was the 'pre-eminent saint' (Qurb al-Zaman) of the age, with the implication that Qaadiriya adherents should abandon their outmoded sect in favor of the new Saaliḥiya brotherhood.

Persons of Qaadiriya persuasion had no desire to follow Sayyid Maḥammad's puritanical order or to heed his uncompromising message. The *'ulema* whom he confronted included the pious Sheikh Madar, the erudite Aw Gaas Maḥammad and the Sayyid's former teacher, 'Abdillaahi 'Aruusi. They must have resented him as an upstart seeking to usurp their place of religious pre-eminence, and the Sayyid's attack on these prominent men could scarcely delight the town's inhabitants, who had high regard for them. In time, the Qaadiriya elders struck back. Commenting on Sayyid Maḥammad's lack of success in his evangelizing efforts, 'Abdillaahi 'Aruusi recorded, with a measure of relief and perhaps some malice, his astonishment at the 'strength of the town's foundations which had prevented Berbera from being turned upside down'.[45] Sheikh Madar warned the Sayyid that in his enthusiasm for Maḥammad Saliḥ, he might be in danger of transgressing the 'way of Islam'. But it was Aw Gaas Maḥammad who may have done the Sayyid the worst damage by calling the dispute to the attention of the administration. He is alleged to have warned the vice-consul (Captain H. E. S. Cordeaux) bluntly: 'This Mullah is brewing up something. If you do not arrest him here and now, some day you will go far, very far, to get him.'[46]

The vice-consul did not arrest the 'Mullah' there and then and, though on hindsight he might have regretted not heeding Aw Gaas's advice, he had no reason at the time to think of the Sayyid as an enemy of the administration. 'So far as the government was concerned,' wrote the administration's chief secretary, 'there was nothing in his teaching at Berbera to which exception could be taken.'[47] The vice-consul thus, not unreasonably, viewed the matter as a religious squabble in which government had no business to meddle. Yet as the religious rift widened, the vice-consul was persuaded, either by his Qaadiriya advisors or on his own appreciation of the situation, to 'close down' the Saaliḥiya's mosque in Berbera. This was the first official act by the government against the cause of the Sayyid and, even so, he might have seen in it the malignant hand of his old *bête noire*, the Qaadiriya detractors.

Tired of preaching to 'bored and unsympathetic audiences'[48] in Berbera, the Sayyid retired into the interior in 1897 to start afresh among his maternal Ḍulbahante kinsmen. On the way he passed by the French Catholic Mission at Daymoole, a few miles inland on the road to Sheikh. The Catholic Mission was established in the Protectorate in 1891 and, with a skeleton staff of three fathers and three sisters, catered to Somali orphans whom they hoped to Christianize. According to local tradition, the Sayyid came upon a party of these orphans who responded to the Sayyid's query of their clan affiliation – the typical Somali query to reveal someone's identity – that they 'belonged to the clan of the fathers'.[49] This encounter is alleged to have enraged the Sayyid, confirming in his mind that Christian overlordship in his country was tantamount to destruction of his people's faith.

Back in the countryside, the Sayyid's fortunes changed for the better. He made his first headquarters at Qoryawayne, a watering place some twenty-nine miles north of ʻAynaba wells. It was here that he adopted the name 'Dervish' for his followers and embarked on his periodic sallies among the pastoral Somalis, preaching religious reform under the Saaliḥiya banner. Unaffected by the new order in Berbera, the pastoral clans proved more attuned to the Sayyid's puritanical message. His influence grew rapidly and in less than two years he brought the Ḍulbahante, the majority of the Habar Tol Jaʻalo and the eastern Habar Yoonis under his sway. Initially, the British found him exercising 'his influence for good'. He settled tribal disputes, prevented the clans from raiding one another and was thought by British officials to be on the 'side of law and order'.[50] The Sayyid was in 'constant communication' with the vice-consul's office and on occasion sent down to Berbera Somali prisoners 'guilty of criminal offences in the interior'.

The apparent amity and good will between the Sayyid and the British came to an abrupt end, ostensibly on account of a stolen gun. On 29 March 1899, the vice-consul sent a peremptory letter requesting the 'immediate return' of a rifle stolen by one Duʻale Ḥirsi, believed to be in the Sayyid's camp. The Sayyid responded just as peremptorily: 'There is no god but God, and Maḥammad is his apostle. Man, nothing have I stolen from you or from anyone else. Seek your wishes from him who has defrauded you and serve him whom thou wilt. This and salaams.'[51] The curt exchange was in fact but a symptom of events which were beginning to set the Sayyid on a collision course with the administration. For the sake of clarity, a slight digression is in order to set these events in perspective. When Consul Sadler returned from Aden in April, he learned of 'conflicting reports current in Berbera concerning the doings of a Mullah . . . who . . . was collecting arms and men with a view to establishing his authority in the southeastern portion of the Protectorate.[52] The Mullah's 'ultimate aim,' concluded the consul, 'was to head a religious expedition against Abyssinia'.

Sadler's assessment contained an important element of truth, an element quite significant to a proper appreciation of the Sayyid's motives but one which has been hitherto overlooked by historians of the Somali Dervishes. This is that the Dervish movement appears to have been originally directed against the Ethiopians rather than the British. And it is one of the curiosities of the history of the British in northern Somalia that they had to bear the brunt of a war that was not meant for them in the first place.

In examining the Somali Dervish struggle, those familiar with European occupation and African reaction will find here none of the catalog of grievances often associated with African resistance and rebellion. The Somalis had nothing in their experience with the British to provoke them into a violent revolt. They do not seem to have suffered under British authorities any grueling physical or psychological trauma – not at least any of the trauma associated with the rising of other eastern and southern African peoples like the Kikuyu, the Shona and the Ndebele, whose resistance to European intrusion was on a scale similar to that of the Somali Dervishes. The Somalis lost no lands to Europeans, were subjected to no forced labor and suffered no disruptive European presence in their midst. At the time of the Somali rising, British presence in Somalia was limited to three forlorn ports on the coast – Berbera, Bulaḥaar and Zeyla' – staffed by a handful of Europeans who had come to the coast at the invitation of the Somalis. They were called upon by Somali elders, religious notables and traders to arbitrate in clan disputes and to keep the peace. What influence these Europeans exerted hardly went beyond the coastal strip. In the interior, where the majority of the Somalis lived, life continued as it had before with its cycle of camel husbandry and hereditary feuds.

The case was of course different with respect to Ethiopian encroachment on western Somalia. Here, there appear to have been genuine Somali grievances. Not that the Ethiopians sought to create particular hardships for the Somalis; nor that Ethiopian colonization was less enlightened or benevolent than the Europeans', as the latter had sanctimoniously claimed. The key difference between European and Ethiopian methods of colonization seems to have hinged on the difference between their technical and economic resources. Unlike the Europeans, the Ethiopians possessed no industrial home base nor a vast accumulation of international monopoly capital to finance their colonial enterprises. While officials of the three European powers on the Somali coast were often bedeviled by lack of sufficient funds, they nevertheless managed, with the help of their international resources, to set up the rudimentary apparatus of administration. Once this was done, they could levy taxes to obtain the necessary funds to administer the colony or protectorate. Furthermore, the European efforts were facilitated by their possession of the ports – and by implication, their monopoly hold on trade – where the assembling of goods in a single spot made taxation a relatively simple task.

The Ethiopians, by contrast, did not have international capital to dip into in extending their influence to the Ogaadeen. Theirs was a subsistence economy and this meant the army of conquest had to live off the land. In the words of a noted Ethiopianist:

> One reason for Menelik's southern conquests was his need to open up fresh lands on which to quarter his growing armies of hungry men

> who were pressing hardly upon the resources of Shoa. During some of these lean periods in the [eighteen-] nineties, Menelik found the cattle seized from the Galla and Somali herds a very valuable asset for his soldiers and people. It is interesting, too, to read that after the Emperor John had despoiled Gojjam so that its *Negus*, Takla Haimanot, could no longer support his own army there, Menelik proposed to him that he should invade Kaffa in order to provide for his soldiers.[53]

To chance upon the path of a traditional military expedition by the Ethiopians was apparently a rugged experience for the civilian population. Oromo and Somali informants recall with particular vividness the 'trail of devastation' which Menelik's robber bands left in their wake in 'Aruusa and the Ogaadeen.[54] Margery Perham echoes indigenous assessment of the harshness involved in the establishment of Ethiopian rule. She observes:

> By the sanction of custom, soldiers on the march ruthlessly took all that they could from the inhabitants in order to save their own supplies. Many European travellers, from the earliest to the latest days, have remarked upon the arrogant and extortionate behaviour of the soldiers. Cattle, mules and donkeys trampled down and ate the crops ... But woe betide those same soldiers if they returned defeated! For then the people whom they had despoiled would turn on them and take their revenge for the injuries they had suffered. It might almost be said that every large-scale campaign in Ethiopia had some of the features of a civil war.[55]

Beyond the traditional sanctions of the army living off the land, Menelik's hordes under Ras Makonnen seem to have had even more pressing reasons to turn their gaze on the 'vast herds' of the Ogaadeen. As a result of the cataclysmic wars in the last two decades of the nineteenth century, the Ethiopian highlands were scourged by a devastating famine in the 1890s.[56] Evidence from the works of Ethiopian specialists Richard Pankhurst and Harold Marcus as well as British diplomats of the day, would seem to emphasize the importance of this famine as a primary impetus to Menelik's move into the Ogaadeen.[57] At a guess based on indigenous evidence, Ras Makonnen exacted in tribute or seized in raid, between 1890 and 1897, 100,000 head of cattle, 200,000 head of camels and about 600,000 sheep and goats from the Ogaadeen Somalis.[58] The Ethiopians appear to have had little use for the camels (whose meat and milk they did not consume) other than to employ them as a bargain with the Somalis who were required to redeem their camels with the payment of cattle and flocks. What the Somalis could not redeem, the

Amharas gave to their Muslim Oromo followers as a reward for their services. The sedentary clans of the Daarood Geri and Bartire on the plains of Jigjiga and the so-called Reer Baare on the lower Shabeelle basin suffered particular deprivations at the hands of the famine-driven Ethiopians. They were periodically infested, their villages burned and their crops pillaged. 'The Ethiopians did not seem to come to the Ogaadeen to govern,'[59] says a western Somali elder from Jigjiga, 'they came to take away livestock.' But the Ethiopians did intend to govern the Ogaadeen, as their unrelenting push eastwards from 1893 onwards was to prove.

Yet the story of Ethiopian–Somali contact in the 1890s was by no means one of steady Ethiopian gains and Somali losses. For one thing, the Bartire and 'Iise Somalis played off the Ethiopians against the Europeans, often to good advantage. In 1891 the 'Iise Somalis allegedly told Capt. Swayne:

> We ask you now to rid us of these Ethiopian intruders. They wish to treat us as they treated the Geri [another Somali clan], to seize our flocks, kill our people and burn our *karias* [villages]. They wish to settle in our country and oust us. We will not have it.[60]

Yet to judge from the intense interaction between the Ethiopians and 'Iises, the Somalis may not have been so hostile to the Ethiopians as Swayne was led to believe. The 'Iises regularly purchased grain at Jigjiga, Ras Makonnen's stronghold, and they may indeed have encouraged him to send his troops to the British zone of influence. The Ethiopian governor, in any event, despatched a small force to Biyo Kaboba, a cluster of wells near the caravan route on the British side of the ill-defined border, and the move precipitated a near-collision between the Ethiopians and the fledgling British administration on the Somali coast.

If the establishment of Ethiopian rule was effected with relative ease in the well-watered northwestern end of the Ogaadeen by the turn of the century, the south-central regions (roughly 80 percent of the Ogaadeen land mass) were another story. Here, the pastoral clans, assisted by vast stretches of impenetrable scrubland, held their own against Abyssinian advances. Except for periodic raids – some of which indeed went in favor of the Somalis – the pastoral clans remained largely autonomous until well into the forties. Douglas Jardine, writing on the British operations against the Somali Dervish leader in 1920, described the Ogaadeen as an 'accursed ... no-man's land populated by fanatical tribes ... the Abyssinians, fearing alike the fevers of the lowland climate and the martial qualities of the tribes, have always steadfastly declined to administer in this zone despite the most urgent representations of our Government.'[61]

To judge from the fierce resistance suffered there by imperial intruders, the Ogaadeen was indeed 'somebody's land'. 'The desert is our birthright,' says an Ogaadeen elder, 'and we have always made the empire-builders' task a bit more difficult for them.'[62]

Although the Ethiopians failed to maintain an adequate grip on the majority of the Ogaadeen Somalis, they nevertheless made their presence felt, keeping up the pressure on the clans through periodic seizures of livestock and the harrying of villages. Thus where the Europeans did not impinge much on Somali life except for a small coastal strip, the Ethiopian presence in the heart of Somali rangelands did constitute a disquieting intrusion. Robert Hess makes a judicious point when he observes that the Ethiopian presence in western Somalia led many Ogaadeen Somalis to join Sayyid Maḥammad's Saaliḥiya order.[63] His view is confirmed by indigenous sources. An 86-year-old Dervish elder related the Sayyid's first message to his inland countrymen in these terms:

> In the name of God the Beneficent, the Merciful. My brothers, I come to you in the name of God who is strong, all-wise and everlasting. It is He who is with me and guides my steps. Infidel invaders have come to surround us. They have come to corrupt our ancient religion, to settle our land, to seize our herds, to burn our *qaryas* [villages], and make our children their children. The End Times are at hand. For what could this general corruption of the earth signify other than to warn us of the approach of the Last Days? The signs are here for him who would be instructed: the Muslim chafes under the tyranny of the unbeliever. Are there any among the Ogaadeen who have not felt the scourge of the Amḥaar [Somali, for Amhara]? Any who have not been despoiled by their odious raids? Not too long ago you heard how the Amḥaar fell on the Reer Amaadin [clan name] and carried off many of their camels in loot. If you follow me, with the help of God, I will deliver you from the Amḥaar.[64]

Insofar as the British came under the category of 'infidels,' the Sayyid's remarks could be construed as anti-British. Clearly though, the gist of his message has an unmistakable focus: 'I will deliver you from the Amḥaar.' It is interesting to note, too, that at this time the Sayyid addressed his audience as 'brothers', thereby presenting himself as one of them. This demonstrates his tact in soliciting the support of the egalitarian pastoralists who might not have responded to his message had they thought he was setting himself above them. When he grew strong in succeeding years, he was to change this strategy and require his followers to call him 'father' (Aabbe).

The reference to the Ethiopian raid on the Reer Amaadin helps to establish a chronological point. From independent sources we know Ras Makonnen made two major raids on the Reer Amaadin near Imay at the headwaters of the Shabeelle River. The one came in 1890 and ended in a complete fiasco for the Ethiopians.[65] The other took place in early 1899 and went well for the Ethiopians, who carried off a vast quantity of stock in booty.[66] As the Sayyid (who left Berbera for the interior in 1897) began in earnest to collect men and arms in 1899, he must have made his speech in that crucial year when his brotherhood had its headquarters in the southeastern edge of the Haud in Ḍulbahante and Ogaadeen territory.

If the Dervish movement was primarily directed at the Ethiopians, as reported by the British consul and corroborated by indigenous testimony, why did Sadler get entangled in what was essentially an Ethiopian problem? This is the question to which we must now turn.

A set of fortuitous circumstances seems to have intervened, forcing the Sayyid and the British Consul to clash with each other. The first hinged on a misunderstanding as to the status of the territory of the Ḍulbahante, the Sayyid's maternal kin. It was here that the Sayyid first gained the allegiance of the men and women who were to make him a 'power in the land to be reckoned with'. But in establishing his power in Ḍulbahante country, the Sayyid had no reason to believe he was infringing on British territory. British imperial title deeds to Somaliland rested on flimsy grounds. They had their origin in a 'handful of treaties with bought-off signatures'[67] which had been obtained from isolated coastal clans. With the Ḍulbahante, there was not even such a treaty. In the dozen years since northern Somalia was officially declared a British possession, colonial contact with the Ḍulbahante consisted of two visits, one in 1895 by a Capt. Welby and another in 1896–7 by Capt. Mereweather. On both occasions 'it was decided not to enter into engagements'[68] with the Ḍulbahante, and the consul was the first to acknowledge his ignorance of these inland people: 'We have no information,' he reported, 'as to the country and character of its inhabitants.'[69]

Under these circumstances, the Sayyid could hardly subscribe to Sadler's claiming the Ḍulbahante as 'an integral part of our protectorate' nor to his proclaiming the Sayyid a rebel when the latter established himself among his kin. Far from being a rebel, the Sayyid saw himself as the legitimate leader of a sovereign people, as he asserted in one of his letters to the vice-consul: 'We are a government. We have a sultan, an Amir and chiefs and subjects.'[70]

Left to themselves, Sadler and the Sayyid might have arrived at some sort of a *modus vivendi*. For a while the consul hoped the movement would 'subside of itself'. This was not happening, yet the Sayyid was not anxious to confront the British, whose power he had had ample opportunity to appreciate during his sojourn in Aden. Sadly for Somaliland, the two men fell victim to factious clan politics. As I have indicated elsewhere, clannish feuding was particularly rife during this period in northern Somalia, with more than twenty lineages at one another's throats.[71] It soon occurred to the antagonists that they could employ the powers of the Sayyid and the administration to good advantage against their enemies if only they could enlist these powers as allies. Sultan Nuur of the Habar Yoonis was a case in point. This wily chieftain used the authority of the Sayyid to oust his rival, Ḥirsi Madar, from the position of '*aaqil* of the clan and to press a backlog of blood money claims against the Ogaadeen which he hoped 'to recover through the influence of the Mullah'.[72] Even while ingratiating himself with the Sayyid, Sultan Nuur was conducting a clandestine raid against the Habar Tol Ja'alo Gaashaanbuur, who were allies of the Sayyid. Soon a situation developed in which the Sayyid and the administration became helpless pawns in the intrigues of warring factions and Sadler could only lament that the country was 'rife with old outstandings [and the clans] find this movement a convenient opportunity for ... releasing themselves from their obligations'.[73] He wrote of the 'bad and suspicious characters who use the Sayyid's name for their own purposes'. The Sayyid, for his part, denounced bitterly the 'liars and slanderers' who sought to misrepresent him. And indeed he was misrepresented on occasion, as, for example, when four caravan escorts sold their rifles to him at hefty profits and reported them in Berbera as 'seized by the Mullah'.[74]

In addition to pastoral guile, the Abyssinian question seems to have kindled the Sayyid's ire against the British. Upon learning of the intended Dervish expedition on the Ethiopians, the Protectorate administration instructed the British Resident in Addis Ababa to 'communicate to King Menelik the religious movement on the borders' of his empire 'which the Mullah ... is conducting'.[75] Menelik undertook 'to stifle the movement should the Mullah cross into Abyssinia'. On arrival in Harar, the British envoy reported satisfactorily that Dejasmatch Biratu, the acting governor, was detailed to deal with the movement. The governor had orders from Menelik to 'do nothing in the Ogaadeen'[76] without the British agent's advice. According to local tradition, the Sayyid was informed of the projected Anglo-Ethiopian cooperation at his expense through his co-religionists in Harar.[77] The Somalis, as we have seen, were at this time feeling the pressure of Ethiopian expansion and the prospect of a community of interests between 'our oppressors' and the British could scarcely endear the heart of the Sayyid to the administration. At least the Sayyid did not hide his resentment towards those who cooperated with the Ethiopians against him. His chief complaint in one of his poems against his own Ogaadeen kin was that they collaborated with Menelik to the detriment of Somali interests:

> They who've gone to the Amharas of Harar,
> Whose father–judge and ruler is Menelik,
> Who'd become servants and toadies of the Abyssinians.
> Let no one else revenge upon them for me,
> Like the prowling lion,
> One day I will jump upon the fence,
> I will descend upon them unawares.[78]

In another poem, he showers praises on his lieutenant, Ḥuseen Ḍiqle, because the latter stood fast for him, while Ḍiqle's relations are denounced as 'ignorant fools' because they 'fled in headlong panic to seek servile protection under the Ethiopian King'.[79]

But even more crucial to the events of 1899 was the paranoid attitude which seems to have permeated British officialdom about Muslim religious movements. They had just put down one such movement (the Mahdist revolt in the Sudan) at a horrendous cost in life and property. Sadler himself may indeed be regarded as the epitome of the prevailing British attitudes. A former career officer of the Indian navy, he brought to Somalia a colonial outlook that was shaped in India. According to Andrew Brockett, the Indian Government had to suppress in the 1890s a series of revolts among the Afridi clans of northwest India led by a horde of 'fanatical mullahs' including 'Sadulah Khan (the Mad Mullah), Ada Mullah, and Sayyid Akbar'.[80] Sadler campaigned against these mullahs, who aroused their adherents into *jihāds* against the British. Given this background, Sadler tended to view the term 'mullah' as a symbol of revolt and fanaticism. Yet the term in its original meaning was harmless enough. It was one of several terms imported from the Indian subcontinent which gained widespread currency in Somaliland in the 1890s.[81] It denotes a Turko-Persian rendition of the Arabic 'maula' meaning a Muslim scholar of theology and sacred law. The epithet 'mad' was first applied to the Sayyid by his Qaadiriya detractors and later given official status in colonial lexicography by Consul Sadler. In a character sketch of the Sayyid in chapter 5, I will take up the question of his alleged madness. I hope it will then become clear that what the Somalis meant in pinning the label on the Sayyid had no relation to what colonial officials assumed it meant. For the moment, I would only surmise that in view of his Indian experience Sadler found the temptation to see in Sayyid Maḥammad another 'fanatical mullah' irresistible.

In that fateful year, 1899, the Sayyid, prodded by the inexorable sweep of fortuitous circumstances, sent on 9 September his famous letter to the authorities in Berbera:

> This is to inform you, you have done whatever you have desired, and you have oppressed our ancient religion without cause . . . Now choose for yourselves. If you want war, we accept it, but if you want peace, pay the fine.[82]

Bad translation in the concluding phrase gave the letter a provocative edge which it is doubtful the Sayyid intended to convey. What came out as 'pay the fine', should have been rendered as something like 'pay the protective tax', and referred to the compensatory tax (*jizya*) in Muslim jurisprudence which a non-believer pays in return for the protection of his person and property accorded him by the Muslim community. As it stood, however, the letter sounded as if the Sayyid regarded British officials as criminal transgressors who should be paying fines for their offenses. Nonetheless, even with the modified version, the Sayyid seemed to imply that he was the sovereign of the land, and the British, protected sojourners. Such a claim, needless to say, would be hotly disputed by his Qaadiriya rivals.

Sadler responded by proclaiming the Sayyid a rebel and warned the 'Friendlies' against any dealings with him. The stage was set for a conflict of twenty years that was to plunge Somaliland into untold misery and was to cost, by a conservative estimate, the lives of one-third of the Protectorate's population.

The concern of the Sayyid with the religious health of his people seems to be central to his grievances against the British. The same concern dominated another letter which he wrote to the chief of the 'Iidagale Isaaq. 'Do you not see,' he complained in July 1899, 'that the infidels have destroyed our religion and made our children their children?'[83] Was the Sayyid goaded into rebellion by a genuine fear that Christian colonization was undermining the integrity of his nation's religion? Such is the impression one would gain from a speech attributed to him:

> Unbelievers have invaded you in your country, to corrupt you and to corrupt your religion, and to force you to believe their own religion, supported by their governments, their arms and their numbers. But your faith in God and in your dignity is sufficient arms. Do not, then, flee from their troops, nor from the greatness of their arms; God is stronger than they.[84]

The Sayyid's encounter with the Catholic Mission outside of Berbera, coupled with his letters and alleged speech, seems to show his central preoccupation with the fate of his country's religion under infidel rule.

It comes as no surprise therefore that some students of the Dervish movement should see in the Sayyid's behavior a sustained 'plan'[85] to rid his country of European Christian rule. Yet the events leading to the Dervish revolt which we have just sketched seem to cast some doubt on this view. The initial phase of the Dervish rising, as reflected by the activities of the Sayyid, seems to have been directed at the Ethiopians, whose colonization had a disrupting impact on the Somalis. In time, the Sayyid did come to see himself and, more important, was seen by others, as a champion of his country's political and religious freedom, defending it against all Christian invaders. Yet if actions speak louder than words, even in religious matters, he was more concerned with the fate of his Saaliḥiya sect than with that of religion *per se*. Although he threatened to drive the Christian infidels into the sea, his first military action, like many of his subsequent campaigns, was directed at his old enemies – in this case, the Aḥmadiya settlement at Sheikh.

Soon after his denunciatory epistle to the British administration, the Sayyid 'arrived suddenly at Bur'o' with a force of 1,500 men equipped with 200 modern rifles and delivered a swift raid on Sheikh, a settlement of *wadaads*, which he allowed his troops to burn and loot.[86] From there he moved westwards bringing the Habar Yoonis Isaaq under his temporary sway and making unsuccessful overtures to the 'Iidagale Isaaq. Rumors freely circulated of his plans to burn Berbera, and the town reacted with panic, the well-to-do merchants hastily evacuating it. He sent his emissaries all over the country and stories reached the coast of all within reach being forced to join his sect. But a great many responded to his message with enthusiasm and it appeared at the end of 1899 that the Sayyid was mustering sufficient forces to make good his threat of driving the infidels into the sea. Then in a moment of blind rage, the Poor Man of God committed the first of his rash acts that was to have serious repercussions for the progress of his cause.

3 THE FLIGHT TO THE OGAADEEN

The nominal sultan (Garaad) of the Ḍulbahante, 'Ali Maḥamuud, had for some time watched with growing unease the expanding power of the Sayyid within the Ḍulbahante. He had baulked at the leadership of the Sayyid, whom he regarded as having surrendered religious duties for political gains at the expense of the Garaad. Initially, the Sayyid sought to allay the Garaad's fears, and for a while the two men made a show of uneasy unity. But at the end of 1899, they clashed over Garaad 'Ali's refusal to go along with the Sayyid on an expedition into Isaaq country. While the Sayyid was away on his Isaaq campaigns, the Garaad allegedly wrote to the British administration, reaffirming his allegiance to the government but complaining of the 'evil influence of this Mullah' which undermined his authority with the clan. The Garaad's overtures to the infidels enraged the Sayyid and he rashly ordered his assassination, which was at once carried out.

The Garaad's murder proved to be a disastrous miscalculation, for it nearly precipitated a civil war within the nascent community. Garaad 'Ali's immediate clan, the Bah-Ararsame, demanded the Sayyid's head in revenge for their fallen leader. The Maḥamuud Garaad, the most numerous of the three Ḍulbahante primary lineages, left the Dervishes in a body, as did other Daarood clans who had been scandalized by the Garaad's murder. Only his immediate maternal kin, the 'Ali Geri, stood fast with the Sayyid. Faced with widespread defection and the threat of Bah-Ararsame revenge, the Sayyid took a precipitous flight to the Ogaadeen, the home of his paternal kin.

The Ogaadeen was one of four political zones in the recently partitioned Somali peninsula: to the northwest lay the French Somali coast, to the north the British Protectorate, to the south Italian Somalia. Italian Somaliland itself consisted of three political regions: the Benaadir coast, the Majeerteen Sultanate on the tip of the Horn and, sandwiched between them, the Hobyo (Obbia) Sultanate of Sultan Yuusuf 'Ali Keenadiid. The Ogaadeen fell to Ethiopia but, then as now, the Ethiopians had difficulty in administering this region. Restrained alike by the fevers of the lowland climate and the martial spirit of the Ogaadeen people, the Ethiopians contented themselves with periodic seizures of the clans' livestock as a symbol of their sovereignty. But as the turbulence of the 1890s led to a devastating famine in the highlands, the Ethiopians turned to the great herds of the Ogaadeen to tide them over the hard times.

Thus when the Sayyid showed up in the Ogaadeen, Ethiopian raids had been occurring there with virulent regularity. It was not therefore an unnatural response on the part of the clans to welcome him as a liberator. In 1900 the Sayyid found a convenient opportunity to impress on the Ogaadeen how useful an ally he could be in times of trouble with Ethiopia. An Ethiopian expedition sent to capture the Sayyid resorted to indiscriminate looting of Maḥammad Subeer camels after failing to engage the Dervishes. The outraged Maḥammad Subeer appealed to the Sayyid, who assembled a force of 6,000 men and on 5 March, stormed the Ethiopian garrison at Jigjiga and succeeded in recovering all the looted stock. Though it was a Pyrrhic victory for the Dervishes, who lost 170 men to Ethiopian rifle fire, the engagement enhanced the prestige of the Dervishes as defenders of the pastoral clans against Abyssinian plunder.

In June the Sayyid followed up his success against the Ethiopians with a raid on the 'Iidagale Isaaq, a British-protected northern Somali clan, and seized 2,000 head of camels in loot. The move on the 'Iidagale was to be remembered as the first raid on a Somali clan and a fellow Muslim people. In pastoral ethos, religious notables are expected, through their moral prestige and pious example, to be the instruments of reconciliation among the clans. This seizure and appropriation by the religious Dervishes of looted stock astonished some Somalis to such an extent that a neutral observer was moved to immortalize the event in verse. In wonder and irony, the poet sang:

> When the Shariif[87] leads the robber-band
> And the learned Sheikh raids the people mercilessly,
> And the herds are seized with the approval and the blessing of a Sayyid –[88]
> Would that I lived long enough
> To witness the end of all these events![89]

Although at the time the Dervishes justified the raid on the 'Iidagale by citing the clan's alleged support for the British, the Sayyid all but renounced this act later as misguided and ill-advised. With an apparent remorsefulness, he reminisced in a poem.

> O Suudi,[90] pray, listen:
> I have no heart for further raids,
> As I still regret the day when intriguers
> Caused me to seize the Dayaḥ-weerar camels.[91]

The Sayyid gained great prestige in recovering the looted stock from the Ethiopians and he used it along with his charisma and powers of oratory to impose his undisputed authority on the Ogaadeen. To harness Ogaadeen enthusiasm into final commitment, he married the daughter of a prominent Ogaadeen chieftain and in return gave his own sister, Tooḥyar Sheikh 'Abdille, to 'Abdi Maḥammad Waal, a notable Maḥammad Subeer elder. It was here that he set out in earnest to create a political structure with governmental institutions, such as an established council of advisors (*khusuusi*), a standing army and a civilian population whose taxes in livestock supported the ruling class.

It would be in order at this point to take a brief look at the structure of the Dervish nascent state. The Dervishes were organized into four main bodies: at the top a sort of ministerial council or *khusuusi* presided over affairs of state. Members of the *khusuusi* were either personally appointed by the Sayyid or by their respective lineages who as a whole had joined the Dervish movement. The *khusuusi* were supposed to be men of impeccable character and selection into the council depended on a range of criteria, including religious (Saaliḥiya) orthodoxy, prowess in warfare, generosity, allegiance to the Sayyid, eloquence and other qualities deemed important by the Somalis.

Next came the bodyguard (*gaar-haye*) who were responsible for matters of security in the Sayyid's household and generally for order in the capital. It was a mark of his political acumen that the Sayyid recruited the bodyguard from servile clans like the riverine Reer Baare and former slaves whom he adopted as sons, provided with wives and endowed lavishly with riches. They were to address him as father (Aabbe) and depended entirely on him for their position in life.

The regular army (*maarra-weyn*) comprised the third principal branch of the Dervishes. Tightly organized – in a manner reminiscent of the Ndebele state in Zimbabwe – into seven regiments, the army was usually settled some distance away from the capital as a precautionary measure against the possibility of its staging a *coup d'état*. Each regiment was commanded by a sort of military governor (*muqadim*) who was appointed by the Sayyid in return for proven loyalty. The number of troops in a given regiment varied from 1,000 to 4,000 with 2,000 men as the average. Each regiment had separate quarters, horses, arms and other provisions.

The civilian population (*reer-beede*) formed the fourth body of the Dervish state. The *reer-beede* were the most unstable segment, consisting as they did of polyglot clans who followed the Dervishes more for political gains – especially the loot which they could exact in the name of Dervishism – than for any firm commitment to the movement. Accordingly, the ranks of the *reer-beede* swelled and shrank in keeping with the fortunes of the Dervishes.

The above remarks will serve to demonstrate something of the militaristic character of the Dervish movement. In function as in structure, the Dervish state was fashioned on the model of a Saaliḥiya brotherhood. It was characterized by the strict hierarchy and rigid centralization of a religious order and in both respects it represented a radical departure from the ephemeral alliances of clan politics. The Sayyid proscribed the tribal identity of his followers in favor of a new identity based on religious ideology. For this reason, he adopted the term 'Dervish' for his followers and issued them with loose robes and a white turban (*duub-'ad*) to mark them apart from other Somalis. He required them to address him as 'father' (Aabbe) or 'master' (Sayyid). The army and the *khusuusi* were supported by tributary donations (*siyaaro*) significantly named after the voluntary charity which Somalis give to mendicant *wadaads*. Trade became the monopoly of the state, with dealing in some items like gold and ostrich feathers designated as a special privilege of the Sayyid's household. The Sayyid, moreover, ran the Dervishes with the autocratic powers of a sheikh, imposing rigid discipline on the day-to-day conduct of his followers. In short, while transforming the Saaliḥiya brotherhood into a highly militaristic state, the Sayyid introduced a new order which was alien to the pastoral Somalis.

Initially, Abyssinian pressure, which the Sayyid appeared to counter, induced the egalitarian clans to submit to his autocratic reign. Predictably, however, it was not long after the impostion of that reign that an anti-Dervish movement got under way among the Ogaadeen. It was led by a Maḥammad Subeer chieftain, Ḥuseen Ḥirsi Dalal 'Iljeeḥ', and grew out of that ever-present pastoral problem: clannish vendetta. After the execution of one of their elders, the Maḥammad Subeer came to the conclusion that under Dervishism they were being subjected to the hegemony of the Sayyid's small Bah-Geri lineage, whom they traditionally despised. Consequently, Maḥammad Subeer elders secretly plotted to assassinate the Sayyid and the entire *khusuusi* council. Word of the conspiracy, however, leaked out before the assassination was carried out and the Sayyid leapt on his swift pony and escaped, but his prime minister and long-time friend, Aw 'Abbas, fell to the conspirators. In the ensuing mêlée, the Dervishes regrouped and succeeded in repulsing the attackers.

Some weeks later, the Maḥammad Subeer proposed to settle up with the Dervishes and with this object in view, sent a delegation of thirty-two men representing the pick of their leadership. On arrival at the *ḥarun* or headquarters, the peace delegation was put in fetters and anklets by the Sayyid, who made their release conditional on the Maḥammad Subeer agreeing to pay not only the blood money of his late friend but also a fine equivalent to the combined blood monies of the hostages. The Maḥammad Subeer refused to meet these terms, which they considered too harsh and arbitrary, and the Sayyid put the prisoners to death. Among those executed was the husband of the Sayyid's sister. In gallant but vain efforts, the young woman tried to persuade her brother to save the life of her husband and when she failed, she would not be dissuaded of her eulogy to him even on pain of death:

> If thy [Sayyid's] stiff dagger kills me,
> If in the decimation of men, I too descend into the dust,
> And if I die – what honor is greater than to follow my beloved 'Abdi?[92]

In pastoral ethos, the killing of a peace deputation is regarded as a most heinous crime and the Dervishes suffered lasting damage to their reputation for the act. The act also adversely affected the position of the Dervishes, for it drove the alienated Maḥammad Subeer into the arms of the Ethiopians and hence dealt a grievous blow to any hope of Somali unity against Euro-Abyssinian colonialism.

Faced with the combined hostility of Menelik and the powerful Maḥammad Subeer Ogaadeen, the Dervishes could not remain in the Ogaadeen and they hastily withdrew to the Nugaal, where the Sayyid propitiated the Ḍulbahante for the moment by a massive payment of blood monies. Dervish re-entry into northern Somalia now caused panic among British-protected clans, who abandoned their pasturelands in the Haud and concentrated their vast herds in the largely barren coast, a situation which soon led to dangerous overcrowding. This impressed on British colonial officials the necessity of military action against the Dervishes and they recommended to their superiors in London the organizing of an expedition to 'put this mullah down' once and for all. But Salisbury, who was already waging two wars in Africa (against the Ashantis and the Boers), was not anxious for a third in Somaliland.

The idea of an expedition to deal with the 'Mullah', however, became feasible when Menelik proposed a joint action with the British at the end of the year. Accordingly, in the spring of 1901, Lt Colonel E. J. Swayne was appointed to head an expedition. Swayne assembled a force of 1,500 Somali troops, officered by twenty-one Europeans. On 22 May he started from Bur'o, hoping to synchronize his efforts with an Ethiopian expedition 15,000 strong which made a simultaneous start from Harar. Both governments were confident that they would rid the country of the Sayyid, who was now dubbed the 'Mad Mullah'. The era of the expeditions had begun.

4 THE INCONCLUSIVE EXPEDITIONS (1901–4)

The history of the operations against the Dervishes has been covered well and it would be redundant to embark on a full-scale narration of them.[93] A few relevant events may be recorded here. The British, with Ethiopian participation and, on occasion, Italian cooperation, sent four major expeditions against the Sayyid between 1901 and 1904 and these either attained inconclusive results or suffered disastrous reverses against the brilliant guerrilla tactics of the Dervishes. At the height of the campaigns, nearly 10,000 British troops, who had come from an assortment of nationalities including Sudanese, Central Africans (Yaos), Indians, Britons, Boers and, of course, Somalis, were deployed against the Dervishes. These comprised, in the words of one official, 'the best seasoned British, Indian, and African troops at the Empire's disposal'.[94] They faced about 20,000 Dervishes, of whom roughly 8,000 were cavalry. So long as the Dervishes stuck to guerrilla tactics they proved invincible, despite their enemy's superiority in fire power and organization. What Sir Charles Eliot said of another ill-fated expedition against Jubaland Somalis could apply equally well to the experience of the British forces:

> It gained no success proportionate to its size or expense, for it was unable to capture or force a battle on the light-footed nomads, who vanished before it in a scrubby wilderness, well known to them though pathless to strangers, while it was on the other hand, exposed to sudden attacks from fanatical desperados.[95]

Reference to a few episodes will provide a better perspective on these expeditions. The first expedition demonstrates the inadequacy of Dervish training in modern warfare as well as their quick ability to learn. The British, unable to force the elusive 'Mullah' to a decisive battle, seized a huge quantity of Dervish stock and placed them in a kraal, in hopes of employing them as bait to attract the Dervishes. The tactic seems to have worked, for on 2 June 1901, some 3,000 Dervishes attacked the kraal. Although the courageous Dervishes made one run after another at the British position, they failed to penetrate the kraal and recover the looted livestock. At the same time, they sustained heavy losses from the well-coordinated enemy fire.

This engagement gave the Dervishes a painful but valuable experience. Henceforward, they assiduously refrained from attacking a fortified enemy position. Instead, they would draw out the British to the dense, waterless bushes of the Haud where the enemy could neither deploy their guns to advantage nor exercise familiar military maneuvers. On the other hand, the Dervishes, divided into small parties under the cover of ideal terrain, maintained light but deadly skirmishes with the British. They often struck at will and harassed British lines of communication with impunity.

This strategy seems to have worked so well for the Dervishes that they managed, in the third expedition, to cut up a strong British force at Gumburu Hill some seventy miles north-west of Gaalka'yo. In one engagement alone, only six survived of a 200-man British contingent. Sheikh Jaama' 'Umar 'Iise described the savage intensity of this battle as well as the tactics employed by the Dervishes:

> Of the great many ponies which the Dervishes brought to battle, they knew which horses were most suited for strenuous action during particular times of the day. They decided therefore to deploy the chestnut horse (ḥamar) in the cool hours of the morning because the chestnut would not stand much heat, and the beige (baroor) in the hotter hours of the day . . . When dawn smiled, the Dervishes said their morning prayer and attacked the British from four directions.

After a while they stopped firing and with guns on their shoulders, delivered a hand to hand combat to the enemy whose fire was falling like raindrops. At eleven in the morning, the first Dervish force withdrew and the second force, fresh and full of dash, took up the field. But few survived out of either Dervish force.[96]

The poet Qaaje Maḥammad 'Iise 'Qaaje-Balas', a private in the British force, summarized the shock of defeat experienced by his men. In the first section of a short poem he dedicated to the occasion, he gratefully acknowledged God for allowing him to escape with his life. He sang:

With this arduous task to put down the Dervishes
I was never pleased.
But evil men aroused my greed
And Allah willed me into it [the campaign],
I desired to seize Dervish camels
But far from realizing my dreams,
I was only too glad
To stagger back alive to my people.
For this I return many thanks to Thee, O God.[97]

Then the poet-soldier turned to ridicule the vaunted might of the British forces:

The English would claim:
'Our Indians will shoot well,
And the Sudanese will deliver a fine charge
And the war-tried Yaos[98] will hold fast.
We will all be ready,
The Dervish horses are feeble,
Their firearms are antiquated ...
With ease we will put them to flight,
Let each one among us
Possess a whole Dervish clan' –
Such exalted claims
Dazzling like a mirage before their miasmic eyes,
Led the English to their downfall.

A supreme propagandist, the Sayyid did his best to play on the doubts and uncertainties of the enemy, as this letter 'to the English People' demonstrates:

I have no forts, no houses ... I have no cultivated fields, no silver or gold for you to take. You gained no benefit by killing my men and my country is of no good to you ... The country is jungle ... If you

> want wood and stone, you can get them in plenty. There are also many ant-heaps. The sun is very hot. All you can get from me is war. I have met your men in battle and have killed them. Our men who have fallen in battle have won paradise. We fight by God's order. We kill, you kill . . . If you wish peace, go away from my country to your own.[99]

These words also reflect something of the Sayyid's profound belief in the rightness of his cause and his deep confidence in the inevitability of ultimate success.

It may be said that a similarly unwarranted confidence led the Dervishes to one of their worst reverses in the fourth expedition. In a subsequent chapter on Sayyid Maḥammad's consummate use of poetic oratory as a political weapon, we will examine the particular features of this expedition and the consequences of the defeat which it inflicted on the Dervishes. For the moment, it need only be said that the Dervishes, buoyed up with the victory of the third expedition, abandoned their former, reliable strategy of guerrilla warfare and sought a head-on confrontation with a strong British force commanded by General (later, Sir) Charles Egerton. Without the benefit of cover, the mass of Dervishes attacked the British position on 9 January 1904 at the plain of Jidbaale. Before the day was out 7,000 Dervishes lay dead. The Dervish army was broken and the Sayyid, a disgraced fugitive, fled to eastern Majeerteen country.

The defeat of Jidbaale seems to have left a permanent scar, some would say a psychic dislocation, on the Sayyid. It is not hard to detect evidence of this scar in his later life and verse, as we shall demonstrate. The reduction of the Dervishes in morale and strength may also account for the Sayyid's willingness to enter into a peace agreement with the 'infidels'. This was the Illig agreement of March, 1905, negotiated with the Dervishes on behalf of the Italian, British and Ethiopian governments by Consul G. Pestalozza, Italian envoy at Aden.

5 THE TREE-OF-BAD-COUNSEL REVOLT

Cautious in their colonial ventures ever since the débâcle of Adowa and busy with a tenuous pacification of the Somali Benaadir, the Italians refrained from engaging in overt hostility against the Dervishes. This fact must have intrigued the Poor Man of God. At war with Ethiopia and Britain, the Dervishes needed the goodwill or at least the neutrality of the third colonial power in the region.

Accordingly, Ḥaaji 'Abdalla Shiḥiri was sent on a mission to Aden to discuss with the Italian consul there the possibility of Italian protection for the Dervishes. The consul showed 'great interest' in the idea and, after further meetings and correspondence with the Sayyid, Pestalozza was persuaded to visit the *ḥarun* to hold face-to-face talks with the Sayyid. This he did twice in 1905. Pestalozza and his party, the first Europeans to set eyes on the Sayyid since his departure from Berbera, were sumptuously entertained at the *ḥarun*, which was now at Illig on the southeast coast of the Italian sphere.[100] The Italian consul succeeded in concluding a treaty of amity and friendship with the Sayyid. This treaty gave the Dervishes (a) a defined territory in Nugaal between the Hobyo and Majeerteen Sultanates, (b) recognition by the powers to govern his followers, (c) religious liberty and (d) freedom of trade except in arms and slaves.

The clause on slave trade may have been added to the provisions of the agreement in order to pander to European liberal opinion at home, since the Sayyid is never known to have trafficked in that commodity. As for firearms, events were to show that he never intended to abide by that prohibition.

Using the peace and the ports which the agreement gave him, the Sayyid began to rebuild his forces and import arms on an unprecedented scale. Outwardly pacific, the Sayyid sent out a network of spies throughout the country who, alternately by threats and promises, sought to undermine Somali loyalty to colonial governments. On another level, the Illig period marks a new phase in the Dervish struggle against colonialism, in which the resistance changed from a war of arms to a war of words. Consequently, it was characterized by a great outpouring of polemical verse and most, if not all, of the Sayyid's best works were produced during this period. Sayyid Maḥammad's ingenious double-dealing with the colonial regimes for a while made uneasy the conscience of some of the more sensitive theologians in the *ḥarun*. These wondered whether it was not unethical for a Muslim to dishonor a solemn treaty, even if it had been entered into with infidels. The question had for some time a deleterious effect on the minds of some, but their scruples were overcome when the Sayyid defended his policy of sharp practice by citing the incongruous, if convenient, example of the early Muslims whom God ordered to break 'covenant' with the treacherous Banū Quraiza of Medina.[101]

Biding their time under the terms of the agreement, the Dervishes put into effect a well-coordinated strategy of sabotage against the colonial administrations, even while protesting friendship with them. Bands of armed looters who passed as 'terrorist thugs' (Bur 'Ad) fanned out from the Dervish capital to loot and terrorize clans loyal to the British and Italians. The Ḍulbahante and Warsangali Daarood played an important role in this program of agitation and disruption. In an attempt to win over the Warsangali, the Dervish Bur 'Ad enabled them to carry out a series of devastating raids against the Maḥamuud Garaad Ḍulbahante, who had earlier defected from the Dervishes. In return, the Warsangali gave the Dervishes free access to their ports at Laas Qoray and Meyt. Other sections of the Ḍulbahante were encouraged to raid the Isaaq. Similar tactics were pursued with respect to the Italian-protected subjects of Boqor 'Ismaan and Yuusuf 'Ali Keenadiid.

Thus employing propaganda and acts of sabotage with equal effect, the Dervishes enjoyed a period of growth and prosperity until 1909. In that year, however, a serious disaffection within the ranks of the *khusuusi* leadership gripped the movement and brought about its near disintegration. 'Abdalla Shiḥiri, the astute envoy who had played a prominent part in the Illig agreement, fell out with the Sayyid, allegedly over a woman whom Shiḥiri loved but who was taken away from him by his master.

Shiḥiri, hitherto an intimate friend of the Sayyid and a veteran Dervish who had taken an active part in all the early fighting, was deeply wounded by the loss of his lady. Disappointed in his master's behavior, he decided to leave the movement. The chance to do so came when he was appointed to head a Dervish trade mission to Aden. Once in Aden, Shiḥiri officially disassociated himself from Dervishism and roundly denounced the Sayyid. Then Shiḥiri made common cause with two prominent sheikhs, 'Ali Nairobi, who was based in Lamu as the spiritual director of Saaliḥiya in southern Somalia, and Ismaa'iil Isaḥaaq of Berbera. The three, no doubt with Anglo-Italian encouragement, went on a deputation to Mecca, where they made strong representations to Maḥammad Saliḥ about the misdoings of his pupil in Somalia. A year later Shiḥiri returned with a letter from Mecca which amounted to a virtual excommunication of the Sayyid:

> I have this news before my eyes – that you and your people have got into bad ways ... I have proofs that you have ceased to abide by the Sharī'a in that you loot and enjoy other men's wives; you shed their blood and rob their property. You can be called neither a Muslim nor a Christian.[102]

Maḥammad Saliḥ concluded that he wished to have 'nothing to do' with the Sayyid. Contemporary sympathizers of the Sayyid dispute the authenticity of this letter, which they regard as a blatant hoax.[103] Whatever the authenticity of the letter, its circulation had a serious impact among the Dervishes. After a copy had been read in the *ḥarun*, 600 conspirators held a secret palaver in the shade of a tree that was to be called the Tree-of-Bad-Counsel (so named because of the conspiracy that was hatched under its shade) with a view to overthrowing the Sayyid. They

The Tree-of-Bad-Counsel ('Anjeel-tala-waa).

considered three proposals: (a) to execute the Sayyid and appoint another in his place, (b) to force him to resign but allow him his life, or (c) to desert the movement *en masse* and hence bring about its inevitable collapse. They could not implement proposals one and two, chiefly because they failed to agree on a candidate to replace the Sayyid, so they settled on plan three, resolving to quit the *ḥarun* with their clans *en masse*.

As the first clans began to leave, the Sayyid was alerted to the conspiracy by one Shire 'Umbaal, who had initially taken part in it but subsequently lost heart. Fighting broke out between troops still loyal to the Sayyid and the rebels who had enlisted the aid of their clans, and the situation soon deteriorated into a major civil war. After a week of intense fighting, the Sayyid emerged victorious, but not before several Dervish clans, like the Reer Samatar Khalaf Majeerteen, were decimated.

Something of the seriousness of the uprising may be appreciated by consideration of three of its ringleaders. One Ḥaaji Ḥasan 'Awl, a military governor reputed to be the bravest man in the movement, was the instigator. The second, Sheikh 'Abdalla Qoriyow, had been the Islamic magistrate of the *ḥarun* and his involvement in the rebellion was a grievous blow to the spiritual prestige of the Sayyid. The third, Faaraḥ Maḥamuud Sugulle, was the Sayyid's brother-in-law and one of the wealthiest of the Dervishes. As punishment for their role in the rising, the first received capital punishment, the second was ostracized from the *ḥarun* and the third placed under house arrest.

The Tree-of-Bad-Counsel illuminates what appears to be a persistent pattern in Sayyid Maḥammad's tempestuous Dervish career. This concerns the fact that whenever there was a major crisis in his life, he tried to employ his poetic skills to weather the storm. It was, moreover, during these periods of crisis that he seems to have produced his most brilliant verse. To paraphrase a knowledgeable indigenous source, the Sayyid's 'creative genius was brought out by his being exposed to heat'.[104]

The Tree-of-Bad-Counsel was no exception. Realizing the gravity of the revolt, the Sayyid composed a series of poems and pithy remarks designed, as an elder put it, 'to silence critics and confound opposition'.[105] One of the poetic proverbs he reportedly coined during the period says:

> O you who grew up in the faith
> And yet would sneak into a conspiratorial tree,
> May Allah destine you to perdition.

Another, obviously intended to overawe his opponents, says:

> O God, rescue us from danger,
> For evil men have stirred a sleeping lion into action!

His best known poem on the revolt, though, is significantly called 'The Tree-of-Bad-Counsel'.[106] It is addressed to Ḥaaji Suudi, one of his disciples who remained steadfastly loyal to the Sayyid throughout the crisis, and the grateful Sayyid possibly chose to alliterate the poem in the letter '**s**' to honor the faithful disciple whose nickname, 'Suudi', began with 'S'. We will see in the next chapter that the Sayyid often addressed his verse to a disciple and that the master–disciple relationship was a cardinal element in his scheme of versification.

Like a poetic contestant before a tribal assembly, the Sayyid presented his case in the manner of an oratorical discourse. Essentially, the argument of 'The Tree-of-Bad-Counsel' is a charge of perfidy. In a deceptively self-pitying tone, the Sayyid complained of the 'odious' fraud which the men whom he trusted as his very soul had perpetrated on him. He promoted these men, he claimed, to elevated positions, gave them wives and wordly possessions, taught them the faith – in short, he took care of them as his beloved children. The charge against them then is one of filial ingratitude, one of the worst sins in the pastoral ethos:

> And I did not expect Qoriyow[107] to sharpen his spear against me,
> And for all my charity, Aḥmad Fiqi[108] did not return a nod of gratitude,

> It is they whom I have fed in the sleepy hours of the night, who now seek my life,
> It is they whom I have given perfumed brides,
> They whom I have given whatever their fancy demanded, who now seek to undo me,
> It is they, even my brother-in-law[109] who has done this evil to me.

The Sayyid went on to give the revolt against him an eschatological significance. 'The End of Time is upon us,' he maintained, because there was not one Somali worthy of trust or capable of keeping good faith. Invariably, every friend he made, he complained, proved to be a 'noxious poison'. In these 'perverse times' of corruption and betrayal, he – the oppressed Poor Man of God – could 'await deliverance only from Allah'. It is not hard to divine from these notes the Sayyid's principal strategy for his defense. Clearly, it was to appeal to the kinder natures of his kinsmen and to justify his behavior in slaughtering during the revolt a great many mullahs and holy men. He attempted to achieve his self-exoneration through the skillful use of an aesthetic craft.

6 TALEEḤ AND AFTER (1910–20)

Despite the Sayyid's notable efforts to mitigate its ill effects, the Tree-of-Bad-Counsel left the Dervishes weak, divided and badly demoralized. In putting down the revolt, the Sayyid had to execute dozens of rivals, many of whom had been prominent Ḥaajis and holy men, and the massacre of these men undermined the prestige of his mission and knocked the moral props from under the movement. Consequently, the Sayyid, deprived of his moral prestige, had to rely increasingly on dictatorial methods to maintain power. Summary executions became common occurrences in the *ḥarun*, and the circle of trusted advisors grew ever smaller. Had the British chosen now to attack the Dervishes or tried to reunite opposition against him, they might have succeeded in their objective of destroying the movement. The option was open to them since the Illig convention crumbled by 1908 and bands of Dervishes were once again openly on the move against friendly clans. But the British had no heart for another military operation. The previous ones had cost the exchequer £2,500,000 and there had been ominous grumblings from a parliament conscious of the taxpayers' censure.

Accordingly, after a series of triangular consultations between London, Cairo and Berbera, the British decided to initiate a further peace overture to the Sayyid in the middle of 1909. Thus Sir Reginald Wingate, military governor of the Sudan, arrived at Berbera in April with a peace mission to the Sayyid. He was accompanied by another 'Sudan hand', Rudolf

Slatin Pasha, and with the combined prestige of the two men who had an expert knowledge of the Sudanese Dervishes, the British government hoped the 'mullah' would somehow be induced to sign a peace treaty. But the Sayyid refused to treat and the men had to content themselves with the writing of a bulky report on Somaliland affairs.[110]

With the failure of the Wingate mission, the British reluctantly decided to cut their losses in Somaliland by withdrawing from the interior and limiting their administration to a few coastal towns. This move, which abandoned the greater part of their sphere, was a tacit acknowledgement by the government of defeat. It was simultaneously decided to arm the Friendlies against the expected Dervish onslaught. When these ill-advised measures were put to effect, they proved favorable to the Dervishes. First, the Friendlies used the arms left them by the withdrawing British not on the Dervishes but against one another. As usual, the clans had a backlog of 'old outstandings' on one another and with a seasonable supply of modern weapons in their possession, they resorted to unprecedented raiding and bloodletting. In the ensuing chaos, entire lineages were stripped of their livestock and reduced to starving destitutes and the period is remembered with infamy as the 'Time of Eating Filth' ('Ḥaaraama-'une').

In 1912, the administration recognized coastal concentration for the failure it was and abandoned it in favor of a new policy which called for a limited involvement in the interior. With this objective in view, a small force of mounted Camel Corps was raised with a view to policing the immediate interior. The force was put under the command of Col. Richard Corfield, a bold if somewhat reckless officer who soon gained the respect and admiration of his Somali subordinates. Highly agile and adopting tactics well suited to pastoral conditions, the Camel Corps scored impressive successes in restoring order in the nearby hinterland. The order was, however, at best tenuous so long as the Dervishes remained at large in the eastern half of the protectorate.

The withdrawal from the interior gave Sayyid Maḥammad a golden opportunity to re-establish himself in the Nugaal and restore his prestige, badly battered by the Tree-of-Bad-Counsel incident. During the three years of anarchy, the Dervishes constituted the only disciplined force inland and the Sayyid put this advantage to ingenious, if rapacious use by seizing unprecedented quantities of livestock in loot. In the closing months of 1909 the capital was moved from Illig in the Italian sphere to Taleeḥ in the heart of the Nugaal. Here three garrison forts of massive stone masonry and a number of residential houses were constructed. The Sayyid, for the first time, built for his exclusive use a luxury-style palace. He strengthened his palace with new recruits from outcast clans and became increas-

The Dervish watchtower (Daar Ilaalo) from a distance, Taleeḥ, northern Somalia.

Silsila: the main Dervish fortress at Taleeḥ, northern Somalia.

ingly less accessible to the public. This was understandable, though not propitious for the resistance cause. Ever since the Tree-of-Bad-Counsel fiasco, attempts on his life had occurred with some regularity. Just the same, the Sayyid continued to have a strong grip on his followers.

The influence of the Dervishes spread rapidly between 1910 and 1914. Following the settlement of Taleeḥ as a permanent capital, other forts were erected at Jiidali and Mirashi in Warsangali country, at Wardeer and Qoraḥay in the Ogaadeen and Belet-Wayn on the lower reaches of the Shabeelle in southern Somalia. Thus by 1913, the Dervishes dominated the entire hinterlands of the Somali peninsula.

In August of that year a Dervish force led jointly by Aw Yuusuf ʻAbdille, the Sayyid's brother, and Ismaaʻiil Mire raided the Habar Yoonis near Burʻo and carried off a vast herd of camels in loot. A contingent of the Camel Corps commanded personally by Corfield gave chase and engaged the retreating Dervishes at Dulmadooba. A fierce battle ensued, which ended in a complete victory for the Dervishes, Corfield himself becoming one of the notable casualties. But it was a Pyrrhic victory. The Dervishes sustained three times as many casualties as their opponents (900 dead). In death, Corfield won the grudging respect and admiration of his foes for his courage and dignified bearing under overwhelming odds, and his fall became an occasion for two of the finest Dervish poems.[111]

Encouraged by their success at Dulmadooba, the Dervishes intensified the pressure on the British. In 1914, a party of forty Dervishes led by Ismaaʻiil Mire, delivered a daring commando raid on Berbera and reduced the city to chaos and terror. The British, preoccupied with the larger matters of World War I, were unable or unwilling to undertake anything more than token efforts designed to contain the Dervishes for the moment.

Meanwhile the circumstances of the war enabled the Sayyid to score a number of diplomatic successes. One was to strike an alliance with the new Ethiopian emperor, Lij Yasu, who acceded to the throne in 1913. Increasingly, Lij Yasu came to manifest pro-Muslim and anti-British tendencies. The possibility of a northeast African empire encompassing Ethiopia and all the Somali regions may have intrigued Lij Yasu. In any event, he proposed to marry Sayyid Maḥammad's daughter, perhaps as a prelude to realizing this dream. But Lij Yasu's hopes evaporated when his Christian subjects, alienated by his Muslim ways, rose in rebellion and deposed him. Before his deposition, the emperor managed to send a German technician, Emil Kirsh, to the Sayyid with the object of making ammunition and repairing guns for the Dervishes. For some unknown reason, Emil Kirsh was badly used by the Sayyid, who imposed on him conditions which induced the German to make a perilous bid for freedom; but, before reaching the coast, he expired from thirst.

The fall of Lij Yasu was apparently a bitter disappointment to the Sayyid. In the aftermath of the war, at a time when the Sayyid was a fugitive in the Ogaadeen, and his state in ruins, he continued to have great admiration for the fallen prince. Referring to the aerial bombardment, he was heard to comment that he did not mind the birds (airplanes) whose droppings fell on his white robe. Rather he was hurt by the damaging imputation to his ancestry which the leaflets dropped from the planes made. 'My origin has apparently been forgotten,' the Sayyid fulminated. 'I am the son of Ras Makhail's brother and I am the cousin of Lij Yasu, the prince of Abyssinia',[112] a claim which the colonial historian of the period dismissed with the rider: 'It would puzzle even a Somali genealogist to discover the common origin of their respective families, unless, indeed, the devil was the ancestor whom both these rascals share.'[113]

The Sayyid also looked for friends among the Ottomans. The Ottoman Sultan, as a universal caliph of the Muslim community, was regarded by the Sayyid as a defender and natural ally of the Dervishes. He had thus appealed to the Turkish commander at Leḥaj for help against the Anglo-Italian alliance in Somalia. The commander, 'Ali Sa'iid Pasha, agreed to provide the necessary help if in return the Sayyid would place his people under Ottoman protection. An agreement to this effect was signed by the Sayyid's envoy, Aḥmad Shirwa' Jaama'.[114] According to Caroselli, the document defining the terms of the agreement did not reach the Sayyid, as it was intercepted on the way by the Italian authorities.[115] However, a Turkish envoy, Mehmet 'Ali, managed to reach Taleeḥ in 1916, where he continued to advise the Sayyid until he was killed by the British in 1920.

The Turkish alliance did not give the Sayyid much in material terms but it offered him considerable aid in the field of propaganda. Turkish agents slipped through Ethiopia into Somalia, where they tried to arouse the Somalis against their Christian overlords. A document purportedly issued with the blessing of the Grand Mufti of Istanbul freely circulated in the Somali interior.[116] A proclamation of *jihād* against Britain, France and Russia, the document urged all Somalis to unite behind the Sayyid who, it claimed, was the appointed representative of the Ottoman Sultan:

> Oh Somali brethren! Let it be known to you that our most honored and respected Khaliifa, the Sultan ... has notified to all the Mohamadans, wherever they may reside, the biggest *jihād* against England, France and Russia ... Concentrate your forces under the command of Sayyid Maḥammad 'Abdullah Ḥasan.

Some Somali sources suggest that Turkish propaganda was crucial in swinging the Ogaadeen behind the Sayyid.[117] How much the Sayyid needed Ogaadeen support became evident when in the closing months of 1919 the British began their final and most effective campaign against the Dervishes.

The Sayyid's diplomatic enterprises and the circumstances of the war concealed a fundamental weakness in the Dervish policy, inaugurated in 1910. This was the policy of fixed residence. In building a fixed capital, with forts to defend and palaces to guard, and in concentrating his troops in stationary fortifications, the Sayyid may have committed the greatest strategic error of his twenty-year resistance struggle. He gave the British the strategic advantage they had long sought: a fixed target to attack. He could no longer boast to the enemy: 'I have no forts, no houses ... I have no cultivated fields, no silver or gold for you to take.' He now had all of these, which the enemy could and did take. The settled life was, moreover, ill-suited to the pastoral Dervishes and they had become inactive and luxury-oriented. 'A sense of moral turpitude crept into Taleeḥ,' says one informant, 'and the Sayyid himself had grown corpulent, dictatorial and over-confident.'[118] Thus, when in the early months of 1920 the British struck with a well-coordinated land, sea and aerial attack, the Dervishes were ill-prepared.

Even more significant for the success of the final expedition was the introduction of the airplane as a combat weapon in warfare. It proved to be a convenient weapon, as one of the pilots put it, to 'bomb the old villain out of his hiding place'.[119] Dervish military leaders were either unappreciative or ignorant of this newly-invented lethal weapon. Hence they seem to have made no contingency plans against an attack from the air. Consequently, when the British delivered the surprise bombing on Taleeḥ and the surrounding forts, the Dervishes not only sustained heavy casualties, but they became demoralized in the face of an attack against which they had no way of retaliating. They thus offered no appreciable resistance. The Sayyid and his reduced followers hastily abandoned Taleeḥ and other Nugaali forts and fled westward into the Ogaadeen. Pursued from the air by planes and on land by a swift mounted force, the fleeing Dervishes offered easy targets to their enemies, but the Sayyid's luck once again held and he managed to elude his pursuers, who failed to kill or capture him.

Once in the Ogaadeen, the Sayyid, unbroken by his staggering losses in Nugaal, employed his old talents of charisma, oratory and knowledge of his countrymen to rebuild his battered forces. In this he was helped by the Turkish propaganda which had done much reconciliatory work on his behalf among the Ogaadeen Somalis prior to his coming. Within six months of his defeat, the Sayyid put together a coalition of Ogaadeen clans, which made him a 'power in the land' once again. He proved this by rebuffing British overtures of peace, which offered him modestly generous terms, including a government subsidy and a land grant in the west of the protectorate where he could settle in liberty with his followers.[120]

The Sayyid humiliated the deputation of notables which brought him these terms and showed his scorn for British overtures of peace by raiding the Friendlies immediately after the deputation had left. Then the ultimate catastrophe struck the Dervishes. A combination of smallpox and rinderpest broke out in the Ogaadeen and decimated man and beast in the Dervish community. At a guess based on an evaluation of indigenous sources, 50 to 60 percent of the Dervishes who had survived Taleeḥ perished during the epidemic.[121] Among the prominent *khusuusi* claimed by the pestilence was Khaliif Sheikh 'Abdille, Sayyid Maḥammad's brother and close advisor.

On the heels of the epidemic came a tribal raid 3,000 strong, armed and organized by the British and led by a Habar Yoonis chieftain, Ḥaaji Waraabe (the Holy Hyena), so named on account of his stormy character. Ḥaaji Waraabe put the remnants of the Dervishes to the sword, carrying off nearly 60,000 head of livestock in booty,[122] but he failed to lay hands on his elusive prize, who had staggered off with a few followers into the headwaters of the Shabeelle River at Iimay. Here, still pursuing the ill-conceived policy of fixed residence, he constructed two forts. He also had resort to his old technique of political marriage and arranged to contract marriages with the princely house of the 'Aruusa Oromo, who had given the destitute refugees some timely protection. This was his last noteworthy act, for shortly after, in December 1920, Sayyid Maḥammad, aged about 64, succumbed to an attack of influenza and died quietly. With his death the most important episode in the history of Somalia for twenty years came to a rather undramatic end. Yet if his life ended quietly, the drama of his influence continues to prosper. In word and deed, the Sayyid epitomized two qualities which are dear to the Somalis: a remarkable poetic talent, especially his zestful political verse, and an unyielding refusal to submit to foreign domination. Having discussed Sayyid Maḥammad's unrelenting efforts to resist colonial imposition, we now turn to a treatment of his other major contribution, notably, his exuberant political verse.

4

Poetic Oratory and the Dervish Movement

1 MAḤAMMAD 'ABDILLE ḤASAN: THE POLITICAL ORATOR

During the twenty-year period of Dervish fighting for independence, Maḥammad 'A. Ḥasan produced the works of poetry which have won for him the reputation of being the greatest Somali poet. By any standard the Sayyid could be judged an artist of great power and by Somali standards as something of a literary master. There is an element of paradox in this observation, as indeed in many other features of Sayyid Maḥammad's complex, at times contradictory, life. Although he lived to be 'one of the greatest Somalis of words' (Somalis speak of 'a man of words' (*nin hadal*) as opposed to one 'of letters', thereby emphasizing the oral character of their verse), there is no record of his having ever composed a word of political poetry until he was a middle-aged man, well into his forties. Indigenous sources hold unanimously that the Sayyid's first Somali poems date from 1904, nearly six years from the inception of the Dervish movement; that a great many of his serious poems were composed between 1905 and 1909, when the Dervishes had settled between Illig and Eyle on the eastern Somali coast between the Majeerteen and Hobyo (Obbia) sultanates.[1] This is not to say that political poetry was not of importance to the Dervish cause before this time. As I hope to demonstrate shortly, high-powered propaganda warfare conducted through the medium of political poetry was a salient feature of the conflict from its early days, and it was utilized by both the Dervishes and their enemies in their fight for the allegiance of the Somali people.

In describing his oratorical verse, his followers speak of it as a 'new and sudden outburst of artistic creativity, a supernatural gift which suddenly descended upon him (waa lagu soo dagey)'.[2] The Sayyid was a master of political manipulation and the corpus of poetry, proverbs and wise sayings which he left behind are permeated with hints and suggestions which encourage his followers to believe and propagate the notion of his sudden inspiration, his possession of a 'divine endowment'. We shall examine this theme in the next chapter.

The first political poem on record involving the Dervish struggle seems, on the basis of internal evidence, to have been composed in 1900, shortly after the Dervish attack on the Ethiopian fortification at Jigjiga.[3] It was not composed by the Dervishes but by their enemies. When the Isaaq poet, 'Ali Jaama' Haabiil (whom we shall come across quite frequently in these pages as the chief poetic antagonist of the Sayyid), learned of Dervish reverses at Jigjiga, he composed his poem 'Maḥammad the Lunatic' ('Maḥammad Waal'), thereby immortalizing in prosodic formula the Sayyid's enduring epithet.[4] With a measure of malice and cynicism, the poet gloated over Dervish losses and scoffed at the 'vaunted martial prowess' of the Dervishes, who bragged of their intent to carry out a successful campaign against the Abyssinians:

> The uncontrollable man – he who'd seek Menelik in battle,
> Who says: 'With my sword I'll smite the Abyssinians',
> Who says: 'I'll give you the Habar Yoonis herds',
> Who'd weave lies around us,
> Who'd take away our minds as if we were brainless camels.

The implication of these lines, obvious in the Somali version, is that the Sayyid promised more than he could deliver: imbued with a false sense of his military resources, he sought out Menelik in battle and lost miserably (historically this is not wholly accurate, of course); he promised his followers the possession in booty of the fabulous herds of Habar Yoonis, a British-protected Isaaq clan, and failed to do this equally miserably; that the Sayyid was a liar 'who'd take away our minds as if we were brainless camels'. Having thus scoffed at Dervish military capability, he turned to ridicule the notion of the Sayyid as a miraculous man of God:

> He who says: 'I'll spear the heavens, and fill the earth with fine pastures',
> Who says: 'Like a ship, my prayer-mat can take you across the sea',
> Oh, how hollow our imagination when we deem the Lunatic Maḥammad our apostle.

Curiously, the poetic response defending the Dervishes did not come from among their camp but from an outsider, one al-Ḥaaj Aḥmad Samatar, a Majeerteen poet who was a resident of Aden at this time. He despatched his poetic reply in the form of an oral epistle which he sent with a dhow returning from Aden, saying:

Is Menelik of your kindred that you should sing praises to him?
As for the cruising ships of the infidels,
Know ye not they are but Allah's brief provisions to the misguided?[5]
If glorious were the infidels, they'd not be destined to perdition;
The things they invent, and the wealth they amass are their damnation;
And the ingenious artifacts their abominable foretaste of ultimate perdition;
This reveling in material things brought the mighty Pharaoh down.

If the meaning of the prayer-mat moving you across the sea escapes your unbelieving mind,
Consider your origin, the very first day when you were created,
In the darkness of the womb the Lord protected you.
How miraculous was your place of origin!
You came into the world by the will of Allah,
O mindless one, make a reflection on this.

Speak not ill of the Sayyid, O brainless one, lest this lead you to Hell,
The ways of the saints, you fool, are dark to you,
And do not take him [the Sayyid] lightly, for unattainable is his likeness![6]

By pastoral standards, al-Ḥaaj Aḥmad Samatar fails to make a successful defense. Although his poem, with its heavy metaphysical-centeredness, may appeal to the pious and the other-worldly, it falls far short of the original poet's attack, especially in its failure to address the issues raised by the attack-poem: Dervish reverses at Jigjiga, the Sayyid's promises which proved hollow in the eyes of the first poet and the charge of insanity in the Sayyid. Nevertheless, the Sayyid was so pleased with Aḥmad Samatar's poetic defense on behalf of the Dervishes that he reportedly made a payment of 150 camels (quite a lavish gift even by today's standards) to its author and the author's brother.[7]

Dervish sympathizers are quick to cite this incident of an outsider coming to their defense as an example of the appeal which their cause had for the Somalis. Opponents of the movement, however, counter that the poet was motivated not so much by an alleged attraction which the Dervishes had for the Somalis as by greed and sycophancy, hoping as he did, they maintain, to obtain material gain by toadying to the Sayyid.[8]

In the following years (1901–1903), the Dervishes fought off three British expeditions, the latter two in collaboration with the Italians and Ethiopians. During this period, the Sayyid does not seem to have joined the war of words. Other men, like the *khusuusi* member, Afqarshe Ḥ. Ismaa'iil and the military governor (*muqadim*), Ismaa'iil Mire, both of whom were poets of note, acted, so to speak, as ministers of propaganda.

In the second expedition (October 1902), for example, the Dervishes scored a notable victory over the British force commanded by Lt. Colonel E. Swayne, which they ambushed at the valley of Eerago in the Haud about seventy miles north of Gaalka'yo. The Sayyid hoped to use his new prestige as a result of his victory over the British to enter into a much-coveted alliance with Sultan 'Ismaan Maḥamuud of the Majeerteen, through whose ports the Dervishes needed to import firearms. Consequently, the Sayyid made overtures of friendship to the sultan, including a proposal to marry the latter's daughter, Qaali 'Ismaan. Although he received 227 camels in advance bride-wealth from the Sayyid, Sultan 'Ismaan remained non-committal on the subject of the proposed marriage alliance. In return, however, he sent to the Dervishes a caravan of forty camels laden with guns and ammunition.[9]

The Sayyid received the sultan's envoys with great cordiality and bestowed lavish gifts upon them. When it was time for them to return, he detailed the poet-in-residence, Afqarshe Ḥ. Ismaa'iil, to issue a valedictory message of solidarity to the Majeerteen court. The resulting poetic epistle falls neatly into four parts. The first wishes the travelers a safe journey home:

> O guests sojourning among us, on the morrow you'll depart,
> *Salaams* be with you as you follow the fleeting dawn,
> Gifts of heart, endearments do follow you,
> Over endless plains and rocky hills, dawn marches and dark hikes.
> Dangerous the road is. May Allah see you through.
> But two eight-days and you'll be at the coast,
> When they who've waited for you extend hearty greetings,
> If they press in on you for news while you are exhausted and unable to speak,
> In your fatigue, pray, do not misrepresent us to the Sultan.
> Uncles,[10] as we've requested, take kind words from us,
> Lest you forget: do greet the Sultan for us.[11]

The second part narrates events about the battle in a manner favorable to the Dervishes:

> Say: on the bed of river Eerago when tumultuous the skies were,
> Rifles and maxim guns, the day bullets were exchanged,
> The day that vultures perched lazily on the ribs of British infidels,
> The day the cowardly whites fell back and fled.

Then follows the central piece of the poem, the crafty attempt to turn a modest battle success into an epic victory which could not be explained except in terms of the divine sanctions enjoyed by the Dervishes:

> A message from Allah this contention was.
> Oh! how the English and the servile Iidoor[12] were humiliated,
> How their flesh and bones were fed to the beasts.
> Say: a line of troops was slaughtered as sacrificed lambs,
> Say: Bad-Eye[13] was struck in the neck in broad daylight,
> Say: the uncircumcised sergeants inferno has claimed,
> And of bullets and guns, a fine haul we made,
> Oh! how the unbelievers fled in headlong panic!
> Brothers-in-law,[14] go and proclaim all this from coast to coast,
> Shout for joy and drive the Italians from your side.

The final section is a piece of fervent sermonizing designed to evangelize for the Sayyid's religious sect, the Saaliḥiya:

> Now, a word to the house of the Sultan:
> This Saaliḥiya religion – it will make us all equals,
> Love and friendship [through Saaliḥiya] Allah will help us exchange,
> Let not Somali gossip-mongers [members of the rival Qaadiriya] drive us apart!

This poem and others which follow illustrate the Sayyid's tendency throughout the early days of the struggle to employ other men to conduct the war of propaganda for him. An earlier example, by no means the only one of its kind, showed how the Sayyid attracted such men of words with impressive material rewards. And this demonstrates the importance he attached to the craft of political compositions. The intriguing question for us in a study of Dervishism is to examine the possible motives the Sayyid may have had in suddenly taking to the production of vast quantities of political verse from 1904 on, thereby becoming his own poet-in-residence, instead of delegating others to perform that task as he had before.

When confronted with such a question, indigenous sources would argue that he did not compose political poetry before this date because he did not know how to, with the implication that he received 'an abrupt inspiration' to versify without premeditation or forethought.[15] This view we may take note of, but would do well to treat with caution and skepticism. Given the strenuous demands which the poetic craft imposes on its practitioners among the pastoral Somalis, men simply do not become celebrated bards overnight.

In the first place, political poetry is a potent tool in socio-political control among the pastoral Somalis and the possession and use of this asset makes for honor and influence in society. The Sayyid knew this and he was likely to capitalize on the prestige of his talent in this regard and to make sure that it was used to underpin his own authority within the Dervish leadership structure. As a result, the composition and use of political verse became, later on, a jealously guarded affair with access limited to a select few. In order to keep their privileged status, these few had to sing praise-songs to the 'father'.[16] They had to display a good deal of self-effacement, dwelling *ad nauseam* on the inferiority of their verse to that of the all-wise Sayyid and their indebtedness to the master for inspiration.

A case in point was Ismaa'iil Mire, a capable military leader and a talented poet. When he, together with the Sayyid's brother, Aw Yuusuf 'Abdille, successfully led a Dervish force against Colonel Corfield's Somaliland Camel Corps, the general, in the great euphoria of the moment, inadvertently dashed off a narrative poem, 'Residing at Taleeḥ',[17] on the history of the expedition, apparently without prior clearance with the Sayyid. Although Ismaa'iil Mire duly gave credit for the victory to his master: 'Cartridges of bullets he distributed among us / Lord, bless him. He prayed to God for us', he was nevertheless asked upon return to Taleeḥ, to 'explain the circumstances of his poem'.[18] The remark was a veiled expression of the Sayyid's displeasure at the liberties which his lieutenant had taken. The Sayyid is said to have added further that Ismaa'iil Mire's poem left something to be desired in that it failed to give a detailed description of Corfield's death. This gave Ismaa'iil Mire a chance to get off the hook. 'Master,' he is reported to have said ingratiatingly, 'I reserved that opportunity for you to compose a poem that would make history for the Somali people.'[19] For the occasion, the Sayyid did compose a poem – which we shall refer to later – and to judge from its enduring popularity, it indeed made something of a history for the Dervishes.

This incident and others of similar nature illustrate the degree of care and jealousy with which the Sayyid sought to control the composition and use of political verse in the movement. The important point to note here is that one way for him to ensure an effective control over this vital resource was to produce it himself, if he had the talent to do so. As an incentive for the Sayyid to enter the literary fray, in addition to his natural interest in controlling the production and flow of political verse, there were the trying events of 1904, the year of his alleged inspiration. In January of that year the Dervishes suffered, for the first time, an almost catastrophic defeat. Forced to a battle at the plain of Jidbaale in the Nugaal valley by General Egerton, commander of the fourth British expedition, the Sayyid chose to face a superior enemy rather than lose face, and the result was an unmitigated disaster for the Dervishes.[20] They lost 7,000 men in dead and injured – half of the entire army which engaged the enemy. The Sayyid himself was given a hot chase under a grueling *Jiilaal* sun by a contingent of the imperial cavalry.

The physical and psychological trauma of defeat left the Dervish cause on the verge of collapse. In addition to the usual problems of morale attendant upon defeat, the Dervishes were subjected to a barrage of harassment and ridicule in the form of taunt songs by hostile clans. The Dervish plight, moreover, was not ameliorated by the spectacle of the Sayyid (the master) who was, despite his vaunted claim to the divine connection of his mission, now a disgraced fugitive.

Fortunately for the Dervishes under these stressful circumstances, the prudent side of the Sayyid's multi-faceted personality took over. First, he reminded his shaken followers that his predecessor, the Arabian Apostle, too, had temporary reverses but ultimately triumphed; there was reason to believe his own mission would follow a similar course. Colonel Swayne, the British commander, complained, 'The Mullah himself made capital out of his reverses by reminding Somalis that Maḥammad had begun in the same way.'[21] Secondly, the Sayyid appealed to a traditional code of ethics which he knew would strike a responsive chord in the hearts of the pastoralists: the notion of unbending defiance in the face of calamitous circumstances, a theme he often stressed in his poems, as this example illustrates:

> If I do not abandon the faith, the guiding truth,
> No matter how infinitely terrible the fire which the Englishman brings upon me,
> By the Lord, I will not quit.[22]

Yet these tactics, designed to hold the ranks of the faithful together, concealed the real shift in strategy which the Sayyid was initiating in the light of grim realities. Realizing that the British infidel could not be driven into the sea by force of arms, he wisely refrained from further suicidal confrontations. But if the enemy could not be defeated by force of arms, perhaps he could be by force of words – by undermining his authority with the clans through the medium of political oratory. And hence the great period of the Sayyid's career as a political orator began, a period in which, as one elder put it, the struggle changed from a 'war of arms to a war of words'.[23]

To give the new approach a chance to work, the Sayyid sought and obtained a 'peace treaty' with his foes, notably the Illig agreement of March 1905, signed on behalf of the three colonial powers (Britain,

Italy, and Ethiopia) by Cavaliere Pestalozza. We noted in the preceding chapter[24] that the Sayyid had no intention of entering into permanent amicable relations with these powers, but merely wanted to use the 'provisions of peace' to regroup and reorganize his scattered forces and, above all, to initiate his new campaign of verbal barrage.

Once he decided to use poetry as a political weapon, the Sayyid brought to his new task a set of qualities which turned his literary barbs into weapons hardly less potent than bullets and which gave him a genuine advantage over his numerous poetic antagonists. In the first place, the Sayyid was a man of experience, what the Somalis call a 'Seer of Time', (*waaya-arag*) who had behind him twenty years of peripatetic wandering when he commenced to give leadership to the Dervish struggle. Thus he began his new career with that seasoned perspective which living in alien cultures brings to one's life, an opportunity his Somali foes did not have.

Secondly, he was a learned man with remarkable erudition in a nation where illiteracy was the dominant norm. An accomplished religious scholar, he could debate on hairsplitting theological and doctrinal points as his Arabic polemic, the 'Letter to the Biyamaal' ('Risāla al-Biyamaal') demonstrates.[25] Although his firm grasp of classical Arabic did not directly bear on his Somali oral verse, it is obvious that he drew on his knowledge and experience of the former for the benefit of the latter. Thirdly, the Sayyid brought from Mecca a dazzling spiritual prestige, not so much because the Meccan sojourn gave him the distinction of being al-Ḥaaj – there were quite a few al-Ḥaajs in Somalia at this time – but because he had studied under and received the 'commission to preach' from the great teacher and mystic, Maḥammad Saliḥ. While the Qaadiriya hierarchy in Berbera did not recognize the spiritual authority of the Sayyid's Meccan mentor, they had to admit grudgingly the persuasive character of Sayyid Maḥammad's message to the Somalis.

These qualities, rare enough individually but unique in combination, received additional vitality from the charismatic personality of the Sayyid himself and from his gift of words. Furthermore, the Sayyid was fortunate to have in Somali a language well noted for its richness of vocabulary, expressive style and adaptability to new ideas, and a cultural tradition highly appreciative of the political uses of the poetic craft. For his part, the Sayyid expanded the horizons of Somali verse by pushing its polemicism to the limits and, in some cases, revolutionized it by inventing new methods and techniques of versification. He composed songs, for example, in all but two (the **kh** and the **y**) of the twenty-one Somali alphabetical sounds, a feat that, on the basis of available evidence, no other Somali poet has accomplished before or since.[26]

In a moment I will treat in some detail the strategy and politics of the Sayyid poetic warfare and the circumstances which prompted his

Somali enemies to consider his literary combat as potent as actual fighting. For a better understanding, however, of the Sayyid's success as a poetic combatant, it would be in order at this point to take a brief look at his poetry to see the principles and characteristics which held it together and made it 'a force in the land to be reckoned with'.

In the eyes of many Somalis, the Sayyid's verse has the 'power,' as one elder put it, 'to kill or give life,'[27] a power which in part derives from the pre-eminent role of poetry in Somali society and in part from the image of the holy mystic which he so consummately cultivated. As we have mentioned earlier, poetry in the Somali context is an invaluable asset deeply rooted in the vicissitudes of everyday life, treasured not so much for its artistic value as for the influential, sometimes sinister, role it plays in molding people's opinions and attitudes. The skilled poet therefore wields formidable power which he can use to ennoble friends and slander enemies. The Sayyid possessed this talent and although he had qualities the Somalis admire in a leader – courage, persistence in the face of overwhelming odds, spiritual power, coupled with a certain degree of recklessness – it was his eloquent verse which articulated these qualities and enabled them to be seen at their best. His impromptu verses recited at his *ḥarun* (headquarters) are likened in Somali metaphor, to 'lethal arrows'[28] which flew across the Somali desert, and came home to the hearts of those who heard them. Uttered by a *wadaad* (man of God), they had the seriousness of a blessing or a curse and caused joy in his camp and consternation within the enemy camp.

Although Somali critics are always impressed by the sweet flow of the Sayyid's verse, its exquisite diction and its power which induced potent emotions in men, they are quick to point out that he was a natural heir to the Somali *gabay*-making tradition. The Ogaadeen have a reputation for their purity of Somali and have produced more of the best known classic poets (Raage Ugaas, Qamaan Bulḥan, Feetin Maḥammad). Since he was born of a Ḍulbahante mother and an Ogaadeen father, it is little wonder that the Sayyid's poetic heritage was cultivated to the full.

2 CHARACTERISTICS OF THE SAYYID'S ORAL VERSE

The principal feature of the Sayyid's verse, which was his own innovation in the *gabay* form, is the triplet stanza. Normally *gabay* lines are grouped in strophes with no set number of lines per strophe. In many of the Sayyid's *gabays*, however, each triplet stanza forms a self-contained unit in theme, while at the same time remaining an integral part of the whole poem. The first line in the triplet introduces the idea or theme, the second develops it and the third contains the conclusion. Thus in the following rough translation of the Sayyid's poem, 'If only' ('Ba'a E Yow

Sheega') alliterating in the letter '**b**', the technique of the triplet stanza may be illustrated:

> *Introduction*: in beauty, graceful bearing, the agile gait,
> *Development*: In canter, the trot, the gallop – for convenience in raiding,
> *Conclusion*: In these ways a horse is ever superior to a mule – if only he were told.[29]

In the first line the poet alludes to something which possesses 'graceful bearing' and an 'agile gait', but we are not told what it is. In the second line, the theme is developed further with the words 'canter', 'trot' and 'gallop'. We now know that the poem concerns a horse. This knowledge – or at least that of a pastoral audience – is further strengthened by the phrase 'for convenience in raiding', since the horse is the principal pastoralist vehicle for inter-clan raiding. The horse and the camel are made for complementary roles, as they say, the former to raid or defend the latter. But, still, we are uninformed as to what it is the poet would have us know about a horse, until we get to the third line, the clincher, which establishes the superiority of a horse to a mule: 'In these – a horse is ever superior to a mule.' Further examples taken randomly from the poem would lend themselves readily to the scheme:

> *Introduction*: If a young, healthy camel just calved,
> *Development*: Rewards not her owner with plentiful milk
> *Conclusion*: Then she'd soon be slaughtered – if only she were told.

> *Introduction:* The stingy man is like an unclean carrion,
> *Development:* He'd extend no hospitable hand to the weary guest,
> *Conclusion*: The miser will be shunned – if only he were told.

> *Introduction*: The slovenly woman, uninstructed by Allah,
> *Development*: However fine the apparel and brilliant sashes you may buy her,
> *Conclusion*: That she'd still lack in grace – if only she were told.

> *Introduction*: The apostate Sheikhs who, like the pagan Indians, reside in the City of the Infidels,[30]
> *Development*: In Allah's Book it is revealed how degenerate they've become,
> *Conclusion*: That they'll be plunged into hellfire – if only they were told.

At times the number 'three' seems to have something of a mystical significance for the Sayyid's literary productivity – the muse, as it were,

– prolong the note slightly
ʬ a slight trill with the voice
/ or \ slide up or down to the next note

Figure 4. *Gabay* musical notation. Each line of the music represents one phrase. Metronome markings are only approximate, as the tempo fluctuates frequently. Many of the minute vocal inflections, both rhythmic and melodic, have been deleted from these musical transcriptions in order that the average Westerner may be able to comprehend Somali chant. (This notation was prepared with the help of Sue Neely, a music student at Northwestern University.)

of his artistic creativity. Not only in his poetry but also in his anecdotes, proverbs and wise sayings, he displays a marked predilection for the formulation of concepts in triplet expressions. A few examples from his proverbs go something like this:

> My son, three do not trust:
> he who tends your camels,
> he who eats (or prepares) your dish
> and he who grows up in your household.[31]

We may blame the note of paranoia and cynicism which the lines convey on the long record of betrayals and internal strife which plagued the Sayyid's household, and which we intend to look at in a subsequent section. In another triplet proverb, the Sayyid says:

> Three I despise:
> the gossip of the Somalis,
> the weakness of the Italians
> and the tasteless manners of the Abyssinians.

In another place, he reflects:

> Three one does not recover from:
> oppression that knows the backing of brute force,
> poverty that knows the destitution of one's home

and childlessness that knows the barrenness of one's procreative faculty.

There is evidence to indicate that the Sayyid was rather strict about the observance of the triad rule and that he regarded it as one of the distinguishing features of his poetry. In his poem, 'Lose not my Utterance', alliterating in the letter 'l', he spells out certain principles and peculiarities which he regards as distinguishing his verse. Thus he exhorts his chief poem-memorizer, Ḥuseen Ḍiqle, to chant 'My Noble Utterance' not in ones, or twos but in threes.[32]

The Sayyid's adherence to the triad technique makes it one of several critical tools the researcher may apply in verifying the authenticity of the body of poems attributed to the Sayyid. If a work purporting to be his departs from the triad design in significant ways, the reader has reason to be alert for omissions or falsifications.

The second principal characteristic of Sayyid Maḥammad's verse is the circumlocutory feature. This technique utilizes what I propose to call, for want of a better term, 'an argument by the back door' or evasive communication. All Somali verse is didactic in the sense that it is composed and chanted in relation to a specific occasion for the purpose of achieving a specific end. A Somali traditional poem has a story to tell, often an argument to advance or a point to make. Characteristically, the Sayyid withholds the point of his argument to build drama and suspense, circles around it, plays, as it were, cat-and-mouse with it and digresses into ostensibly irrelevant moralizing. The strategy is to disarm the opponent with a verbal barrage, to charm him with the range of his knowledge and the eloquence of his utterance. He then makes a precipitous descent from the lofty world of philosophizing into the practical one of bickering, stating his case in a line, more often in an ironic twist of phrase that is usually difficult to refute. To illustrate this point, we may take the Sayyid's poetic diatribe, 'The Parching Heat of the Wind',[33] on 'Ali Jaama' Haabiil, a prominent poet spokesman of the Habar Awal section of the Isaaq clan-family, whose people persistently opposed Dervishism. Until his premature death some years before the collapse of the Dervish movement, 'Ali Jaama' Haabiil delighted in exchanging poetic duels with the Sayyid as, for example, this passage illustrates:

> Inasmuch as you attribute words of wisdom to me, it is for me to spear this Mullah;
> For Allah hath removed wise counsel from the Reer-Ḥamar thief:[34]
> Of free women, he cohabits with seven;
> And a thousand devout worshipers he butchered as one would a he-goat;

And caravans are given the safety of Allah,
But he wantonly cuts the tendons of weary travelers and engorges their dates.
He's battened on the weak and the orphan,
Call you this Italian-infidel a Mahdi? How puzzling the thought![35]

We may note in passing that the Roman Catholic priest who first translated this passage into Italian in the 1910s, took exception to the use of the word 'Italian' in this unflattering context and bowdlerized the line to his satisfaction by replacing 'Italian' with 'Jew'.[36] But the distortion could not successfully be concealed since 'Italian' (Talyaanni, in Somali) plays an important role in the alliterative scheme of the poem, a function which 'Jew' (Yahuudi) could not perform.

The 'Parching Heat of the Wind', the Sayyid's reply, is a poem of seventy-two lines, only one line – the last – of which addresses the issue at hand. The rest is a jumble of philosophical observations on nature, culture, history and, of course, invective against enemy clans. A few examples:

The scorching flame of heat belongs to the parching wind.
The thunder, lightning – the blinding flash – belongs to the torrential rain,
An overcast sky, a land filled with rainwater belongs to Haradigeed pools.

The distant murmur belongs to a hungry lion, perhaps a raging sea, maybe, to fired bullets;
When dust rises from the fury of the battle, the forward charge belongs to the valiant
As the backward flight belongs to the craven coward.

False hope belongs to the Somalis who've gone astray,
Words of wisdom belong to the saintly Dervishes –
The men who've become refuge to the faith – dignity belongs to the Shirshoora.[37]

In this manner he continues to range far afield, holding the hearer in suspenseful anticipation while probing him for sympathy through the eloquence of language. Then he suddenly leaps to the attack: 'And filth belongs to the donkey and to foul-mouthed 'Ali Jaama'!'

3 THE COMPOSER OF ORAL EPISTLES

It is necessary to devote a passing comment to the third major characteristic of the Sayyid's verse, namely the epistolary nature of his poetic compositions. The great mass of Somali oral poetry is message-oriented, composed to disseminate information and to facilitate the external relations of the clans. In one of its multi-dimensional functions, poetry is for the pastoral Somalis what the radio and press are for industrial societies: it plays the role of broadcasting. (This point was also brought out by Andrzejewski and Lewis.)[38]

The Sayyid consummately cultivated and utilized with great effect the communicative or transmitting function of Somali verse. Aware of the importance of public opinion in an egalitarian society, he designed his verse in the manner of exhortative epistles to appeal or abuse, to enhance or discredit. As a result, the majority of his poems are addressed to 'somebody' – to colonial officials and their Somali collaborators whom he tried to discredit, to neutral clans whom he hoped to attract, or to his followers whom he tried to encourage. Epistolary poems are composed in a characteristic style which identifies (usually by name) (a) the messenger or transmitter to whom the publicizing of the poem is entrusted, (b) the party to whom the message is meant and (c) finally, the message itself. Thematically, verse epistles may be described as a private lament and public complaint, and their objective is often to appeal to three types of audience. On one level, the composer appears to pour out intimate feelings and emotions, laying his heart bare to a confidant, the one to whose care the poem is committed. The master – disciple relationship between composer and memorizer gives the verse epistle an air of familiarity, delicacy and a graceful simplicity:

> O Ḥuseen, by the will of the Lord, let not your mind vanish,
> May the Lord accept my prayer for you,
> Live for a while yet, for you're a man in whom I trust,
> Yet if you die – I am certain that you'll join the ranks of the blessed;
> You'll go up, up to be with the disciples of Fragrance,
> And you'll enter the gates of heaven . . .
> Now hark, your task is a little word I'd entrust to you,
> Beloved, you'll not forget my words,
> Listen, then, to the chant of my prayer.[39]

The Ḥuseen to whom the poem is addressed is Ḥseen Ḍiqle, a *khusuusi* member who served his master with unwavering allegiance throughout the long struggle. He was the chief of a retinue of aides whose principal task was to commit the Sayyid's verse to memory and propagate it throughout the Somali peninsula and even beyond to Arabia and Egypt.

The disciple is the first audience and the guarantor of the survival of his master's precious legacy. The rest of us who hear or read the poem are treated as bystanders, and while the composer appears oblivious of our presence in his intimate communication with his protégé, he is in fact very much concerned to draw our attention. We are his second audience and it is us he intends to move and win over to his cause. So we are allowed to listen in (to eavesdrop, perhaps) and to share the secrets of the master, with the tacit knowledge in pastoral ethos that the privilege of participation in his inner thoughts imposes on us a moral obligation to respond to the urgings of the poem. A moral web is thrown around us and neutral we cannot be.

The third audience of the verse epistle are the people concerned with the issues expounded or argued in the poem. The Sayyid began, as we noted above, with a few supplicant pleasantries, flattering to the addressee-confidant but morally obligating to us. The supple pleasantries, moreover, correspond to the salutation in a letter, and after he disposes of these in a few lines, he introduces the main subject of his composition, which in the case of the poem at hand is a wide-ranging complaint against British-protected clans whom he charged with moral abhorrence and religious apostasy. To their shame and damnation, these clans sided with the Euro-infidel against a fellow Muslim and a kinsman:

> They who've refused the ordinance of their creator,
> Who've heaped insults on the prophets and saints,
> Who've become the progeny of the Nazarenes, and fostered kinship ties with the whites.
>
> Who've sought, on their own volition, to serve the Kaffir-whites,
> Who were not under duress but fawned after the whites,
> Who've chosen to become the offspring of the base Nazarenes.
>
> They who've gone to the Amharas of Harar,
> Whose father-judge and ruler is Menelik,
> Who've become servants and toadies of the Abyssinians.
>
> Who've turned the English against us,
> Who've brought, at Afbakayle, the stinking infidel upon me,
> They who visited afflictions upon me at Oodagooye and Daratoole woods.
>
> They who out of jest decimated the brethren,
> Who've plunged unkind spears in the Lord's anointed [the Dervishes]
> And who, with gusto, rained maxim guns on my men.
>
> In my cry their name was on my lips when other men lay asleep,
> They sold me out and ate the price of my life . . .
>
> They've done all this to me, they cannot deny,

Let no one else revenge upon them for me,
One day, like the prowling lion, I will jump upon the fence, I'll descend upon them unawares.

4 THE SINGER OF POLEMICS: DIATRIBE, CURSE AND EXHORTATION

Consideration shows that the uses of the Sayyid's verse were also traditional: to influence the opinions of a body of kinsmen. He employed his poetry to inform, to persuade, to attack, to exhort, to curse, to appeal and above all, to enhance his position. Of the 120 poems which have so far been collected and verified as his, almost two-thirds are poetic diatribes attacking colonial infidels and their Somali collaborators.[40] Nearly all of his poetry was composed during the struggle (1900–1920) and almost every poem makes at least one direct reference to it. Even the seemingly apolitical praise-song which the Dervishes sang for their master, Maḥammad Saliḥ: 'Oh miraculous man of God, Sheikh Maḥammad Saliḥ, the helper, Maḥammad Saliḥ',[41] eventually assumed the role of a war-song, which the Dervishes chanted when charging into battle and was said to strike terror into the hearts of Somali British collaborators.

Although many themes underlie the poems of the Sayyid, it appears that his major topics relate to diatribe, exhortation and curse. Poetic diatribes are by far the most numerous and best remembered.

Produced during the war, these poems are belligerent in tone and incisive, reflecting the spirit of war:[42]

Until I had driven long spears through the shameless Reer Hagar,[43]
And until the shedding of their thick blood had been celebrated with rejoicing,
And until they had been massacred and destroyed utterly,
And until my task had been fulfilled, I would not have given up Haddaysane.[44]

There is also the vulgar element in the Sayyid's poetic diatribes and this seems to be an accepted part of his style. He was wont, it is said, to boast: 'Allah taught me the art of acrimony and abuse', a reference to the Qur'anic precedent where God, of course in the mouth of the Prophet Maḥammad, inveighed against a Meccan opponent of the Muslims in this exceptionally virulent language:

He who is given to much swearing, feeble in faith, decrepit of mind, disgraced man of scandal ... gossip-monger in the face of corruption ... niggardly in giving and hinderer of people from coming

> to the faith ... inveterate oppressor ... steeped in sin ... argumentative, having a protruding belly ... a bastard adopted to an alien race![45]

The Sayyid receives high marks for his malevolent pronouncements from B. W. Andrzejewski and I. M. Lewis who maintain that 'by any literary standards he must be judged to be a master of invective, ridicule and scorn'.[46] Despite his skill as a master polemicist, the Sayyid's passionate dislike of the British, coupled with the poet's intoxication with language, at times entangled him in disastrous excesses which all but overwhelmed his argument, threatening to defeat the very cause he had sought to advance. A poem to the 'English Woman' represents the use of such fulsome language. An epigram which borders on the obscene, it is presumably meant for Col. Richard Corfield's sister who, after the officer's fall in an engagement with the Dervishes at Dulmadooba in August 1913, raised funds for a monument erected in his memory on the spot where he died. The Sayyid's graphic description of the lady's physique in rather unflattering terms is likely to be judged an unnecessary manifestation of rancorous zeal. But the 'English Woman' is an aberration.

Despite his penchant for cynicism and the heaping of invective, ridicule and scorn on his foes, he did this, for the most part, in a way that did not diminish the artistic value of his verse. Consider, for example, the Sayyid's feat in sustaining the studied ridicule in these lines taken from an epistle to British-protected clans:

> Ye have mistaken the hell-ordained and Christians for the prophet,
> Ye have shamelessly groveled after the accursed,
> Were you noblemen (as you claim) ye would loathe the white infidels.[47]

An exposition of the Sayyid's acrimonious style may predispose us to judge his caustic verse as the idle fulmination of a sour-tempered old warrior, embittered by failure and frustration. Such a judgement, however, would rest on an erroneous interpretation of the Sayyid's method and ideas. Polemicism, to re-emphasize the point, is central to Somali notions of versification and there is nothing wrong with abusive verse so long as it is, in the words of the Sayyid himself, 'done with proper style'.[48] This means that in the arcane tastes of pastoral literature, there is a 'proper way to abuse' and to articulate literary propaganda so as to be effective, and judged by these criteria the Sayyid stands unassailable, a point which even his bitter foes would allow.[49]

The practice and craft of poetic curse, of lashing out against one's foes and engaging in ruthless character assassination through poetry is a frequent occurrence, a weapon commonly employed in the political relations of the clans. Hence, when the Sayyid cursed, it was not out of ill-will or purposeless rancor, although this may have played a part, but out of a conscious determination to utilize a national resource in which he happened to be well endowed by nature – the Sayyid cursed for a cause.

By contrast, exhortation poems are intended to keep the flock together. They sharply contrast the nobility of the Dervish cause with the baseness of colonialism, the righteousness of Islam with the duplicity of the Christian infidel. The most important function of exhortation poems, however, seems to be to silence the critics of the Sayyid within the Dervish leadership and to perpetuate his grip on the movement. The task of staving off opposition within the movement had become increasingly urgent and difficult to achieve, especially after the suppression with great harshness of the so-called Tree-of-Bad-Counsel revolt.[50] In putting down the revolt, the Sayyid executed dozens of rivals, many of whom had been prominent Ḥaajis and holy men, and the massacre of these men undercut the prestige of his mission and knocked the moral props from under the movement. Consequently, the Sayyid showed after this episode growing signs of insecurity. This had been justified by the ever-dwindling number of trusted counsellors and the numerous attempts on his life.

This sense of insecurity prompted the Sayyid to produce 'Alas, My Wives', a poem composed after he had escaped an assassination through food poisoning by one of his wives. In it he attacks his wives as 'the basest of womankind' and pleads with God to save him from their 'bloody snares':

> My wives all – they are the basest of womankind,
> Everyone married to me is a glowing ember of hell,
> Alas, decency dwells not among my hags!
>
> Inveterate spendthrifts, they save not for the future ...
>
> Let them not pour out for me cupfuls of fresh milk,
> Let them not feed me dates and delicate dishes,
> Let them not warm me up in the biting cold of the Dayr season.
>
> Since they shy not away from swearing, anger, blasphemy,
> In their wiles, they seek to undo the innocent,
> O how they'd savor my blood! Lord, deliver me from them.[51]

The Sayyid then turns to the praise of his new spouse, his first cousin, 'Aasha Yuusuf, whom he ennobles in glowing terms:

Had I but found one like my cousin for a wife I wouldn't be smitten with grief,
Now that I have her, I spurn all the biting curs [his other wives],
And that is why, of all women, I choose my cousin!

In courtesy, understanding, goodness – nay, in unoffending quietude,
In the setting of porch-mats, in the making of the sublime dwelling, curtains and all,
Excellent in serving the dish; in purity of heart obedient, upright:
All these and many others she is
In deference to Allah, who made her thus – she is the noblest of women.[52]

The exalted sentiment which the poet expresses for his new spouse conceals more mundane motives, notably the fact that the marriage to his cousin was prompted not so much by the urgings of the heart as by the cold calculation of the mind: after a close brush with death through food poisoning, he could trust only a near relative to prepare his dish.

5 POETRY AS A TOOL IN THE LONG STRUGGLE

I hope the preceding notes have served to show something of the depth and range of the Sayyid as an artist and a polemicist, as well as the involvement of his verse in the intimate interplay of people and events. I now turn to a discussion of the ways in which the Sayyid used his verse to achieve specific political ends. To do this I would refer to a series of interrelated episodes to demonstrate the very real connection between the Sayyid's poetry and the vicissitudes of the resistance struggle. One such episode is the battle of Jidbaale which, though not the only one to do so, shows admirably the relevance of poetry to battle.

Militarily, we noted above, Jidbaale represented an unmitigated disaster for the Dervish cause. Demoralized and disorganized, the Dervishes were forced to disperse all over the Nugaal and the Haud after their resounding defeat by the British expeditionary force. Not only did they sustain heavy casualties (7,000 to 8,000 in dead and injured) but also the loss of 20,000 of their best war-horses.[53]

The Sayyid and what was left of his battered troops were within easy grasp of the advancing British cavalry when a gracious offer came from Sultan 'Ismaan Maḥamuud inviting the Sayyid to retreat into the eastern Majeerteen country under nominal Italian protection. This offer was accepted with relief by the hard-pressed Dervishes but the Sayyid viewed it with cautious eye, for the goodwill of 'Ismaan Maḥamuud, a man noted for chicanery and Machiavellianism in his dealings with the Dervishes, could not be taken for granted. Might he not be luring them into his camp in their hour of weakness to pay off old scores? After much heart-searching and hesitation, and against the advice of important members of the *khusuusi* (inner circle of advisors), the Sayyid embarked on a long, weary trek to 'Ismaan Maḥamuud's territory.

Meanwhile Cavaliere Pestalozza, Italian Consul at Aden and Italy's chief envoy to her Somaliland territories, learned of the latter's friendly overtures to the Sayyid. According to local sources the Consul, fearing that an undesirable Dervish–Majeerteen alliance might result, threatened 'Ismaan Maḥamuud with naval bombardment.[54] The threat of Italian armed intervention cowed the Sultan, who immediately began a war with the disarrayed Dervishes. Terrible casualties were inflicted on both sides, including the massacre of women and children. At about the same time the British, in cooperation with the Italians, stormed the port of Illig, the last Dervish stronghold along the coast. As if this were not enough misfortune, 400 warriors of his own Ogaadeen clan deserted the Sayyid *en masse*. Faced with hostility on all sides, deprived of livestock, his few survivors diminishing by the day, the Sayyid became a fugitive, and it seemed that the Dervish cause was on the verge of collapse. At this dismal point, the Sayyid turned to his last resource, to the power of his mouth. He composed a number of poems designed to put his case before his countrymen. The best remembered of them is the 'Jiin' or 'Jiinley'.

Filled with archaisms, discontinuous in thought progression and morbid in tone, the 'Jiin' can only be fully grasped by the contemporaries of the Sayyid. Thematically, it embodies what I. M. Lewis calls 'a duality in Somali notions of power'. On the one hand, force is commonly revered and is usually a decisive factor in inter-clan conflicts, and on the other: 'the weak and those who for other reasons cannot have direct recourse to war are protected by supernatural sanctions. Somalis seek strength in everything, and where it is not found in physical force it is sought in the supernatural sphere.'[55]

The spiritual power which the Sayyid invokes in the 'Jiin' derives from two pillars: Islam and *ḥeer* (traditions). By Islamic teaching, all Muslims are brothers and are under obligation to assist one another and to follow the path of righteousness. In the words of B. W. Andrzejewski and Muuse Galaal, who made a similar observation in a treatment of three Somali poets:

> Any intrigue, instigation, double-dealing and hypocrisy are regarded as particularly heinous sins, which are often punished in this world. Injustice done to a brother Muslim is considered even greater if he

> is bound to the evil-doer by bonds of kinship, and the closer the degree of kinship the graver the offence. Thus the transgressor not only has to bear the burden of guilt, but suffers from anxiety that at any moment retribution may come upon him in the form of one misfortune or another.[56]

The 'Jiin' can in fact be fittingly called the 'Lament of a Kinsman'. Alliterating in 'j', the poem dwells on two themes: the deception of 'Ismaan Maḥamuud and the desertion of the Ogaadeen warriors (the poet's own kinsmen). The first part condemns the cowardly desertion of his relatives who to their eternal shame abandoned a kinsman at his most extreme hour and sought servile security under the Ethiopian king. Such men, the Sayyid charged, deserve disgrace on earth and damnation in the other world:

> Oh! Ḥuseen,[57] it is unworthy of honorable men to speak words of worthless banter,
> You are my comrade.
> You have not joined the ignorant who fled in headlong panic,
> You've not gone to the Amhar king when your relatives had departed.
> Those who sought protection under the infidels are kinsmen of Hell;
> By the Qur'an they are Hell-ordained.[58]

The second section reveals the treasonous deception perpetrated on the 'trusting' Dervishes by the Majeerteen Sultan. The Sayyid argues that he was comfortably settled with his Dervishes, enjoying peace and prosperity, teaching and practicing the true religion when the dissembling 'Ismaan Maḥamuud invited the unsuspecting Dervishes and treacherously fell on them:

> Attended by an assembly of friends and relatives in my home,
> With no one daring to utter an evil word against me,
> Lying comfortably on my mat, bent on the study of the Faith,
> Meditating with the dignitaries in my *ḥarun*,
> Receiving at a sign from me whatever my heart desired,
> Alas, the jinni has deceived me of my sceptre.[59]

The poet then proceeds to present a graphic description of the long, weary trek. He vividly details the privations they suffered and the menaces they met on the way: thirst, starvation, injury to the body, beasts of prey, poisonous snakes, marauding *midgaans* and outcasts – only to be pounced on, upon arrival, by the murderous Sultan. The havoc this long trek wrought on the Dervishes is borne out by Douglas Jardine who wrote: 'The direct line of the Mullah's flight was marked by a trail of dead men, women, children, camels, cattle, goats and abandoned water-vessels and household utensils.'[60]

The poet concludes his lament:

> Ah, I would not have gone if a message had not come to me from a Sultan;
> The flesh would not have moved had he urged me to stay;
> It is out of love that I blundered into the seas of the Genies.[61]
> Instantly I leapt upon hearing the din of the Majeerteen message,
> It is the fool who seldom realizes when he is being lured into a trap,
> As for me, the man with the fawning countenance brought this evil upon me.

The poem was publicized and it spread rapidly across the desert, pricking the conscience of those who heard it. 'The enemy,' said Aw Daahir Afqarshe, 'defeated him in the battlefield but the Sayyid defeated them by his mouth.'[62] The clans are said to have become 'disgusted' and 'horrified' at the dishonorable treatment the Sayyid, a fellow Muslim and kinsman, was accorded. And according to Aw Daahir Afqarshe, a cry of 'shame' was soon heard in the country. For although a great many Somalis had learned by bitter experience to hate and fear the Sayyid and in spite of the fact that many had been victims of Dervish deprivations, they were moved by his verse. The Sayyid's charisma, his claim to supernatural powers, and the tacit conviction among most Somalis that he was in fact fighting the cause of Allah against an infidel power, instilled reverence in the minds of the people, friend and foe alike. But when these noble qualities and objectives were skillfully articulated in a medium which of itself affects the Somalis in strong ways, the result was truly persuasive.

The 'moral outrage' prompted by the publicizing of the 'Jiin' at least in part translated itself into action. Many of the Ogaadeen who had earlier deserted returned to him, especially those of his immediate Bah-Geri lineage. Those who feared to return sent presents of livestock and rifles.[63] It is also said 'Ismaan Maḥamuud faced rebellion by his morally affronted subjects. Reportedly, he sought to propitiate the Sayyid by proposing to reopen his ports for Dervish importation of firearms. The proposal fell through though, possibly because the wily Sultan never intended to carry it out.

From the conclusion of the Illig agreement in 1905 to its collapse in 1909, the Sayyid fought the propaganda war, and the prime weapon at his disposal during these years was his mouth. The policies which he pursued and which his poetry reflects are well summarized by Jardine:

> Whilst refraining in his own interest from committing any overt act of hostility, he took advantage of the respite afforded by the Agreement to collect together again his scattered forces. Outwardly pacific, he ... organized a widespread service of secret agents whose *duty it was to undermine the loyalty of our tribes.*[64] (Emphasis added)

'To undermine the loyalty of our tribes' through political poetry was the centerpiece of the Sayyid's policy, and the political verse produced during this period includes such outstanding works as the 'Jiin', 'This News from Beyond the Seas' ('Warka Badah laga Keenayo'), the 'Blessings of the Lord' ('Bishaarooyinkii Eebahay'), 'Time Everlasting' ('Ka Sabaan Ka Sabaan Baan') and the 'Sound of Flying Gravel' ('Ḥiin Finiin'). The central message of these poems is twofold: (a) a concerted effort to persuade the clans to abandon their allegiance to their respective colonial governments in favor of the 'good cause' and (b) to foster an aura of personality cult around the Sayyid with a crafty view to discouraging any potential challenge to his leadership from the ranks of the Dervishes. There is a third class of verse which served as policy declarations or proclamations of edicts, a kind of state-of-the-union address. Both the 'Time Everlasting' and the 'Scourge of Infidels' ('Gaala-Leged')[65] would fit into the latter category.

Indigenous testimony would seem to recognize the period of poetry as a period of 'unprecedented prosperity'. Sheikh Jaamaʿ writes: 'In the years of coastal settlement, the Dervishes grew from strength to strength ... Wealth and weapons poured into their hands, and God favored them with charisma, power and influence.'[66]

The prominent clans won over to the Dervish cause during this period include the Warsangali Daarood, with whose sultan, Ina ʿAli Shire, the Sayyid contracted a marriage alliance, sections of the Ḍulbahante who defected from the Dervishes after the defeat of Jidbaale, and the princely house of the ʿUmar Maḥamuud Majeerteen, the Reer Islaan. In addition, Dervish influence spread to the lower reaches of the Shabeelle River, where they threatened the Italian Benaadir coast. Here, the recently converted Jidle clan killed Sheikh Uways I, the spiritual leader of the rival Qaadiriya, in 1909.

In the Warsangali, the Sayyid secured a convenient access to arms through their port of Laas Qoray and in a spirited exchange of letters and verbal messages, the British consul Cordeaux urged him, in deference to the peace agreement, to cease his seditious 'propaganda'[67] among a government clan. To this Sayyid Maḥammad replied by composing the 'Send me not to the Ogaadeen', an oratorical poem in which the poet 'neatly counter[ed] each charge made against him and 'turn[ed] it into an attack upon his accusers'.[68] With respect to the Warsangali, the Sayyid declared rhetorically:

> Concerning your demand 'turn aside from the Warsangali', I have a complaint:
> If they prefer you, then they and I shall be at variance,
> It is not in my nature to accept people who cringe to you.
> But if they are Dervishes, how can I turn aside from them?
> Do you also share their ancestry from Daarood Ismaa'iil?[69]
> Are you trying to steal towards me through my ancestor's genealogy?[70]

Although concealing his identity lest he provoke hostility with the British, the Sayyid made good use of the Bur-'Ad (roving bands of robbers) to prod along those clans who proved unsusceptible to words alone. Thus he unleashed a combination of Warsangali and Bur-'Ad raiders on the Jaama' Siyaad Ḍulbahante and the raiders reduced the clan to destitution. Similarly, he made repeated forays into the Majeerteen sultanates of 'Ismaan Maḥamuud and 'Ali Yuusuf where the Dervishes perpetrated genocidal attacks on the 'Iise Maḥamuud sublineages. Conveniently, he used the thousands of captured stock to reward his followers and to pay the lavish bride-prices for the multiple political marriages he sought to contract. The Sayyid was sufficiently pleased with the effects which the union of the sword and the poem were having on the country to sing:

> Let my soul proclaim the good tidings from the Lord;
> When the din of battle was heard a hundred times,
> The princes of the unbeliever-whites lay dead in the dust,
> From them I captured the many guns in my possession.
>
> Defeated, the English now bring us tributes;
> From Bullahaar[71] comes the rich token of their submission;
> As for the Italians – behold, they come as Dervish allies![72]

The display of pomp and bravura in these lines betrays the Sayyid's ingenious use of ordinary events to enhance the prestige of the Dervishes. The Illig agreement provided for a free flow of trade between the Dervishes and the British and Italian colonial authorities, and in fulfillment of this provision, the colonial authorities allowed the Dervishes to import commodities through their ports. Shrewdly, the Sayyid turned the colonial gesture into an acknowledgement by the Europeans of his suzerainty over them, the commodities being a 'rich token of their submission'. This line of argument was quite plausible to ordinary Somalis who had little or no knowledge of the inner mechanics of the agreement. He then went on to brag:

> I decimated the low-caste Majeerteen,
> Behold, the hyena feasts on the flesh of their fallen dead . . .
> And the vulture on the valiant among them . . .
> And their hapless remnant now pleads: 'Pray, let's eat some grain.'

Following the successful marriage alliance with the Warsangali, the Sayyid made a similar bid to Islaan Faaraḥ, the chief of the powerful 'Umar Maḥamuud lineage of the Majeerteen. Wary of any close dealings with the Dervishes ever since the poet, Shire Idaad, stigmatized them as a 'black magic sweeping the earth' from whom 'not a path has escaped', the Majeerteen chieftain was rather reluctant about treating with the Sayyid. But to directly rebuff him would no doubt have brought the wrath of the Dervishes on his clan, a matter that would entail dreadful consequences. So Islaan Faaraḥ sent an oblique response 'agreeing' in principle to the proposed marriage but requesting to have, among other valuables, Ḥiin Finiin, a swift pony, dear to the Sayyid's heart, in bride-wealth. The Majeerteen hoped the Sayyid would refuse to part with his favorite pony, a circumstance that would allow him to bow out of the proposed marriage without offending the Dervishes.

With the arrival of the oral epistle, it was now the Sayyid's turn to become crestfallen. To surrender his 'beloved beast' would be a terrible loss but not to do so would be even worse, damning as it was likely to be to his vaunted reputation of generosity. After much hesitation and heartache, the Sayyid decided to surrender the beast, but not before composing the 'Ḥiin Finiin' ('The Sound of Flying Gravel'), a somber reply named after the horse. Andrzejewski and Lewis, who produced a fine translation of the 'Ḥiin Finiin', perceive it, correctly in my view, as the poet's 'lament' of his 'loss'.

> Long life, Faaraḥ! Men are entitled to straightforward and respectful words.
> And I am a respectful man except when I am slighted,
> And friendship and openheartedness was my wont until the hateful envy of the infidels was unleashed upon me,
> And you have come to me bearing a message which a man of authority has written.
> Had you yourself sought from me countless wealth and livestock,
> I would not have hesitated in meeting your request,
> And indeed I intended to present you with a gift of fine camels from the herds,

And I meant to order thousands of those fine beasts to be driven into a corral for you,
But when you decided upon Ḥiin Finiin you made me heavy with pain.[73]

The poet then proceeded to detail Ḥiin Finiin's exceptional qualities:

And he is bay; for in colour horses are not equal.
The gallop, the trot, the canter, the walk,
To whichever you turn him he is without equal.
Oh, you the straight-limbed one; this beast is without peer;
And whenever he comes into my thoughts my love for him is rekindled,
And nothing except the letter of my faith surpasses my love for him.

Then follows a description of the uses which he intended to make of Ḥiin Finiin:

It was upon him that I intended to make a feast of my enemies for the hornbill[74] (the witness of death),
On him in the *Ḥays* rains I intended to attack from Ḥalin,
And between here and the coast to loot camels,
And on his back I meant to cut off the testicles of the menstruating infidels.

True to habit, the Sayyid turned to the subject he best knew how to handle, namely, vilification of his enemies whom he attacked as 'shameless' and 'evil-doers skulking about the world' who would jump at any chance to slander his reputation:

But always in the world there are evil-doers skulking,
They spread slander like the [base] Isaaq,[75]
And I fear that they will spoil my reputation;
And alas, to a man of honour slander is ever shameful,
And as a pilgrim I cannot in these times afford miserliness;
Instead of being talked about behind my back, I am now free from blame ...

At last the Sayyid is said to have turned over the reins of the horse to the Sultan's representative and concluded dramatically:

It is Ḥiin Finiin that you hold on a rope,
And all the other beasts shy away from him with reverence.
Since the Sultan to whom I owe respect has insisted on having it,
Take its bridle; I would not have honoured another man with it!

In return for his poetic pains and the surrender of his property, the

Sayyid did win his bride but not the power of her clan, who a year or so later fell out with him and left the Dervishes *en masse*.

To put the Sayyid's poetic combat in wider perspective, it may be helpful to discuss it in relation to that of the legion of poetic antagonists who did literary battle with him. The most notable among these are the two poets, 'Ali Ḍuuḥ of the Ḍulbahante clan and 'Ali Jaama' Haabiil of the Habar Awal Isaaq. Throughout the long struggle, these two maintained virulent literary duels with Sayyid Maḥammad, managing, on occasion, to more than hold their own. As a member of the 'Ali Geri sublineage, 'Ali Ḍuuḥ was a distant maternal uncle of the Sayyid. Like many of his kin, 'Ali Ḍuuḥ was an ardent follower of the Sayyid in the early phases of the struggle but later defected to the British sphere, whence he did much damage to the Dervish cause by concentrating his heavy literary guns on them.

The Isaaq poet, 'Ali Jaama' Haabiil, was, on the other hand, a resident of Berbera. Urbane, pious and of an unusually handsome physique, 'Ali Jaama' Haabiil utterly lacked those traits that would be vulnerable to slander by the Sayyid. He was clean, according to many observers, in 'both body and soul'. This lack of 'slanderable' quality in the Isaaq poet much vexed the Sayyid. Legend has it that he sent spies to Berbera with instructions to 'dig out dirt' on Ali Jaama' Haabiil in hopes of employing whatever skeleton – to use a modern phrase – could be found in the Isaaq's closet as material for his acrimonious epistles.

The crestfallen agents returned to their master with the report that indeed 'Ali Jaama' Haabiil was a 'man of impeccable stature',[76] in respect both of living habits and of physical appearance. They noted, however, that the Isaaq had a minor blemish to his physique, notably a yellow discoloration on his front teeth. And this blemish, such as it was, was to serve as the take-off material for the Sayyid's 72-line diatribe, 'The Parching Heat of the Wind', alliterating in the letter '**h**'. In 'The Parching Heat' Sayyid Maḥammad, with an injurious tongue and an embittered spirit, presented a genealogical catalogue of opponent clans for abuse and ridicule.

Only one line of this malevolent invocation is devoted to the Isaaq poet, 'And filth belongs to the donkey and to foul-mouthed 'Ali Jaama'', an apparent reference to the plaque on the latter's teeth. The brevity of the attack, however, gains effectiveness from its juxtaposition with the catalogue of tongue-lashing on other clans. The formalization in poetry of such abuse makes it belong to a class of defamatory verse, remembered and re-applied to new situations long after the original one had faded into oblivion.

In his response, 'Ali Jaama' concentrated his attacks on the two areas where the Sayyid was most vulnerable: (a) the Sayyid's indiscriminate 'raiding' and 'butchering', as he put it, of defenceless Muslims and (b) the Sayyid's well-known weakness for the fair sex. On the former, 'Ali Jaama' charged the Sayyid with one of the most heinous crimes in Islamic teaching, namely, the seizure and plunder of the property of orphans, as well as the callous slaughter of pious Muslims:

> And a thousand devout worshipers he butchered as one would a he-goat;
> And caravans are given the safety of Allah,
> But he wantonly cuts the tendons of weary travelers and engorges their dates.
> He's battened on the weak and the orphan
> Call you this Italian-infidel a Mahdi? How puzzling the thought:[77]

The accusation is that anyone guilty of such atrocities as 'Ali Jaama' claims to be regularly committed in the name of Dervishism could not be a genuine *wadaad* (man of God) but rather a vicious charlatan. By all accounts, the Sayyid had his share of the poet's weakness for pleasures of the flesh, and the 'beauty of women' received persistent attention both in his poetry and life. He is said to have contracted at least a dozen marriages, some of them, no doubt, politically inspired, while others testified to his 'keen eye for the fair maiden' ('bikrad bili' leh'). Since in Islam a man may marry no more than four wives at a time, the Sayyid was obliged, in an attempt to facilitate his multiple nuptial transactions, to marry and divorce frequently and this may have contributed to the instability, marital infidelity, internal strife and even death which from time to time afflicted his household.[78]

Thus we should understand, even if we are a little dismayed, when the Sayyid advises us 'not to trust him/her who grows up in your household' or cries out in verse that 'Every one married to me is a glowing ember of hell.'

It is this theme, the Sayyid's weakness for light pleasure, which his poetic antagonists constantly hammer at. 'Ali Jaama' accuses the Sayyid of being a libertine and an adulterer – 'Of free women / he cohabits with seven' – while 'Ali Ḍuuḥ went even further and charged the Sayyid with incest:

> And the women you consort with are fifteen ...
> Like a fattened ram among sheep in heat
> He tires not of lust, the lecherous infidel;
> In a crimson shawl and silken veil many an innocent lass night-visited him,

And lo, Rooḥa [the Sayyid's sister] has come to the office, testifying to partnership of lust . . .[79]

'Ali Ḍuuḥ further accused the Sayyid of drunken habits, a flight of imagination which could only have been concocted by an intemperate gush of resentment:

The Lunatic Maḥammad did not make me drink wine with him as he had done to the Khayr people,
Nor have I partaken of vinegar, the bitter thing, with him,
He did not turn my head, as he had the learned elders addicted to the crumbs of his table,
I've looked into his character and found him a worthless ruffian,
I have left him, the adventurous gambler, let calamity come upon him.[80]

'Ali Ḍuuḥ also did his measure of cursing:

Would that, O Maḥammad, a hissing ember of hell descended upon you,
Would that your chest and delicate organs were embraced by inferno,
O thou hairy one, let Allah destine you to perdition,
As you've earned, let Allah burden heat upon you.
Of the Shuun people [Ethiopian] and a whiskered Amḥaar you are.[81]

The charge against the Sayyid of womanizing is credible enough, that of wine-drinking less credible, unsupported as it is by any evidence, though curiously enough it has persisted through the years. A fake poem, for example, which came out in the 1960s purporting to be the Sayyid's, glories in the consumption of liquor, as this excerpt seems to indicate:

Beloved, my son, give me of this thing,
The thing that transports me into the status of a prudent elder . . .
But a sip of it and lethargy flies from the eyes,
It turns not my head, nor makes me insane,
But only removes mercy from the heart![82]

The alleged author of this counterfeit poem, 'Abdisalaam Ḥ. Aadan, is a contemporary Isaaq poet who has won fame, some say notoriety, for his crafty, though hilarious, imitations of Dervish poets for the purpose of burlesquing and trivializing their poetry.[83] Here, 'Abdisalaam arranges his parody on the Sayyid in triplet groupings to make it credible, thus cleverly meeting the physical, structural requirement of a triad. He even manages to construct into his poetic scheme one of the

Sayyid's formulaic devices of addressing his poem to a confidant, the 'Beloved, my son' who starts off the first line.

It is, however, on the semantic structure that he stumbles. It is clear, for example, that the 'thing' is the subject of 'Abdisalaam's versicle. Yet the 'thing' (whatever it is) is not developed as we would expect the Sayyid to develop it, but rather described with every line revealing something new, some unique property about it: (line 2) 'transports me into the status of ... elder'; (line 3) causes 'lethargy' to fly from the eyes; (line 4) does not turn the poet's head or make him insane, etc.

Although such description as the poet provides puts us in a position to render an informed guess, it never enables us to know exactly the identity of the 'thing'. Such an exercise in obscurity would be likely to ruffle, perhaps provoke the suspicion of, those accustomed to the Sayyid's clear, declarative style which never leaves the hearer groping in the dark as to the identity of its subject. Thus in an outwardly similar construction by the Sayyid, we have:

> Beloved, my son, there is a type of desire that fosters mortal offenses in men,
> But towards you I am gently disposed, because we are relatives,
> However harsh my treatment of others, to you I'll always remain kind.[84]

Here the subject of the triplet is the 'you', the addressee of the first line who receives a clear warning about the dire consequences of certain 'mortal' desires. In the second, the 'you' is carried on to be informed of the poet's gentle disposition toward him because 'we are relatives'. In the third, the thought is brought to a conclusion by the declaration that however severe the poet's mistreatment of others, he will always 'remain kind' to the 'beloved son'.

The Sayyid, at his best, thus utilizes the technique of sustained development, selecting a design and holding on to it. 'Abdisalaam, the burlesquer, by contrast, utilizes what may be termed the technique of sustained parallelism, with each subsequent line adding to what preceded it but never building on it. It is a subtle but an important difference.

Another opponent poet, the Isaaq Jeeni-'Ade, made a damning comparison between the Dervish government and that of the English, maintaining that life under a Christian ruler was infinitely preferable to the bloody anarchy which, he charged, characterized the Dervishes:

> Of water, the reliable trickle is better than the untested gush of the fount,
> An obedient wench is better than an intemperate woman of class;

And an unyielding camel which supports her suckling
Is better than a mean-tempered camel of much milk,
And an adversary is better than kinsmen who abandon fellow kin.
It is better to have none than to be afflicted with in-laws of bad manners,
Better than a murderous Muslim is a Christian who protects your woman and child![85]

The polemic was second nature to the Sayyid and he was more often than not able to 'outdo' his opponents but whenever a certain missive proved particularly offensive to his honor, he would organize a punitive expedition against the clan of the offending poet. He would also direct a response to each individual attacker so that the resulting poetic exchange became what the Somalis call a 'chain' (*silsilad*), a series of polemics. In addition, he would compose a blanket answer to the 'Somalis', a term of derision reserved for non-Dervishes. In the following passage of proverbs with its typical circumlocutions, he attacks colonial-protected clans as 'peons and houseboys' of white men:

A liar I despise,
A miser I despise,
And I despise him who eats polluted food.

A tobacco-chewer I despise,
I despise compulsiveness in men
And fat without strength.

I despise an uncourageous man of small lineage,
I despise a tool that doesn't obey its user . . .

A white man's peon I despise
And his houseboy I despise . . .

An unjust king I despise,
A flag without an army I despise
And a city without rule I despise.[86]

It is clear that the combined weight of his legion of attackers was having a corrosive effect on the Sayyid, and on occasion he betrayed the extent of his bitterness against his accusers. In 1908, he wrote to the Commissioner of Somaliland that one of the prime causes of the disturbance of the peace was the insults, intrigue and envy directed at him by poets of government clans: 'Being cursed [he complained] is harder for us to bear than having our necks cut off . . . I am considered (by opponents) and called a bad man, such as 'old singer', 'looter', 'disturber of peace' . . .[87]

Poetic oratory and the Dervish movement

If the British-protected 'Ali Jaama' and 'Ali Ḍuuḥ could attack the Sayyid from the relative security of Berbera, other poets were not so lucky. 'Ol-u-Joog Aadan Jugle, who belonged to the more inland Habar Yoonis Isaaq, despatched a vitriolic versicle to the Sayyid, the key line of which read: 'Even the Sayyid is in mortal fear of stirring our camels / which've come down to pasture on the Seeto plains.' Evidently, the Sayyid took a deep offense at the imputation of personal cowardice to him for he is said to have assembled his warriors and fulminated: 'Is there not one among my cowardly followers who can defend me against this low-caste Habar Yoonis poet?'[88]

Although the Sayyid's response, 'This News from Beyond the Seas', constitutes, literarily, one of his outstanding poems, it reveals the depressed mood he was in at the time of composing:

> This news from beyond the seas, imparted to me of late by the villagers,
> This news from the low-born Habar Yoonis which reached me in the East saddens me.
> He who believes the Dervishes to be any longer men of valor is mistaken,
> The valiant among them are no more, only the rabble remains,
> These lads – who swagger and sway – they've lost the fighting mettle.
>
> I fret in fury while my men languish in stupefying fear,
> They cower and cringe in terror ever since the defeat of Buura hills,[89]
> The rout of Jidbaale's turned them into a miserable lot of nursing maids.
>
> Oh, how the heart, my heart aches as if I've engorged the fat tail of sheep,
> The throb of pain is upon it
> And the body shrinks from sadness and weeping.
>
> Afflicted and dust-ridden, I lie, humiliated by the uncircumcised unbeliever [the English],
> The liver shivers, I quake for the men the infidel killed in wanton jest,
> Behold, the hyena feasts on the flesh of my fallen comrades.[90]

The poet continued to pour out his lugubrious jeremiads, regretting the loss of his brave warriors who had been killed in the wars and dwelling on his dark contention that those who remained of the Dervishes were no longer men but 'nursing maids'.

His object in composing 'This News from Beyond the Seas' was to arouse his men into a renewed martial spirit, and he was not disappointed.

Shortly after the publicizing of the mournful composition, 600 Dervish warriors went on a secret expedition, sworn to 'avenge themselves on the slanderer of their master'.[91] Marching under cover of night and keeping their mission completely secret, they reached the plains overlooking the town of Bur'o three months later. Here they surprised and put their taunter's clan to the sword. With a ferocity savage even by Dervish standards, they are said to have 'destroyed every living thing they chanced upon which they had not carried off in booty'.[92]

The Dervishes seized 20,000 camels in loot (a loot known as Daboolane) and among the Habar Yoonis dead they left behind were the clan's chieftain, Aḥmad Shire and his brother.

With the safe arrival of his men and the booty, the Sayyid composed several taunt songs, the most notable among them being the 'Herald of Good Tidings', 'Mahade Haw Sheego', alliterating in the letter '**m**'. Apart from being of considerable literary quality, this poem has a significance which lies in its author's awareness of the international dimensions of the conflict. As the Sayyid saw it, the blow against the Habar Yoonis Isaaq, a British-protected clan, was not only a blow against the English but also a victory for the Muslim community the world over. Thus the epistle is addressed to Egypt:

> This, my song, I will send to Egypt,
> I'll send it in a ship, a ship which will tear through the rolling waves,
> And will plunge through the tangled maze of sea life.
>
> Let it voyage from here to Aden . . .
> And when it reaches the port and fastens anchor to unload,
> Let it place my greetings on the right hand of the Muslim faithful,
> Let it take my affection to him who is not a servile servant to the heathen-whites.[93]

The eighty-four lines of this poem which are extant reveal the Sayyid employing all the major ingredients of his technique: the triad, the evasive verbosity and the verse epistle, as well as a high-minded blend of the didactic with the artistic. With gleeful effusions, the Sayyid narrates fully the Dervish victory over the Habar Yoonis and inflates it, for propaganda effect, into an epic triumph with international dimensions.

The Sayyid's rejoicings, however, were to prove premature. A few years later (around 1915) the Dervishes were stripped not only of what they had robbed from the Habar Yoonis but of much of their original stock by the Sultan 'Ismaan Maḥamuud, the wily chieftain who may be said to have played a significant role in the fall of Dervishism. Miinanle, as the herd of Dervish stock seized by the Majeerteen came to be known, was proclaimed the biggest camel theft in the annals of stock-rustling among the pastoral Somalis. The significant thing, for the purpose of this discussion is that this, too, was allegedly provoked by poetry.

The two Majeerteen sultanates of 'Ismaan Maḥamuud and Yuusuf 'Ali Keenadiid had fought desultory wars ever since the 1880s when Yuusuf 'Ali Keenadiid, Sultan 'Ali's father, in a succession struggle, broke off from his cousin's territory and founded his mini-state of Hobyo, further south along the coast. Pestalozza concluded the Illig agreement partly to place the Dervishes as a buffer state between Italy's two warring princelets on the Somali coast. On the rumor that 'Ismaan Maḥamuud was preparing an expedition against Hobyo, 'Ali Yuusuf prompted his court poet to compose a damning epistle on Sultan 'Ismaan which was issued and publicized, cunningly enough, as the work of the Dervishes. Keenadiid's object in originating the incisive missive was to arouse hostility between the Sayyid and Sultan 'Ismaan, in hopes of deflecting the latter from the proposed expedition, and he was successful. Before the Dervishes had any knowledge of the existence of the poem or the opportunity to deny being its source, Sultan 'Ismaan, who was incensed at being attacked as 'not a prince but a mere fisher' (*kaluun dabato*) – the consumption of fish is despised by the pastoralists – fell on the unsuspecting Dervishes and made off with 50,000 head of Dervish stock.

The Dervishes under the military command of 'Aamir 'Agoole, Sayyid Maḥammad's uncle, made protracted attempts to recover Miinanle but never succeeded in doing so, although they had repeatedly harried the Majeerteen. Henceforth, the Dervishes remained mortal enemies of the Majeerteen sultanate and the Sayyid composed at least half a dozen poetic laments, regretting the loss of his precious herds and singling out his lieutenants' lack of vigilance as the blame for the misfortune.[94]

We have said that the period of poetry was, on the whole, a period of Dervish prosperity and it is this prosperity which underlies the composition of the 'Time Everlasting', a song of military display or, in the words of a Dervish elder, a 'showing of the teeth' (*ḍoola tusad*).[95] For five years following the Illig agreement, the Sayyid fought a literary war in which, to judge from the growth of Dervish strength and influence, the Dervishes recovered from the reverses of Jidbaale. 'Viewing a military parade and seeing the coming of fighting age of the orphans whose fathers were killed in previous battles',[96] the Sayyid ordered the military maneuver to impress on his foes that he had not only the strength but the determination to resume the armed phase of the struggle. A few sample illustrations from the 'Time Everlasting', though in an inadequate translation, reveal his mood of defiance:

Must I from time everlasting
Maintain servile politeness,
Abstain from evil words,
And observe the peace?

Must I from time everlasting
Coax into false calmness
The husbandless wife and the fatherless child?

Must I from time everlasting
Fear to face [out of shame]
The weeping of the women
And the clamor they would make?

Must I from time everlasting
Implore every morning that comes round
For restitution for my men
Who've been wantonly slaughtered
And my property
Which has been confiscated?

Must I from time everlasting
Again and again cry out:
'Pray, Officer Swayne,[97] let's leave each other alone'?
But leave me alone he would not.

The 'Time Everlasting' belongs to a category of verse in which the Sayyid attained fame for his description and praise of the horse: its uses in warfare, its nobility in the animal species and the 'sheer magnificence' of its physical beauty. A rendition in English of the Sayyid's verse on the horse would be likely to yield an interesting and rewarding result, though such an effort does not belong here, and it is hoped that others who possess literary ambition will undertake the task.

In 1909, as in other years, the Sayyid proposed and events disposed. Just as he was about to resume the armed assault to complement the literary assault on the 'unbeliever', there occurred a convulsive episode which shook up the Dervishes, nearly cost the Sayyid his leadership of the movement and occupied his poetic and political energies for the next four years. This was the Tree-of-Bad-Counsel revolt discussed in the preceding chapter. In this aborted coup, 600 conspirators tried unsuccessfully to oust the Sayyid from power following the outright repudiation of him by his Meccan master, Maḥammad Saliḥ.

The uprising, whose suppression precipitated the ruthless slaughter of scores of religious men and Dervish notables, destroyed the moral basis of the movement, and it could be said with fairness that ever after this incident the Sayyid ruled more by coercion than by persuasion. Henceforward, he behaved like, and seems to have become, a mere warrior chieftain.

The series of apologetic poems in which he tried to absolve himself of responsibility for the disaster and to gloss over its evil effects are referred to as the 'Chain of the Tree-of-Bad-Counsel' ('Silsilada 'Anjeel Tala waa'). The chain includes the 'Alas, My Wives' discussed in an earlier section, the 'Bad Tree' ('Anjeel Tala waa'), the 'Rising Fury' ('Saha Ka'ay'), the 'Voice of Verse' (''Od Gabay') and the 'Hyena among the Goats' ('Ḍurwaa Ariga'). In them the Sayyid attempted to justify, with mixed success, his harsh conduct towards the conspirators: the summary executions of the ring leaders (many of whom were prominent mullahs and al-Ḥaajs) and the dispossession and banishment of the rest, as morally sound and politically imperative. Politically imperative, maybe, but hardly a moral victory. He tried to discredit the rebels as apostates, spies, malcontents and greedy men who sought to advance personal ends at the expense of the cause. How could anyone blame him for preventing these ravenous hyenas from devouring the flock? In the amusing song, the 'Hyena among the Goats', he prompted his aide, Ḥuseen Ḍiqle, to hold a mock but telling poetic contest with an imaginary hyena over the question of who has the right to consume the flocks – flocks understood in this context to stand metaphorically for the Dervish faithful. Ḥuseen Ḍiqle sang:

> O, Hyena, the flocks belong to God,
> To God and to the Master,
> The flocks belong to armed warriors,
> It is the Dervish warriors . . .
> Before a hidden club strikes you,
> Flee, flee for your life.[98]

The hyena, in the mouth of the Sayyid, replied:

> A word with you, O man of little knowledge,
> Earlier you said, 'The flocks belong to God.'
> Why do you say now 'The flocks are ours?'
> Would you speak with two mouths?
> Are you like God? Or would you claim to be stronger than he is?
> Can you prevent, O, you lowly son of Adam, my livelihood?
> Did not the Lord give the breath of life to both of us?
> Or would you think the great Lord (respecter of no persons) to be partial to you?

Why would you whine and whimper if I should find one day a morsel of bread
To break my fast?

This poem belongs to a poetic genre which the pastoralists call 'converted' or 'hidden' (*qafilan*) verse. Impregnated with social ambiguities and contradictions, such material calls on the poet to treat it with a great deal of tact, in particular, to handle ambiguities in ambiguous language, so as to avoid the embarrassment and even the socio-political crisis which the elucidation of hitherto 'hidden' things may entail. On one level, for example, the hyena accuses his poetic opponent, Ḥuseen Ḍiqle (here representing the human family) of arrogance, vanity, selfishness and other evil emotions associated with the human species.

On another level, the hyena may be seen as representing the rebels and Ḥuseen Ḍiqle as an obvious spokesman for his master. It is the rebels' intention, then, to challenge the Sayyid's arrogation to himself, indeed his monopoly, of the leadership of the movement. Their protest is a protest against the tyranny of one-man rule, in particular, when that man has lost the moral credibility to lead – as had the Sayyid, in their view, the moment he was disavowed by his teacher.

On yet a third level, and probably the one most tenable in a content analysis of the whole poem, it may be seen as a statement of clannish politics. Traditionally, the hyena is associated with the Ḍulbahante as a sort of metaphoric totem. In terms of agnatic kinship (the Somalis are patrilineal), the Ḍulbahante belong to the Harti cluster of clan families including the Majeerteen and the Warsangali. The Harti, though too numerous and too unwieldy to act together politically, regard themselves as kinsmen in relation to the Ogaadeen, the Sayyid's paternal kin and the other main branch of the Daarood clans.

If it was the Ḍulbahante who constituted the central pillar of the Dervish force, it was also from them that the ringleaders (with the exception of Aḥmad Fiqi and 'Abdille Qoryow) of the attempted coup sprang. In the poem, the hyena admonishes both the Sayyid and his aide to quit the territory of his cousins and to go to their Ogaadeen kinsmen.

The Sayyid was certainly alive to the paradox and the precariousness of his position from a tribal viewpoint – aware, too, of the circumstance that his power rested on the Ḍulbahante with whom, tough he was maternally attached, he did not share paternal ties. This may in part account for his sustained requirement that upon entry into the Dervish ranks all his followers should renounce their former kinship obligations in favor of allegiance to him and to the new cause. 'Ali Ḍuuḥ, the Ḍulbahante poet and the Sayyid's perennial foe, on the other hand, sought to exploit the situation in the opposite direction by striving relentlessly to expose the Sayyid as an outsider and an impostor who had no right to exercise leadership among 'Ali Ḍuuḥ's kin. So he maintained in this excerpt from a poem in which he attacked the Sayyid as a 'hairy sorcerer'.[99]

> I'll sing and sing till I've caused my kin to quit you *en masse*;
> You fool, they who've made you mighty were not of your flesh,
> As well aware, you, the hairy sorcerer, must be that your elders belong to the Adan-Ḍagaḥ[100]
> And your kin to the Reer-Ḥamar [101] dogs.

The last, though important, series selected for comment is called 'Corfield's Chain' ('Silsilada Koofil') and it began in the spring of 1913. As the title implies, the chain concerns Col. Richard Corfield of Somaliland, and his death constitutes the central event in the series, although the first poem was composed some months before the colonel's fall. Sent to Somaliland to organize a camel constabulary and establish order after two years of unprecedented anarchy in the interior, Corfield proved to be a man of courage and dash, gradually winning the respect of friendly clans whose confidence in the government had been badly shaken. He did much to 'restore order', to keep the trade-routes open in the vicinity of Berbera and to put an end to internecine fighting between the Habar Yoonis and Habar Awal clans.

But Corfield had a streak of the madcap in him – rash, arrogant and tactless, he treated the Somalis with great highhandedness, subjecting them to summary confiscations, jailings and banishings. It was after one such incident that the first of the series, a curse versicle or 'stabber-poem', was pronounced on him by an Isaaq poet, one Ina Weesa-ḥume, whose herds had been seized and sold at an auction by Corfield:

> When the Sayyid strikes ... and you pursue him to rescue the herds,
> Would that you and your party had perished in the pursuit,
> Would that your maxim guns had stopped firing ...
> Let the men of God hungry for infidel blood hack you to pieces,
> As you're partial in judging, let your mouth be cut off,
> You've reduced my kinsmen to poverty,
> Would that you were cut off before the *gu'* rains.[102]

We may note here that the Somalis attach significance to the coincidence of the curse on Corfield and his death a few months later. They do not in fact speak of it as a mere coincidence but as something of a cause and effect, believing, as they do, in the power of the poetic curse to influence events.

Corfield's success with the friendly clans may have given him a false sense of invincibility, for he was drawn into an engagement with a large Dervish raiding party at Dulmadooba near Oodweyne on 9 August 1913. Although the constabulary fought courageously, they were overwhelmed and savagely cut up, Corfield being killed in action. The Dervishes sustained considerable losses but proudly carried off the looted stock and Corfield's severed arm as a war trophy.

On arrival at the *ḥarun*, Ismaa'iil Mire, one of the commanders of the raid, composed a *gabay*, the second in the series, 'Residing in Taleeḥ', celebrating the success which attended his operation. We observed earlier that this poem seems to have been composed without the Sayyid's permission, for it evidently got its author into trouble with his master. The Sayyid is said to have censured his disciple by delivering a critique on the poem, praising it as a work of an accomplished *gabayaa* (poet), but mildly protesting that the *gabay* did not include vivid details concerning the manner of Corfield's death. Ismaa'iil Mire observed with convenient humility that his was the work of amateurish enthusiasm but that he hoped the master would compose a poem worthy of the occasion. More Dervishes joined Ismaa'iil Mire imploring the Sayyid to recite a *gabay*, whereupon he reportedly burst into hysterical laughter, stroked his fuzzy beard with unwonted animation and addressed a valedictory message to Corfield's severed arm.[103] The resulting poem named 'Koofil', a Somali corruption of 'Corfield', should therefore be viewed as an epistle sent to the souls in the Other World:

> You have died, Corfield, and are no longer in this world,
> A merciless journey was your portion.
> When, Hell-destined, you set out for the Other World
> Those who have gone to Heaven will question you, if God is willing;
> When you see the companions of the faithful and the jewels of Heaven,
> Answer them how God tried you.
> Say to them: 'From that day to this the Dervishes never ceased their assaults upon us.
> The British were broken, the noise of battle engulfed us;
> With fervour and faith the Dervishes attacked us.'
> Say: 'They attacked us at mid-morning.'
> Say: 'Yesterday in the holy war a bullet from one of their old rifles struck me.
> And the bullet struck me in the arm.'
> Say: 'In fury they fell upon us.'
> Report how savagely their swords tore you,

Show these past generations in how many places the daggers were plunged.
Say: '"Friend," I called, "have compassion and spare me!"'
Say: 'As I looked fearfully from side to side my heart was plucked from its sheath.'
Say: 'My eyes stiffened as I watched with horror;
The mercy I implored was not granted.'
Say: 'Striking with spear-butts at my mouth they silenced my soft words;
My ears, straining for deliverance, found nothing;
The risk I took, the mistake I made, cost me my life.'
Say: 'Like the war leaders of old, I cherished great plans for victory.'
Say: 'The schemes the djinns planted in me brought my ruin.'
Say: 'When pain racked me everywhere
Men lay sleepless at my shrieks.'
Say: 'Great shouts acclaimed the departing of my soul.'
Say: 'Beasts of prey have eaten my flesh and torn it apart for meat.'
Say: 'The sound of swallowing the flesh and the fat comes from the hyena.'
Say: 'The crows plucked out my veins and tendons.'
Say: 'If stubborn denials are to be abandoned, then my clansmen were defeated.'
In the last stand of resistance there is always great slaughter.
Say: 'The Dervishes are like the advancing thunderbolts of a storm, rumbling and roaring.'[104]

The 'Epistle to the English Woman', intended for Richard Corfield's sister, is another in the series and I have already cited this work as an example of polemical excesses which nearly overwhelmed the otherwise valid points in the poem.

Corfield's biographer, H. F. P. Battersby, seems unwittingly to have entered the poetic contest. Although there is no evidence that he was aware of the literary warfare at work on the Somali side, he opened his biography with a poem by a certain Sidney Low that admirably fits into the vitriolic properties of pastoral polemicism. A blend of passionate eulogy and bitter criticism, 'Beyond these Voices' is the author's attempt to defend his subject against defamation by officialdom – Corfield was attacked by the Colonial Office as rash and overbold – and to pay tribute to a 'gallant soldier' who admittedly fell as 'Englishmen should fall' in an 'obscure desert', while serving the empire:

We strive to pierce the veil, and deem,
Not wholly vain it is, the dream

That they who pass beyond our ken
Hear echoes from the world of men.
Ah, wistful hearts! Ah, straining eyes!
Do ye not know that death is wise?
That death is merciful to spread
His veil between us and our dead?
Lest they should taste the keener sting,
To hear Earth's evil rumours ring;
The cankered taunt, the venomed lie.
The honour stained they held so high.
May we not praise him: young and brave,
Who lies there in his desert grave?
May we not say that, after all,
He fell as Englishmen should fall?
No! We must deprecate and scold;
Hint he was rash, was over-bold;
Throw lurking shadows round his name,
Deny him his poor meed of fame.
Then rest, O valiant soul! Nor know,
We rate your gift of life so low;
And Death be tender still, and keep
Our shameful voices from your sleep.[105]

To reassert here the seriousness with which Somalis view the poetic curse, and the mixture of awe and contempt in which they hold the composer and user of curse, would be to restate the obvious. What needs to be re-emphasized, perhaps, is the tacit ethical code that poetic invocation of evil should be used sparingly, if it must be used at all. There is about the curse an element that boomerangs, a sort of 'he who lives by the curse shall perish by the curse'. And so it was, in the view of some Dervish observers, with Maḥammad 'Abdille Ḥasan.[106]

According to Ismaa'iil Mire, the Sayyid's right-hand man who was lucky enough to survive the violent demise of Dervishism, the collapse of the holy war was directly attributable to the Sayyid's heavy-handed treatment of the Ḍulbahante Khayr people, a clan of mullahs whom Somalis believe to enjoy divine protection. From 1916 onwards, the Khayr people were repeatedly harried by the Dervishes, as were most clans in northeastern Somalia, partly to give an edge to the Dervishes' new policy of what might be termed 'subjugation by force'. In his 'Road to Harar' ('Jidka Adari Loo Maro'), composed around 1914, a poem, as one observer put it, 'dripping with blood',[107] the Sayyid declared that henceforward he would make the Somalis 'pay him homage by the point of the spear' (waran 'aaradi). And the violent chaos which followed showed that his was far from being an idle threat. In the relevant portion of his 'Reward of Success', Ismaa'iil Mire claimed:

> Again and again the Sayyid made war and people helped him;
> Thousand upon thousand, all with white turbans, he brought to the battle of Beerdiga,
> But what brought his downfall was the day he destroyed the Khayr people.
> Oh men, pride brings disaster: let that be remembered![108]

Few could have been more aware than Ismaa'iil Mire, the Dervish warrior who experienced at first hand the cataclysmic early months of 1920, that what brought Sayyid Maḥammad's 'downfall' was the combination of British might and a smallpox epidemic which ravaged the Dervishes by turns. Yet Ismaa'iil Mire, like many other observers of the movement including contemporary ones, would seem to place more weight on the transcendental cause of the collapse than on the immediate: the Sayyid, they would maintain, disobeyed the divine mandate by ordering the indiscriminate massacre of *wadaads* and innocent folk.[109] This charge against the Sayyid of estrangement from the 'proper' course and of incurring concomitant divine displeasure is reflected in the work of the Ḍulbahante poet, Ḥasan Shiil, whose stabber-poem is associated in the minds of some with the fall of the Sayyid. Stripped of stock by the Dervishes, the poet fled to Hobyo with a band of refugees where he is alleged to have despatched his epistolary malediction around 1918:

> O Lord we pray to thee
> Bring death on the man [the Sayyid],
> Or make him insane,
> Or guide him to the true faith,
> Or turn him over to
> The infidels that seek his life.
> Lord, do not choose this man
> Above all thy people.[110]

Indigenous sources who tend to place faith in the efficacy of the poetic curse are quick to make a mystical linkage between this and similar invocations of evil brought on by Dervish excesses and the demise of the movement the following year. While making a seasoned assessment of the real causes which terminated the struggle – war, internal strife, pestilence – they nevertheless point to the curse as a contributing cause. To them, the relationship between the actual cause and the transcendental does not involve an absolute dichotomy, but rather a situation in which the one serves as the agent of the other. Through their intemperate use of power, these sources would argue, the Dervishes incurred a curse – therefore, catastrophe came upon them.

It is the description of this catastrophe which constitutes the central message of 'The Will' ('Dardaaran'), Sayyid Maḥammad's last poem, composed in the closing months of 1920 shortly before his death.[111] 'The Will', as the title implies, is a testimonial epistle, relating a frighteningly realistic account of the Dervish losses to the last British expedition and to the subsequent outbreak of the disastrous epidemic. It ends with a somber, though strikingly prescient, prediction of colonial triumph over the Somalis. There is also an element of the 'Jiin' in 'The Will', the old warrior, at once combative and self-pitying, striving to alert his countrymen to the imminent catastrophe through the poetic word. After describing in vivid detail what he lost in men and property, the Sayyid posited a defiant challenge:

> A beating we took, forced to flee, to swim in haste across the river,[112]
> Stripped of stock, we reel, reduced to destitution.
> Rejoice, then, you lackeys who remained behind.
>
> And an argument I will return to these people who revel in ceaseless banter,
> Oh men, foolery leads to mental deterioration,
> Yet some love to indulge in profitless disputation.
>
> I, on my own volition, chose to fight the infidels,
> It was I who said to the filthy unbeliever: 'This land is not yours.'
> It was I who sought and found the prophet's guidance.
>
> It was I who rejected again and again the infidel's offer to buy me out,
> It was I who refused to sell my faith to gain the gates of hell,
> And it was I who desired no status in the first of the two Worlds.[113]

Then once again the old apostle of acrimony raised his head:

> It was I who would not pack transport camels for the expeditions of the heathen,
> It was I who would not carry their compass when they go to raid,
> And it was I who would not go before the white man as guide and scout.
>
> It was I who would not assist the dirty unbeliever,
> I who would not succor the uniformed whites,
> I who would not be, like the greedy Iidoor,[114] the white man's burden-bearing beast.
>
> It was I who would not enter the house of pigs nor of dogs . . .

Then the master-manipulator of clan politics sought to exploit the tribal differences of his opponents with a view to dividing the enemy alliance:

> O the pity the Daarood know not the trap being laid for them,
> The fools, they drummed and danced with joy when I was defeated,
> The fools, they sighed with relief: 'Lo, the *Wadaad* flees westward.'

In this triplet the Sayyid was making a direct reference to a taunt song by his implacable enemy, 'Ali Ḍuuḥ, who, upon hearing of the defeat of the Dervishes, gloated over their fall with injurious malice: 'How delightful it is to savor the defeat of your oppressor / Behold, the Mullah flees with the west wind.' In the response, the Sayyid was craftily trying to remind the Daarood 'Ali Ḍuuḥ that the defeat of the Sayyid who, as a fellow Daarood was after all a kinsman, might well usher in a domination of all the Daaroods, including 'Ali Ḍuuḥ's clan, by their ancient rivals, the Isaaq.

Finally, we hear the voice of the ardent nationalist who, contemptuous of clannish politics and petty feuding, was aiming at higher things, notably, to awaken his sleeping countrymen to the loss of their land and liberty:

> Oh, hear me, hear me, fellow Somalis
> Or refusing to hear, say comfortingly to yourselves: 'Let the madman rave.'
> Here, my will to the prudent man, let the fool ignore it:
>
> There never was a gain in treating with the whites;
> You soften up to the unbelieving white man and he is bound to deceive you,
> One day you will come to regret the *dirhams* [money] he is pouring over you.
>
> First, he'll disarm you, he'll turn you into womenfolk,
> Next, he'll commit you to his prison wards,
> Then, he'll say to you under duress: 'Trade in the land for a little mammon.'
>
> Last, he'll place a heavy load, like a pack donkey's, on your wretched backs;
> Since in my flight I've gone beyond the plains of Iimey[115] and the hills of Harar,
> What good will your gloating do you, your gloating over my predicament?
> Behold, tomorrow he'll descend over you with his colonizing tools.[116]

It is hoped that despite the loss in translation of the alliteration, rhythm and meter, something of the majesty, the truly moving power of the original comes through to the reader. The Sayyid did not live long enough to savor the effects, if any, that 'The Will' had on his countrymen. Whether it would have succeeded in deflecting the disaster, as did the Jidbaale series, or would merely have fallen on deaf ears, given the hardships which latter-day Dervishism caused in the land, is a matter for conjecture. 'With his death,' says an Ogaadeen elder, 'we sustained the contradictory feelings of gloom and relief. Gloom that in his passing we lost an indefatigable fighter of imperialists, a great nationalist, a pillar of Islam and a brave kinsman. Relief that the terrible man, the hairy Mullah was no more.'[117]

The significant thing is that Maḥammad 'Abdille Ḥasan repeatedly sought to achieve in verse what he had failed to achieve in arms. The examples of Jidbaale, of the Tree-of-Bad-Counsel, of the Corfield series – in short, the constant poetic battles have, it is hoped, presented the reader with sufficient material to appreciate the importance of the poetic word to the success of Somali Dervishism. When defeated, the Sayyid dipped into his reservoir of rhymes at once to boost the morale of his broken army and to reduce his enemies to confusion. When victorious the poetic word was equally efficacious to celebrate the victory, and more important, to solemnize it so that it became history. 'Victory without verse,' said Aw Daahir Afqarshe, 'was no victory but merely an ephemeral event.'[118]

Both functions – inspiration of the faithful and denunciation of the foe – were necessary for the success, in fact the peculiar durability, of Somali Dervishism for the words of the poet were far from being idle utterances. They were no less important than the actual fighting, as the instances above have demonstrated. Even when his verse reflected the feeble and self-pitying cry of a discredited old warrior – which is in effect what the 'Jiin' is – the Sayyid exercised profound influence over the hearts and minds of his countrymen through his rare powers of the tongue. Given the peculiar ways in which poetic diction influences the Somali environment, the Sayyid had the power, at least symbolically, to give life or withhold it, to save or damn, and to inspire men with that loyalty which enabled them to invoke his name not only in the heat of battle but at the cold hour of execution.

5

Myth and the Mullah[1]

No character in recent Somali history has drawn so much attention from both foreign and indigenous writers as the Sayyid Maḥammad 'Abdille Ḥasan, known in colonial literature as the 'Mad Mullah'.[2] Yet, paradoxically, few have been misinterpreted and misunderstood more than this enigmatic sheikh who caused untold trouble for the British administration in northern Somalia, restricted the Italians to the south and harried Ethiopia's forces in the west for two decades (1900–20). The Sayyid and his movement have been so condemned on the one hand and adulated on the other that it is hard for the student of Somali Dervishism to avoid either the unrestrained bias of anti-Dervish literature or the equally uncritical pro-Dervish publicity.

In the past, Western literature, British in particular, depicted Sayyid Maḥammad 'Abdille Ḥasan as a 'monomaniac a libertine, a profligate, and a cut-throat tyrant', whose 'oriental mind saw sensual pleasures as the natural rewards of earthly power' and whose fanatical movement 'spelt economic stagnation for Somaliland and ruin for its inhabitants'.[3]

Recently, however, another interpretation of the Somali Dervishes has gained momentum. The latter, chiefly propounded by Somali national leaders and popularized by historians, portrays Maḥammad 'Abdille Ḥasan as 'a visionary, the father of the modern Somali nation',[4] blocked at every turn by imperialist machinations in his attempts to unify the Somali nation. With the struggle against colonialism and the concomitant achievement of independence, it was only natural that Somali leaders should look back in their history to find a national hero whose legacy commands a continuing vitality for contemporary Somalis and for the task of nation-building. Maḥammad 'Abdille Ḥasan is the only figure since the Garaad Ḥirsi 'Wiil waal' ('Crazy Boy') of Jigjiga (*ca.* 1800–50), and before him the sixteenth-century Muslim leader, Aḥmad Gurey (Maḥammad Gran), whose prestige cut across tribal lines.[5] He has therefore been chosen to bridge the discontinuity between present nationalism and early twentieth-century resistance groups – hence the overstated tribute to the man and his movement.

1 THE CHANGING IMAGES OF THE MULLAH

The controversy in the historiography of Maḥammad 'Abdille Ḥasan begins with the traditional, Western, pejorative title, the 'Mad Mullah'. Although they did not invent the term, colonial writers certainly welcomed it as a fitting epithet portraying what they thought to be the man's manifest irrationality. In reviewing British literature of the period, one comes to realize how easy it was for the British imperial temper and taste to view Maḥammad 'Abdille Ḥasan as a madman and, worse still, as an outlaw-chieftain of an isolated band of cut-throat robbers who supposedly had no appeal to the Somalis and no significance to the history of Somalia.

Italian colonial opinion was a shade gentler to the Sayyid. In contrast to the British, the Italians did not characterize him as a monomaniac, but rather as a misguided savage prompted by an ideal to embark on an ill-advised course. Robert Hess quotes a revealing passage from Francesco S. Caroselli stating that the Italians found the Somali Dervish leader 'a little African Napoleon . . . equal to the great Corsican perhaps only in his hatred of the English'.[6]

The colonial image of Maḥammad 'Abdille Ḥasan changed abruptly in the wake of an independent Somalia and the consequent rise of Afro-centric historiography. Under the new interpretation, the term 'Mullah' has given way to 'Sayyid' (master). Likewise, the Dervish warriors are now called freedom fighters. The temptation is thus to err towards the other extreme, that of overstating the merits of the man and his movement. Demonstrative of the new trend is the banishing of the term 'Mad Mullah' from the vocabulary of contemporary historians and the introduction of terminology more appropriate to a nationalist hero, such as 'an African Napoleon'.[7] Thus, after the efforts of I. M. Lewis,[8] Robert Hess and, recently, B. G. Martin,[9] the user of the word 'Mullah' in reference to the Sayyid runs the risk of being charged with historiographical infidelity.

The term 'Mad Mullah' had a rather innocuous beginning. Contrary to the common assumption held by many contemporary historians, its roots go back to Somali rivals of the Sayyid rather than to his colonial detractors. The label 'Mad Mullah' ('Wadaad Waal') was given to him by the inhabitants of Berbera who belonged to the Muslim religious order of Qaadiriya.[10] The Sayyid, as representative of the new and more puritanical Saaliḥiya sect, was embroiled for two years (1895–7) in a disastrous theological dispute with Qaadiriya notables, and it was they who not only gave him the enduring epithet but drove him out of town in a less than honorable fashion.

The adjective 'Mad' was later given an official status in colonial writing by J. Hayes Sadler, the first British Consul General of the Somaliland Protectorate, who wrote in July 1899, that 'reports from the Dolbahanta, apparently on good authority, are to the effect that the Mullah has gone off his head'. Sadler added later on in a leisurely manner: 'The general opinion about the man is that he has gone religious mad.'[11] The term 'Mullah' itself, as we have seen, was one of a group of words imported from the Indian sub-continent which gained widespread currency in Somaliland in the 1890s.

It appears that what Somalis had in mind in coining the phrase had no relation to what the British thought it meant. When Somalis speak of someone as being mad (*waalan*), they may be expressing a variety of concepts, beginning with the recklessness characteristic of the 'mad brave' (*geesi waalan*). The renunciation of worldly concerns in favor of a transcendental mystery characteristic of the Muslim mystic (Sufi) is a similar concept, as is being slightly touched, a little queer but not really mad (*salaaf*). Finally, genuine insanity must be mentioned. Some of these traits are admired in a leader, especially those of the 'mad brave' and the mystic. The *wadaad waal* of the Somalis combined the inner serenity of the Sufi with the death-defying recklessness of the warrior.

At one end of the spectrum of the nationalist literature are the works of such Somali writers as Aḥmad 'Abdallah Riirash[12] and Sheikh Jaama' 'Umar 'Iise,[13] whose accounts of the Sayyid and the Dervishes tend to border on panegyrics. To them, the Sayyid is a founding father. In assessing his career, these Somali writers are inclined to compare Sayyid Maḥammad 'Abdille Ḥasan to Prophet Maḥammad of Arabia.[14] To fortify their argument of the heroic qualities of the Sayyid, they point to the 'three things' which the Sayyid shared with the Arabian Apostle: the name, the age (at which they began their respective ministries) and the propensity to wage *jihād*. The dutiful Sheikh Jaama' has even undertaken a spirited effort to bowdlerize the Sayyid's poetry, pruning away obscenities from some poems while suppressing from publication others which could not be so redeemed.[15]

At the other end of the spectrum of the literature sympathetic to the Dervishes, are the works of Professors Robert L. Hess and I. M. Lewis, two circumspect authors whose accounts are quite clearly the outcome of careful research. Lewis' work came out in 1965 and was part of his general effort to reconstruct Somali history from the late nineteenth century to independence – to my knowledge, the only such effort by a contemporary author. With a judicious combination of archival and field research,

Lewis deployed here the same levelheaded critical judgement that made his *Pastoral Democracy* a landmark in the study of northern Somali pastoralism. Taken together the two books present the most useful account of Somali Dervishism. Hess's came out in 1968 as one of the political biographies of six Eastern African leaders.[16] The reader who wishes to have a brief but competent summary of Somali Dervishism would do well to start by consulting their timely essays. While we remain indebted to their notable achievements, it may be in order to point out that both authors give us, on occasion, sufficient grounds to quibble.

Lewis at times reveals his professional bias: as a social anthropologist, he has a measure of difficulty in resisting the temptation to explain the Dervish movement in terms of 'kinship' ties and 'political marriages'.[17]

Professor Hess's work, on the other hand, may be said to stem from the 'archival connection', and is characterized by a limiting dependence on documentary sources, and, in particular, on Italian archives. Hess was one of the first contemporary scholars of the Horn of Africa to gain access to the Italian archives and he used this opportunity along with his proficiency in Italian to increase our knowledge of Italian colonialism in Somalia in general and the Italian viewpoint on the Dervishes in particular.

B. G. Martin and 'Abd as-Sabūr Marzūq[18] (the latter an Egyptian author) may be considered as belonging to a separate category in their interpretation of the Dervishes, in the sense that both emphasize the 'religious connection' in the rise of Maḥammad 'Abdille Ḥasan. In their studies of the movement, one detects echoes of J. Spencer Trimingham's interpretation of the role of Sufi brotherhoods as being instrumental in late nineteenth-century Islamic revivalism in Africa. Behind the rise of the Somali Dervishes, they see a rise of militant Islam in Northeast Africa (a point also brought out by Hess) which they treat as part of a general religious reawakening, 'an anti-Western ferment running through African Islam',[19] provoked in part by the imposition of Euro-Christian rule on Muslims and Muslim lands.

The comparison between Marzūq and Martin stops here, for the Egyptian is essentially a traditionalist, a chronicler more than an interpreter, seeming to give a disconcerting stress to the miraculous and the mystical in the Somali leader. Martin, by contrast, provides a perceptive assessment as well as an erudite narration of the Somali resistance struggle and he is cautious in both, examining the movement along with other African movements of its genre, such as the Uwaysiya of Sheikh Uways Maḥammad of East Africa, the Sanusis of Libya and the series of North African and West African reformist *jihāds*.

Martin had access to some of Sayyid Maḥammad's Arabic works, mainly his two polemical epistles, 'Risala Biyamaal' ('Letter to the Biyamaal') and the 'Qam'i al-Mu'anidin' ('The Suppression of the Rebellious'). His chief contribution, however, seems to be his grasp of the subtle shades of doctrinal differences and trends of thought in various schools of Islamic mysticism, such as the Wahhabi-influenced cluster of neo-Sufists (Aḥmadiya, Sanūsiya, Tijaniya) as opposed to classical Sufism (Qaadiriya-related). His attempt, furthermore, to interpret the Sayyid's intellectual development in the light of neo-Sufist influence and his elucidation of the concept of intercessory powers of saints (*tawassul*) as having been the basis of much of the doctrinal conflict between the Qaadiriya and Saaliḥiya brotherhoods, yield, in my view, fruitful results.

Martin, however, fails to address the dimension of the Saaliḥiya brotherhood which seems to me to have been of more importance to the success of the Dervish movement. This is the organizational dimension. While correctly perceiving the radical innovation in the form of centralized, hierarchical organization which these mystical orders represented, he stops short of stating the important implication of such an innovation for the Somali movement: that in converting the Saaliḥiya brotherhood into a political movement, Sayyid Maḥammad adopted its hierarchical model which enabled him to create a large-scale organization. This allowed him to surmount the great weakness in Somali clan politics arising from the traditional absence of any centralized political authority.

The socio-political structure of the Dervishes, as noted earlier, resembled to a marked degree that of a Muslim brotherhood.[20] The Sayyid distinguished his followers, whom he called Dervish or 'ikhwān' ('brethren') from the clans, whom he called 'Somalis'. For him the latter term evidently carried a derogatory connotation, reminding him of pastoral egalitarianism, clannishness and decentralizing tendencies.

By now the reader may be inclined, with some justice, to regard my approach to the study of Maḥammad 'Abdille Ḥasan as the 'literary connection'. And such an inference, though not wholly accurate, would not be unjust in view of my sustained emphasis on the Sayyid's oratorical powers as in large measure explaining both the surprising durability of the Somali Dervishes in the face of overwhelming odds and Sayyid Maḥammad's continued grip on the reins of power despite numerous attempts within the Dervish leadership to unseat him. While recognizing the multiple factors which went into the making of the complex character and circumstances of the Sayyid, I have tended to stress his powers of persuasion along with his religious prominence as playing key roles in his success in forging, out of a multiplicity of clans hitherto at war with one another, a united, fighting front – a front which demonstrated a remarkable cohesion for twenty-two years, during which numerous military reverses were sustained.

The spiritual prestige and oratorical finesse with which the Sayyid seems to have been blessed are two assets essential to success in Somali pastoral society. The one, namely religion, gave him the legitimacy for leadership and the other, namely political oratory, gave him the practical tool to exercise leadership. To generalize, the pastoral Somalis are by temperament easily moved, and British colonials had occasion to regret 'excitability'[21] as 'one of the besetting sins' of the Somalis. A politician endowed with poetic oration and a proper set of spiritual credentials is thus in a strong position to excite their imagination, and to capture their hearts and minds.

2 THE MASTER POLEMICIST

Sayyid Maḥammad 'Abdille Ḥasan was possessed of those qualities which make for powerful influence. His gift for public speaking, his ability to fuse thought and feeling into verbal expression are proverbial among the Somalis. As for poetry, a field in which he faced a legion of notable competitors from among his countrymen, some say he was 'peerless'[22] and his 'noble lines' which are commonly quoted throughout the Somali peninsula provoked strong emotions in the past as they continue to be a source of inspiration for many today. In this connection, J. Spencer Trimingham is correct for the most part, I believe, when he observes that Maḥammad 'Abdille Ḥasan 'was a master of eloquence and excelled in the art of composing impromptu poems which so readily inspire and inflame the Somalis'.[23] To be sure, the Sayyid's verse did inspire and inflame the Somalis, but it was far from being an 'impromptu' art, representing as it did a conscious production of a complex form of literature which sought to fuse ideas with verbal beauty in such a manner as to produce certain effects in the hearer. Behind the seeming spontaneity and vitality of the reciter of pastoral verse are the composer's long hours of patient labors. The Sayyid was fond of observing, it is said, that he composed his verse to 'show the truth of his position'[24] and the 'falsehood' of that of his opponents.

I have said that Sayyid Maḥammad's oral poetry was committed verse and that it was utilized in accordance with traditional poetic uses: either to enhance his position or to discredit that of his opponents. That he was able to do this reveals as much about the Sayyid's oratorical powers as about the influence of verbal communication among his people. Yet to assert here the power of the spoken word among the pastoral Somalis is hardly to make a unique claim for them. Words, in print or spoken, have continued to prove powerful in all of mankind's societies, from the ancient Greeks to the present. It is in recognition of this power that modern governments have come to rely so heavily on the artful use of words in their public relations activities, to sell their policies to their own peoples, to promote the interests and aspirations of their nations to other nations, and to fight off hostile propaganda. It is the power of words which gives so much influence to the ultimate persuaders of modern society, the press and related media of today's mass-consumer cultures. In the words of a former director of the US Information Agency: 'If this country believes that the end of the day will be carried not by force of arms but by force of persuasion, the job we do is key to our survival. I for one am persuaded that we have no alternative; we must persuade or perish in the attempt.'[25]

The expanded democratization of the political process and the corresponding rise in the importance of public opinion for politicians may have given special significance to the role of words as persuaders in the West. Yet the American's observation may well hold true for virtually all egalitarian societies, modern or primitive, industrialized or economically backward. Where the citizenry must be persuaded rather than coerced, the skilful use of words has proved essential to politicians.

What seems to give some uniqueness, or at least a sense of particularity, to the case of the Sayyid and the Somalis concerns the art medium which the Somali leader harnessed to exercise his verbal skills. The employment of poetry for the purpose of 'public persuasion', in effect for propaganda uses, may provoke a reflex suspicion in many, in view of the bad name which the Nazis have given the word 'propaganda'. Yet one man's propaganda may be another's 'truth', and the Sayyid for one, was inclined, it is said, to observe, apparently with deep conviction, that in his poetry he labored for the 'sincerest expression of truth'.[26] The pursuit of this goal, the 'sincerest expression', on occasion runs riot with the Sayyid, as we have seen, leaving an unpleasant stultifying effect on his lyrics, bringing to perilous heights the element of the preachy, the self-righteous, and the piously indignant. Thus the imposition of the 'truth' on the poems, at times, denies them the opportunity to breathe freely, to speak for themselves. Slaves to the Sayyid's version of the truth, they are in danger of being smothered by righteousness.

Despite his professedly steadfast dedication to an 'honest' exposition of the truth, the Sayyid's acrimonious method of obtaining that objective is likely to ruffle the advocates of the doctrine of 'art for art's sake' – the notion that the 'creative process' is something too personal and, by implication, too 'noble' to be subjected to collective or mass enterprises.

In the extreme manifestations of this doctrine, good poetry, or for that matter good art, is equated with individualistic art. Detached, standoffish and often opaque, this kind of art is viewed as a highly 'individual skill'[27] pre-ordained, as it were, to be the exclusive possession of a favored few, the cultured elect, and has therefore nothing to say to or about simple folk and their ways.

An argument about the origin, growth and 'proper' role of literature does not belong here; though it may be in order to note simply that a cross-cultural examination of the subject may well reveal that social or political commitment in the arts does not necessarily preclude quality, that poetry need not be detached from vital community concerns in order to be good and that one of the ancient, perhaps chief, functions of the creative skills has been to instruct, to guide men and women to the 'truth'.[28]

In any event, even among modern thinkers of Europe and America where, by and large, the view of 'art for art's sake' has come to hold sway, the Sayyid would find an occasional comrade. One such comrade was Lenin, the Russian thinker–revolutionary–statesman, whose advocacy of the concept of 'Socialist Realism'[29] or 'party-mindedness' and whose call for the subordination of letters and images to the imperatives of the party betrays much kinship to the Sayyid's relentless attempts to exploit 'my mighty tongue' for the holy war.

The question of 'message' in poetry does not appear to have exercised Sayyid Maḥammad's mind – he had inherited a poetic tradition, a way of art in which the 'message' is central to verbal creativity. His chief concern was to humiliate his opponents by 'out-arguing them' and the principal function of his poetry was to refine the quality of the contest by formalizing the language of argument. In the discussion of the institution of *godob* (blood and speech vendetta), I pointed out how the formalization of language through poetry represents power, mainly because poetry gives language a power that prose does not, that among the pastoral Somalis an attack in verse is considered as injurious as a physical attack.[30] Thus to vilify a man in verse is to violate his soul, to shatter, as the pastoralists put it, his 'mirror of honor'.[31]

Thus while the Sayyid may give the glory to God for the origins of his acrimonious style – 'Allah taught me the art of abuse' – he was in fact more indebted to the pastoral traditions of poetic combat which taught him the usefulness of 'out-arguing' an opponent. Pastoral poetry thrives on pastoral speech vendetta.

An examination of his verse reveals that he intended to convey three types of power as the cardinal virtues of his poetic art. The first was what we may term the 'elemental power' – fire, water, wind, wild beasts and so on. Based on a claim to sheer physical ferocity, this kind of theme is often dealt with in the 'boast' sections of his poems.

Boasting is so regular a feature of Somali traditional verse that almost every pastoral poem contains a boastful part, often the introductory section or that next to it, in which the poet employs high-flown, grandiloquent language to praise his poetic merits. The strategy is to intimidate one's opponent through grandiose self-praising.

Such a tradition seems to have suited the Sayyid's temperament and he sought to overawe his enemies through the use of verbal extravagance, which, of course, he could frequently back up with the sword. A passage from 'The Scourge of Infidels' illustrates the use of elemental power:[32]

> Say: these, my four lines betoken the potency of my poetic ways,
> Say: as I let them roll down the hills,
> They come to the ear as the boom of heavy guns and the thunder of fired bullets,
> Say: they engulf the opponent with darkness as of torrential rains,
> Say: they come with the rumble of thunder and the flash of lightning,
> Say: they strike with the force of gale winds and the gathering clouds of rain,
> Say: they are the fury of the floods and the hurricane sweeping by ever so closely,
> Say: they are the quaking sea, the raging waves and the roaring rapids of Eyle.[33]

Water, wind, and fire – while these are terrible forces possessed with power at once fierce, impersonal and unpredictable, they also represent a benevolent power without which life could not exist. As they are the agents of death and destruction, so are they the source of life and prosperity. The poet claims that his words possess similar properties: gentle and life-giving to friends but death-dealing to enemies.

In another poem he likens his power to the ferocity of the lion and the fury of fire burning out of control:

> If the blaze of the fire I kindled does not consume them . . .
> If the English dogs do not flee in headlong panic . . .
> If I do not send Igarray[34] and other traitors to the Other World . . .
> If I do not cut off necks as the prowling lion,
> If all these things do not come to pass,
> Then, let it be said that I am not a true Muslim![35]

Then there is the mystical power which Somalis associate with his person and poetry. In chapter 2. I outlined five categories of curse which the pastoralists recognize as having potent effects: the curse of all living but powerless beings against powerful and oppressive ones, the curse of God, angels and prophets against sinners and troublemakers, the curse of parents against unruly children, the curse of the man of God against offending individuals and groups and, finally, the curse at the command of the poet. Both as a poet and a man of God, the Sayyid was said to command all these categories of curse, and numerous stories are related of how he disabled enemies by pronouncing a stabber poem on them or by merely 'concentrating an angry look on them'.[36] Typical of the poetic curse is the following versicle which he reportedly pronounced on his brother-in-law, Faaraḥ Maḥamuud Sugulle, who defected from the Dervish cause after the disaster of the Tree-of-Bad-Counsel:

Oh, you Twisted Lip, the traitor,
Twisted Lip, the ruffian,
If you say, 'I would have worldly gains',
May Allah deny you even a donkey;
And if you say, 'I would have faith',
May the Lord blind you to it;
And if you say, 'I would run for war',
May the Lord hobble your legs.[37]

The deserter had an inauspicious chance encounter some years later with a party of Dervish scouts, who recognized him and had him executed. Although Faaraḥ Maḥamuud Sugulle fell to what we may call cold-blooded assassination, indigenous sources would make much of the Sayyid's curse which mystically 'hobbled his legs'[38] and rendered him unable to flee his foes.

Finally, there is the spiritual power which, the Sayyid claimed, set him and his poetry above all others. On numerous occasions, in his correspondence with the colonial powers and rival Somalis, he referred to himself as the 'Poor Man of God',[39] and the phrase does a great deal to shed light on the Sayyid's thinking about the long struggle and the part he played in it. He seems to have seen himself as a sort of 'lone voice in the wilderness', a martyr–champion defending the cause of God against an alliance of infidels and apostate Somalis. He was afflicted and persecuted on all sides, he claimed, because of his steadfast dedication to the truth. Yet, he argued, although he was outnumbered and outgunned by the enemy, he was confident of ultimate victory because the source of all power was on his side. Thus, in 'The Scourge of Infidels', he shifts back and forth between the image of weakness in worldly terms and that of strength through God:

O Lord, we are endangered on all sides,
Threatened we are, for the nations have joined in alliance against us,
Lo, even the Greeks[40] would point their lethal arrows at us.

And we did nothing to earn their hatred, only out of wickedness they'd oppress us,
If they had any cause to attack us, we'd understand and be satisfied;
Lord, they persecute us because we called on them to come to the faith.[41]

Yet it does not take the 'afflicted man of God' very long to be transformed into a holy fighter (*ghāzi*) leading the divine host against unbelievers and backsliders:

And I'll react against the malice and oppression unleashed upon me,
Yes, I am justified to smite, to sweep through the land with terror and fury,
And I'll go out to make the country free of infidel influence.

I am a man frenzied by indignation, who will not spare even a little maiden,
And whatever destruction I wrought will be sheer pleasure to me,
And he upon whom I fall will be the unfortunate of the land.

Like a handful of grain I'll scoop up the cowardly Ogaadeen,
And if I do not halt the ceaseless jabs upon them,
By the Lord's will, they'll be reduced to nothingness; they'll shrink as dried-up pools.

His contention that he was in league with God, and his opponents with the devil, was probably Sayyid Maḥammad's most effective argument, the 'cutting edge' as an unsympathetic observer put it, 'of his malicious tongue'.[42] This observer continued:

> Concealing his true and life-long ambition of imposing his illegitimate authority under the banner of an alien sect in the country, he wore the cloak of religion and nationalism, two ideals which he worked with great propaganda effect.

To judge from his verbal techniques, the Sayyid knew how to 'wear his cloak' to advantage, marshaling in his poetic oratory those elements of the struggle on which there was almost unanimous agreement and which were bound to undermine the position of his opponents: thus, he would taunt them:

If the land is your land, why aren't you its government?

If Islam is your religion, why submit to infidel overlords?
And why consort with hairy, English dogs?

The hopeless fools you are, how much goodness you've missed! . . .[43]

The Sayyid thrived on controversy and his loftiest moment came, one would think, when he was on the attack, demolishing 'somebody' or his ideas. Yet it would be wrong to assume that he pursued argumentation for its own end. Given the power of poetic formalization in pastoral ethos, to out-argue one's enemy was more than the winning of a mere verbal contest. It was tantamount, in Sheikh Jaama''s words, to winning 'half the physical battle'.[44]

3 THE MYSTIC WARRIOR

If, as Sheikh Jaama' maintains, poetry was 'the central principle which brought the Dervishes together, kept them integrated and gave the movement a dynamic sense of direction,'[45] it was hardly the 'center' of Sayyid Maḥammad's life. The Sayyid's experience was rooted in several 'centers' which sometimes seem to have worked against one another to produce the 'tensions and contradictions' which were said to characterize his life. If he was a pastoral poet of polemics, he was also a Sufi (mystic) and a warrior.

Central to the various elements which produce the Sufi way of life is the abiding desire on the part of the mystic to 'enter into fellowship'[46] with God. The practices used to reach this objective have come to assume different shades in different regions and cultures of the Muslim world. The essential component is 'self-denial', the Sufi's attempt through ascetic practices and habits to liberate the immortal spirit from the mortal body. The central objective is to purify the soul from the 'carnal self' so that the soul now freed from the shackles of the flesh is 'able to receive Divine illumination'[47] and to 'attain to the life in God, that unitive state in which the soul shares, here and now, in eternal life'. The seeker may go through a series of enlightening transformations, leading him upwards to 'knowledge' and 'perfection' until, ideally, he has attained to the 'blissful union' with the Deity, when he becomes the 'Friend of God' (Waliya Allah). The prominent features of the stages which a Sufi may pass through in his search for inner light are summarized by Margaret Smith and they include:

> repentance (*tawba*), patience (*sabr*), gratitude (*shukr*), hope (*raja*) and fear (*khawf*), poverty (*faqr*), asceticism or renunciation (*zuhd*), the merging of the personal will with the Will of God (*tawhīd*), dependence on, and trust in, God (*tawakkul*), love (*maḥabba*)—

including longing for God (*shawq*), fellowship with Him (*uns*) and satisfaction with all He desires (*riḍa*).[48]

The Sufism which Sayyid Maḥammad inherited seems to have been partly influenced by these strains of early Islamic mysticism, but his was also a reformed mysticism, mainly the result of the nineteenth-century Muslim revival in the form of reformist brotherhoods which, according to B. G. Martin, received some influence from the puritanical doctrines of the Arabian Wahhabis. In contrast to the broad, on occasion allegorical, interpretations of the Qur'an and the Traditions favored by earlier Sufis, neo-Sufists tended to take a stricter, more literal approach in their interpretations of the faith. Neo-Sufism was, moreover, characterized by a militant puritanism, a concerted spiritual effort to return to the basics of the Shari a. We had occasion to note how the Sayyid's attempts to 'purify' the faith from what he declared to be Qaadiriya heresies entangled him in his unhappy quarrel with the inhabitants of Berbera.

The Sayyid's mystical imperatives clashed with his pastoral guile and pragmatism, to produce what one source called the 'tempestuous personality'[49] which he came to manifest at times. Mysticism demanded a life of quiet and contemplation; the role in which circumstances cast him demanded constant action and involvement. The troops had to be fed, and that called for perennial raiding of stock. Strategies had to be devised and battles fought, and that called for endless maneuverings. Conspiracies needed to be guarded against, and this called for occasional execution of rivals. New recruits were to be enlisted, and that necessitated an unethical use of propaganda and publicity.

The Sayyid wanted wholeheartedly to satisfy both the pious tranquility of his faith and the stormy duties of his career as a warrior chieftain, and the dogged pursuit of these contradictory objectives led him, on occasion, into 'erratic behavior', which his enemies were quick to exploit as a sign of his manifest deception, or, worse still, as an incontrovertible 'proof of his madness'.[50] He maintained, evidently with conviction, that he was the 'Poor Man of God' who loved nothing more than to 'renounce this world'[51] in his single-minded pursuit of 'higher things'. Yet he did not abstain from fulminating at 'this very world', threatening to 'sink my spear'[52] in the Somalis who had refused to join the cause. On one occasion he would be declaiming that 'nothing pained him more'[53] than to cause even a mild hardship to others, while on the next he would be on the move with the 'cavalry of terror', not sparing 'even a little maiden'.[54]

To his enemies, this – the inconsistency of word and deed – seemed all of a piece: he was the charlatan *wadaad* who wore the cloak of religion to achieve his goal of 'unabashed lust for power'.[55] The British sought to debunk his 'fraudulence' or 'insanity' by making much of the Sayyid's alleged claim that he could 'turn bullets to water'[56] and could hear with his 'own ears' what was being said about him in Berbera, a couple of hundred miles away. But for a Sufi to claim attributes of omnipotence, omniscience and omnipresence was scarcely to betoken fraudulence or madness on his part, since he was operating, as Sufis often do, on a plane of reality where the real and the supernatural have a way of merging into each other without any apparent transition, in a world of 'miracles' and 'strange happenings' wholly perplexing to 'ordinary mortals'.[57] The Sayyid may have been convinced, even as he tried to convince others, of the sanctity of his person. He is said to have attributed his 'miraculous' ability to survive dangers to a life-saving gift he received in his seeker days, an enchanted book from a divine agent (who 'appeared' to him first in the form of a lizard and later as a lady) whom he had gallantly saved from death by thirst. The Sayyid may have believed in this tale, for indeed it is not out of character with other miracles he attributed to himself.

To the secular eye of the historian, this tale seems much in keeping with countless others of the Sayyid's deft tricks of psychic manipulation designed to foster in the Somalis, friends and foes alike, a belief in the invincibility of the 'divinely inspired' *wadaad.* He seems to have achieved some success in this, for there are some indigenous sources who, even today, cite this alleged 'protection of his person' by higher powers as the reason for his nimble talents in escaping the numerous attempts on his life.[58]

The Sayyid's allegiance to the mystical tradition had practical, on occasion, inauspicious, consequences for the movement. Against the advice of his generals, for example, he insisted on outfitting the troops with a white turban (*duub-'ad*), as was customary with Sufi traditional costume, and the implementation of the ill-conceived injunction marked his men out and made them an easy target for enemy fire. Although his military advisors are said to have repeatedly pleaded with him to discontinue the use of the 'suicidal uniform',[59] he would not yield to their remonstrances, on the grounds that to do so would be, in his mind, to violate the Sufi way.

At the battle of Jidbaale, he had allegedly ordered the army to be arranged into two divisions of 6,200 men each, so that the number of each division would 'coincide with the number of verses in the Qur'an'.[60] The mystical stunt might have proved harmless enough, had it not led to a heavy concentration of the men in one spot, and this together with the 'white heads' of the Dervishes is said to have helped the heavy guns of the enemy to strike with deadly accuracy.

The Sayyid was given, it is said, to dreams and midnight revelations which, though boosting his prestige as a divinely inspired sheikh, occasionally undermined a rational execution of the struggle. He demanded his followers to call him 'Sayyid' (master), or 'Aabbe' (father) which must have struck the egalitarian pastoralists as an odd requirement. They were to greet him and one another on formal occasions with a praise ode (*dhikr-as-salaam*) to his spiritual Master, to maintain a strict observance of the five daily prayers, to recite regularly the esoteric creed of the sect, and to uphold the practice of other mystical deeds which were difficult or impractical to comply with. And he punished severely for lack of compliance.[61]

Poet, mystic, warrior – he strove earnestly to be true to all the ideological cross-currents of his life, and when the urgings of these impulses coincided, he appeared to be an extraordinarily gifted man, equally endowed with poetic creativity, political craftsmanship and an impeccable, spiritual integrity. But when the underlying compulsions clashed, their strains became easily visible, making him appear somewhat erratic and unstable, an eccentric but amiable master to his followers, a vicious fraud to his foes.

The Sayyid's inner tensions, which no doubt influenced his outward behavior, made him vulnerable to misunderstanding and misinterpretation and prompted his enemies to describe him in contradictory terms. They condemned him by turns as a 'corrosive ascetic' and a 'sensuous libertine', a 'glamorous romantic' but nonetheless a 'consummate scoundrel', a 'megalomaniac' whose 'unbounded hunger for power' drove him to 'kill and maim innocent women and children' and an ardent resister of colonialism 'who will forever live in the hearts of his fellow countrymen . . . as a national hero', a 'madman' but one who was nevertheless 'accursed with a madness that was akin to genius'.[62]

While notable for the tone of rancor with which they were written, the contradictory adjectives would seem to signify something of the complexity and multifariousness of the Sayyid's personality. He tried to please the several masters of his life. That he subjected himself to the exacting discipline – no less exacting than the one he subjected his followers to – which enabled him to impose order on his intermixture of fierce emotions so that he managed to carry on with his arduous task for twenty-two years, should serve as a lasting monument to the strength of his character. His contradictions were the contradictions of a complicated personality. And while they do much to expose his frailties as a human being, they should do little to diminish his deserved reputation as one of the greatest Somalis of this century.

4 SAYYID MAḤAMMAD'S LEGACY: AN APPRAISAL

Douglas Jardine's assessment sixty years ago of the Sayyid as 'forever living in the hearts of his fellow countrymen . . . as a national hero' has proved highly prescient, in view of the exalted position which Sayyid Maḥammad's legacy occupies in the Somalis' history of struggle for independence. That the Sayyid's image as father-founder of Somali nationalism overshadows his other, no less noteworthy, achievements has a certain measure of irony about it. For whatever courage, charisma and destiny made of his later career, he was first and foremost a man of religion.

From early in life when he began, like his forefathers, as a roving holy man, till his return to Berbera as the envoy of his Meccan mentor, to the waging of the holy war, the Sayyid's enduring passion had been to attain spiritual perfection. A corollary of his unrelenting quest for spiritual knowledge was his desire to regenerate his people's devotion to Islam. His perception that the 'spiritual laxity' of the rival Qaadiriya, protected by Christian overlords, stood in the way of spiritual reform fired his religious and patriotic sense of obligation and prompted him to conduct a *jihād*.

The national struggle which resulted from this momentous decision was thus primarily to achieve this end. Although he informed the British government of his intention to create his own sovereign state, he did not in fact establish a state structure which would survive his death. Although he harnessed to good advantage such favorable factors as the Somalis' antipathy to Euro-Abyssinian colonization and the hierarchical Saaliḥiya model, to forge out a national movement, yet topography, tradition and the pressure of hostile circumstances militated against the establishment of a durable state apparatus. And while he shared power with the ablest among his lieutenants, the government of the Dervishes remained fluid and personal in character.

From a practical standpoint, the Dervish movement was less than a dazzling success. Not only did the Sayyid fail in his stated objective of ridding his country of infidel rule, but his efforts may actually have served as a catalyst for the consolidation of colonial hold over the Somalis. Yet, if the overwhelming motivation to reform religion unwittingly cast the Sayyid in the role of a national resister, the challenge of the task unleashed in him qualities of leadership and literary talents which made far greater contributions to the Somali cause than the movement had done. In the first place, the Sayyid expanded the literary frontiers of the Somali language. In utilizing poetics as a political weapon, the Sayyid was inspired, during the course of the struggle, to produce a magnificent body of oral poetry which has greatly enriched the Somali poetic tradition. It would doubtless have come as something of a revelation for British colonial officials to learn at the time that the man they dubbed the 'Mad Mullah' was doing for his language something comparable to what Shakespeare had done for theirs, and that the very poetic messages which, in their ignorance of the culture, they dismissed as incoherent, would become classics for the Somalis.

In the second place, the war, though destructive of life and property, broadened the Somalis' perspective, making them alive to the possibility of enterprises worthy of pursuit beyond the tribe. By bringing together the man of religion and the spear-bearer, the farmer and the pastoralist – men and women from diverse clans – into a common bond, the Dervish experience had a detribalizing effect. It forced its participants to see themselves as 'Dervishes' rather than as representatives of disparate clans. Hence, one of the long-lasting effects of the Dervish conflict was the development of pan-Somali ideas, from which the subsequent struggle for independence drew much inspiration. 'The very idea of the nation',[63] says a contemporary elder in a sentiment no doubt shared by many Somalis, 'was inspired by the Dervish example.'

Grudgingly, the British came to acknowledge his dynamism and tenacity of purpose. Wrote Jardine:

> Faced by a European power, which was at once strong and anxious for peace, he was never tempted to abandon his ideals and come to terms. Even when he lost everything but his personal freedom, he scorned and scoffed at the extremely favourable peace terms that were offered to him . . . No misfortune broke his spirit . . . On due reflection, one must confess there is something to be said for the man who does not know when he is beaten.[64]

Long before the doctrine of 'black consciousness' was in vogue, Sayyid Maḥammad was an African leader who was a conscious black man, as his defiant verse clearly demonstrates:

> It was I who would not assist the unbelieving whites,
> I who would not be . . . the white man's burden-bearing beast;
> It was I who would not enter the house of pigs nor of dogs . . .

The Dervishes may even have lent some inspiration to other resisters of colonialism in east and southern Africa. At least one militant group of Rhodesian blacks called attention to the Somali resistance in attempts to unify their own opposition to white settlers. 'If Lobengula had wanted to,'[65] declared the speakers of the first black Rhodesian trade union in

June 1929, 'he could have called on every nation to help him. He did not. That is why he was conquered. In Somaliland they are still fighting. That is because they are united. Let us be united.'

Manifestly, the Sayyid was aided in his task by his religious prestige and gift of political oratory. Yet it is doubtful that these factors would in themselves have been sufficient to overcome the political disunity and clannish discord inherent in the very fabric of Somali pastoralism. It took Sayyid Maḥammad's powers of charisma and personal resourcefulness to channel Somali discontent into a national front. While the movement was supra-tribal, nevertheless, it must be pointed out that the Sayyid exploited Somali clannishness when it seemed profitable to do so, taking good advantage of his paternal ties with the Ogaadeen on one occasion, and his maternal ties with the Ḍulbahante on another. Sometimes he also played on the ancient rivalry between these Daarood clans and the Isaaq, as evidenced by his poem, 'The Will':

> O the pity! the Daarood know not the trap being laid for them [by the Isaaq].
> The fools, they drummed and danced with joy when I was defeated,
> The fools, they sighed with relief: 'Lo, the Wadaad flees westward.

His scathing poetic attacks on the Isaaq people – 'the fate of the Isaaq is to remain forever as stupid as donkeys' – is not to be interpreted as a particular ill-will which the Sayyid had against this clan, but as mainly due to a fortuitous circumstance: as a coastal people, the Isaaq were more firmly under the colonial administration than were the inland Ogaadeen and Ḍulbahante peoples. Hence, they had little choice but to oppose him. The Sayyid's right-hand man, Ḥaaji Suudi, was an Isaaq, as were many in the *khusuusi* inner circle of advisors. His Ogaadeen kin, too, came in for their share of poetic tirade when they offended the 'Poor Man of God' – 'Like a handful of grain I'll scoop up the cowardly Ogaadeen' – as did the Ḍulbahante – 'Until I had driven long spears through the shameless Reer Hagar (Ḍulbahante lineage).'

On the negative side, the war exacted a terrible toll from the Somalis, both in life and property. The twenty-one years of the Dervish eruption are generally remembered as a time of untold misery, a period, in the words of the poet, of 'universal perdition'.[66] The Dervishes are likened to a 'black magic sweeping through the land' from which 'not a path hath escaped'. Raiding livestock with impunity on account of their superior force, the Dervishes helped to break down the moral sanctions regulating the external relations of the clans. Thus in the general demoralization of the land, the strong plundered the weak at will and the pastoral pastimes of feud and vendetta were unleashed with unprecedented ferocity, turning northern Somalia into a land of 'prey and predator'.[67] By a conservative estimate, the Dervish revolt and the colonial campaigns to put it down together caused the destruction of 200,000 lives, a casualty figure which must have had a terrible impact on a population that barely numbered a million.[68]

Of even more serious consequence for long-term Somali welfare, was the fact that the high cost of the war prejudiced the British Crown against the economic development of the Protectorate. Somaliland, as I have stressed, came into British possession as a distant 'outpost of the Indian Empire'. The British reluctantly occupied the Somali coast mainly because they wanted to keep their traditional supply of meat for the Aden garrison from falling into French hands. Later the Protectorate came in handy when the British found they could use it as a bargaining chip with Ethiopia for higher imperial stakes. The high cost of suppressing the Dervishes encouraged even further the tradition of neglect and marginality with which Britain treated her Somaliland possession. Lamented an administrator of the Protectorate soon after Dervishism came to an end:

> All available Government funds have been expended on the maintenance of military forces to meet a situation happily unparalleled elsewhere in British Africa. Nothing has been left for education, for the encouragement of agriculture, for development, or even a survey of the country's mineral resources ... In the Sudan, the final destruction of the Dervish power left the country with 500 miles of railway, 900 miles of telegraph, and a flotilla of Nile steamers wherewith to promote economic development. But the greatest boon of all was the establishment of Gordon College ... It is Somaliland's misfortune that her twenty-one years' war left her with nothing more than a few ramshackle Ford cars.[69]

The Dervish conflict also seems to have established the Somalis in British eyes as the 'bad natives' of British East Africa. From the early nineteenth century onwards, British–Somali contacts were dominated by a series of misunderstandings, mutual suspicion and violent confrontations. Some of the spectacular events of the unhappy British–Somali relations include the pillaging by Somali tribesmen of several British vessels shipwrecked on the coast in the early nineteenth century, the devastating raid, again by Somali tribesmen, on Richard Burton and John Speke's ill-fated expedition to the Nile at Berbera in 1854, the attack on a British garrison in the 1890s by 'Iise Somali spearmen and the protracted violence which greeted the British in their attempts to subdue the Jubaland Somalis at the turn of the century.[70] To each of these incidents the British responded with massive reprisals.

British colonial attitude toward the Somalis was partly shaped by these and similar incidents. The prolonged Dervish conflict, along with the general 'unruliness' of the pastoralists who showed no perceptible reverence for British imperial might, helped to mark out the Somalis in colonial eyes as a 'bad breed of natives.'[71] They were found to be 'treacherous, fanatical and vindictive.' The prevailing counsel for British officials whom misfortune destined to take charge of managing the Somalis was to minimize any involvement in the affairs of these 'wild' clans so as to 'avoid getting killed'.[72] The result was a general colonial antipathy toward the Somalis.

> It is certain [wrote Sir Charles Eliot with a touch of Victorian paternalism] that the average Englishman has little sympathy for the Somali. He tolerates a black man who admits his inferiority, and even those who show a good fight and give in; but he cannot tolerate dark colour combined with an intelligence in any way equal to his own. This is the secret of the universal dislike of the . . . Somali among East African officials.[73]

The Somalis may have paid a high price for their recalcitrance, not only in the form of economic and educational stagnation, but, more seriously, in the establishment of what I. M. Lewis calls a 'tradition of Anglo-Ethiopian collaboration against Somali interests'.[74] At any rate, there was no voice sympathetic to the Somalis in British officialdom, no Bishop Oldham, as in the case of Kenya, to raise a protesting voice against the British Government's casual but systematic cessions of Somali pasturelands to Ethiopia.

Yet it would be unfair – and empirically untenable – to judge Sayyid Maḥammad and his movement by events which at best have tenuous links with his resistance struggle. To suggest that passive acceptance of British colonialism would have made English friends for the Somalis is to engage in flimsy theorizing, too speculative to be of consequence to this discussion.. The Sayyid is today a towering figure in Somali eyes, the hero of Somali nationalism and one of their finest poets. If he failed in his objective of ridding his country of alien rule, his failures are regarded as 'failures of the tragic hero' – at once sad and inspiring.

The Sayyid was more than a nationalist. He was a poet of awesome artistic force, too, and his contribution to the heritage of Somali pastoral verse is judged by many Somalis to be infinitely superior to his nationalist contribution. He inherited a poetic tradition throbbing with life and vitality, and he did much to advance the frontiers of that tradition by transmitting to it in image and metaphor the versatility and sophistication of his educational and travel experience. It should be noted here that the Sayyid's period, in the history of Somali oral literature, produced pastoral bards of extraordinary craftsmanship, probably the single most concentrated outburst of talent in one generation. And when we think of bards like Raage Ugaas, Qamaan Bulḥan, 'Ali Ḍuuḥ, Salaan 'Arrabay and 'Ali Jaama' Haabiil, we are reminded of the stiff competition which the Sayyid faced in the field. Nevertheless, although many Somalis would admire the craftsmanship of these men and would recognize their talents – individually or collectively – few would quarrel with the assessment of an educated Somali who spoke of the Sayyid as the 'high priest of Somali oral verse in this century'.[75]

Owing to the strong connection between politics and oral poetry in pastoral tradition, the Sayyid deployed his verbal arts to great political advantage, using it to humiliate his (Somali) enemies and to enhance his power and prestige in the land. A thoroughgoing traditionalist, he showed in his verse the two sides of the pastoral bard: the artist and the polemicist striving with each other for mastery of the poet's soul. His deep antipathy towards his country's colonizers, together with his contempt for their Somali collaborators, at times overwhelmed the artist in him, giving the polemicist a free rein. Manifestly, the Sayyid's deeply flawed, even obscene poems – as for example 'The English Woman' (also called 'Corfield's Sister'),[76] 'Ḍiima', a rude attack on the Sayyid's wayward wife of the same name, and the equally vitriolic diatribe, 'A Prince's Daughter' ('Ina Boqor') on Sultan 'Ismaan's daughter whom the Sayyid spitefully castigated after she rebuffed his amorous advances – represent clear instances of polemical rancor. Inevitably, the quality of his verse suffered during these periods of excess and bitterness. But fortunately for Dervishism (and for the Somali poetic heritage) the Sayyid for the most part kept on a firm leash the polemical animal stirring menacingly within him, and the great mass of his poetry will not disappoint the seasoned listener. Indeed, in some poems – 'The Scourge of Infidels' ('Gaala-Leged'), 'The Double-Dealer' ('Musuqmaasuq'), 'The Herald of Good Tidings' ('Bishaarooyinkii Eebahay'), 'A Hymn of Thanksgiving' ('Mahade Haw Sheego'), and 'The Will' ('Dardaaran') are notable examples – the grand themes of death and freedom which underlie them inspired the Sayyid to a grandeur of language and evocative power which surely must rank as splendid achievements by any literary standard. When rhythmic vigor and sweeping cadences blend well with flashes of insight – as they do in these poems – the Sayyid achieves virtuoso effects, and even moments of sheer delight. On such occasions we cannot but forgive his touching vanity exhorting us to 'hold fast to my noble utterance/Lest thou perish'.[77]

Notes

Introduction

1 Leo Tolstoy, *What Is Art? and Essays on Art*, trans. Aylmer Maude (Oxford: Oxford University Press, 1930), p. 227.
2 From the Sayyid's poem, 'The Scourge of Infidels' ('Gaala-Leged'), a Somali version of which appears in Sheikh Jaama' 'Umar 'Iise (Aw Jaamac Cumar Ciise), *Diiwaanka Gabayadii Sayid Maxamad Cabdulle Xasan* (Mogadishu: Wakaaladda Madbacadda Qaranka, 1974), pp. 223–30.
3 The 'sense of mission' in the Sayyid's thinking is discussed in chapter 5.
4 From the Sayyid's poem, 'The Will' ('Dardaaran').
5 Tolstoy, *What Is Art*? p. 232.
6 Ibid., p. 125.
7 I take up again in the opening pages of the first chapter the question of the description of the Somalis by outsiders as a 'nation of bards'. For the moment, the interested reader may refer to the brief but perceptive anthology of numerous Somali poets by B. W. Andrzejewski and I. M. Lewis, *Somali Poetry: An Introduction* (Oxford: The Clarendon Press, 1964).
8 For an articulate expression of this view, see Margaret Laurence, *A Tree for Poverty* (Nairobi: Eagle Press, 1954), pp. 1–3.
9 Margaret Laurence, *The Prophet's Camel Bell* (London: Macmillan, 1963), *passim*.
10 T. O. Ranger coined this phrase in his two-part article, 'Connexions between "primary resistance movements" and modern mass nationalism in East and Central Africa,' *Journal of African History*, 9, Nos. 3 and 4 (1968), 437–54; 631–42.
11 T. O. Ranger, *Revolt in Southern Rhodesia: A Study in African Resistance* (Evanston, Illinois: Northwestern University Press, 1967).
12 As a sample of the challenge to Professor Ranger's ideas on resistance, see Robert W. Strayer *et al.*, *Protest Movements in Colonial East Africa: Aspects of Early African Response to European Rule* (Syracuse, New York: Eastern African Studies Program, 1973).
13 Carl G. Rosberg, Jr and John Nottingham, *The Myth of 'Mau Mau': Nationalism in Kenya* (Cleveland, Ohio: The World Publishing Company, 1970).

Chapter 1

1 Richard Burton, *First Footsteps in East Africa* (2 vols., London: Tylston and Edwards, 1894).
2 M. Maino, *La Lingua Somala – Strumento d'Insegnamento Professionale* (Alessandria: Ferrari, Occella & Co., 1953).
3 Margaret Laurence, *A Tree for Poverty* (Nairobi: Eagle Press, 1954).
4 B. W. Andrzejewski and I. M. Lewis, *Somali Poetry* (Oxford: Clarendon Press, 1964).
5 Somali Government, *The Somali Peninsula: New Light on Imperial Motives* (London: Staples Printers, 1962), p. v.
6 The ratio of nomadic to urban Somalis has not as yet been reduced to reliable statistics but the official 'guess' is two nomads per one urban person.
7 Said S. Samatar, 'Gabay-Ḥayir: a Somali mock heroic song', *Research in African Literatures*, 11, No. 4 (1980), 450.
8 The Benaadiris essentially constitute the four coastal, southern Somali towns of Mogadishu, Merca, Brava and Kismaayo. Unlike other Somalis, the Benaadiris have been an urban community for centuries and are distinguishable from the pastoral Somalis by linguistic and economic differences.
9 See, for example, William Morgan, *Population of Kenya: Density and Distribution* (Nairobi: Oxford University Press, 1966), *passim*.
10 I. M. Lewis, *A Pastoral Democracy* (Oxford: Oxford University Press, 1961).
11 Enrico Cerulli, *Somalia: Scritti Vari Editi ed Inediti* (Rome: Istituto Poligrafico dello Stato), vol. 1 (1957); vol. 2 (1959); vol. 3 (1964).
12 Lewis, *A Pastoral Democracy*, pp. 4–7.
13 The Somali version of this prayer goes as follows: 'Ilaahow in bog ku socota iyo in baaba'o ku socota iyo in boodda naga najee. Ilaahow, habbadii kal iyo mooye ḍeḥdooda ku barida naga yeel.'
14 A town in the Ogaadeen, a region in Eastern Ethiopia currently disputed by Ethiopia and Somalia.
15 Shabeelle River, whose verdant basin is inhabited by Somalis who resent Ethiopian overlordship in their traditional pasturelands.
16 The central plains of the Ogaadeen.
17 This note and similar ones below are based on a 6-month period of field work (1977) in Somalia and Kenya which I conducted as part of the research for my 1979 history dissertation (Northwestern University), a project whose outcome forms the core of this book. The project was funded jointly by the Social Science Research Council and Northwestern's Graduate School. The part of these notes (hereafter to be called Fieldnotes) utilized for this book will be cited as follows: first, I cite the name of the informant, the word 'Fieldnotes', then the place and date of interview. Thus, in the present example: Sheikh 'Aaqib 'Abdullahi Jaama', Fieldnotes, Mogadishu, 10 April 1977.
18 The Somali says: 'Nabigii baa isagoo 'araysan oo kaba la' maray dulkeena. Markaasuu habaaray, markaasaa ḍulkii noqday qodaḥ, ḍagaḥ, iyo qorraḥ: The prophet, angry and without shoes, passed through our land. He cursed it: hence, the scourges of drought, stones and thistles.'
19 D. A. Low, 'The Northern Interior', in *History of East Africa*, ed. Roland Oliver and Gervase Mathew (3 vols., Oxford: Oxford University Press, 1963), vol. 1, pp. 301–5.
20 E. E. Evans-Pritchard, *The Nuer: A Description of the Modes of Livelihood*

and Political Institutions of a Nilotic People (Oxford: The Clarendon Press, 1940), pp. 16–50.

21 Sheikh Jaama' 'Umar 'Iise, Fieldnotes, Mogadishu, 8 February 1977.

22 During my childhood, we didn't drink water and didn't miss it for months, as camel milk is both nutritious and thirst-quenching. On occasion it is even used for bathing. It is also fed to less hardy animals like horses.

23 'Goodir' is also the Somali name for Greater Kudu.

24 I am not sure how much a baby camel weighs. As a teenager, I used to carry them over a distance of about seven miles a day, a rather exhausting task, but I did not think much of it then.

25 Unlike sheep and goat or cow milk, camel milk produces hardly any butter when it is churned. That it is highly nutritious is indicated by the fact that nomads who consume it as a staple food do not diminish in strength when they have a sufficient supply of it. They are usually taller and skinnier than cultivators and townspeople, but they are no weaker and their powers of endurance border on the phenomenal. A pastoralist is capable of marching several days, covering great distances, with little or no food and drink. This firsthand observation is confirmed by the findings of scientific study. See, for example, Ivo Droandi, *Il Cammello: Storia Naturale* (Florence: Istituto Agricolo Coloniale Italiano, 1936), *passim*.

26 For more about Somali camels, see Lewis, *A Pastoral Democracy*, pp. 35–88.

27 'Ha targaafo sida tooja geel tuurin baw Qoran e' from 'Ali J. Haabiil's poem, 'Ma talyaanigaasaa mahdi ah'.

28 Cattle also play a major part in the Somali economy in the south.

29 It turns cold at night, especially in the early morning when the camp starts marching, and terribly hot in the day. In the night, we used to dig a hole in the sand and bury our bodies up to the head to keep ourselves warm.

30 Lewis, *A Pastoral Democracy*, pp. 2–3.

31 Evans-Pritchard, *The Nuer*, pp. 20–50.

32 'Geel hadba ḥeruu ku jiraa,' ama' Geel ama ḥera Isaaq ama ḥera Ogaadeeen buu jiraa.'

33 Aḥmad Guray (1800–1850), best known for his self-pitying verse on ageing.

34 Name for camel.

35 Water made holy by the blessing of a *wadaad* or a man of God, deemed to be efficacious in preventing diseases and other misfortunes.

36 An anonymous poet of the 1850s.

37 'Hagoogan' means in Somali 'to cover one's face', and Somalis say he who shared in the booty of Hagoogane camels covered his face with pride, while he who missed that great event covered his face with anger and remorsefulness.

38 'Sidii geel ḍukaan qaba miyaan 'aday ka ḍuubnaaday.'

39 'Sidii geel ubakii laga ḥiray miyaan ololay oo reemay.'

40 'Geelaa haduu daranyahay laba nin doogtaayee.
Waḥ kaloo la darandooriyaa dama' ma yeeshaane.'

41 'Hadalkaagii waan u guuḥay.'

42 Ralph E. Drake-Brockman, *British Somaliland* (London: Hurst and Brackett, 1912), p. 199.

43 As an example, see Raage Ugaas's *geeraar*, 'Tribute to a Beloved Beast', Yuusuf Meygaag Samatar, Fieldnotes, Mogadishu, 26 March 1977. Cf. Sayyid Maḥammad's praise *geeraars* of horses in Sheikh Jaama' (Aw Jaamac Cumar Ciise), *Diiwaanka Gabayadii Sayid Maxamad Cabdulle Xasan* (Mogadishu:

Wakaaladda Madbacadda Qaranka, 1974), pp. 134–6, 272–3, 295–8 and 314–15.

44 Douglas Jardine, *The Mad Mullah of Somaliland* (London: Herbert Jenkins, 1923), p. 33.

45 L. S. Amery, 'Thought and Language' in The English Association *Presidential Address* (London: n. p., 1949), p. 7.

46 Maurice Bloch, ed., *Political Language and Oratory in Traditional Society* (London: Academic Press, 1975), p. 28.

47 Asmarom Legesse, *Gada: Three Approaches to the Study of African Society* (New York: The Free Press, 1973), pp. 207–29.

48 Laurence, *A Tree for Poverty*, p. 1.

49 J. W. Kirk, *A Grammar of the Somali Language* (Cambridge: Cambridge University Press, 1905), p. 170.

50 Maino, *La Lingua, passim.*

51 Laurence, *A Tree for Poverty*, pp. 1–2.

52 The terms I have employed to designate these categories of offense are those in use in the Ogaadeen. There may be variant words to denote the same concept in other regions.

53 Ma'alim 'Abdullahi Ḥ. Rabaḥ, Fieldnotes, Machakos, Kenya, 7 January 1977.

54 'Ali Ḥammaal, an Isaaq poet. In Somali, the line goes like this: 'Gooddiga Ban 'Awl buu fakhrigu, geed ku leeyahay e.'

55 Maḥammad Ḥaji Ḥuseen, 'Sheeka-Ḥariir' ('Man of Beautiful Story'), Fieldnotes, Mogadishu, 6 February 1977.

56 Ibid.

57 A notable incident of political slander by *afmiishaars* occurred during the political elections of the soon-to-become-independent British Somaliland Protectorate. In a bitter political campaign in the closing months of 1959, the Somali National League (SNL) led by Maḥammad Ibraahim 'Igaal, accused Michael Mariano, leader of the opposition National United Front (NUF), of being an anti-Islamic imperialist stooge. This devastating propaganda is thought to have played a major part in SNL's sweeping victory.

58 Sheeka-Ḥariir, Fieldnotes, Mogadishu, 6 February 1977.

59 Andrzejewski and Lewis, *Somali Poetry*, p. 45.

60 I was often made aware of my inferiority in memory when I took notes in an interview. At one interview, I nearly lost my informants' respect when they noticed that I could not load my camera without referring to the instructions.

61 Sheeka-Ḥariir, Fieldnotes, Mogadishu, 6 February 1977.

62 Ibid., 7 February 1977.

63 Ibid., 10 February 1977.

64 'Daaqato' (Somali for 'pastoralist') and 'Beerato' ('farmer') are generic terms referring to the cultural and economic modes of the feuding clans whose ethnic names are withheld for the following reason: as part of the Horn of Africa's war-torn Ogaadeen, the clans and their homelands are, at the time of writing, caught up in a ruthless conflict between Somali guerrilla fighters and Ethiopian authorities. To reveal their identities would be to expose them to dangerous and needless reprisals by either – or both – of the conflicting parties.

For much the same reason, the two principal speakers at the Daaqato meeting are identified by their descriptive nicknames rather than their real names. However, the reader with academic interest in knowing their real identities (as those of the feuding clans) may consult my fieldnotes deposited (1979–80) at the Africana branch of Northwestern University Library (Evanston, Illinois) where special permission allows scholars to have access to them.

To explain the circumstances which led to my having a firsthand knowledge of the Daaqato–Beerato feud, I should say that I lived in the town of Qallaafo–along with other members of my family – at the time the feud occurred there and was therefore an eyewitness to the events described. A fortuitous but fortunate circumstance motivated me to follow these events with special interest: my father, Sheikh Samatar Maḥammad, who was the Islamic magistrate of the town, was invited by the elders of the Daaqato to attend their meeting in the hope of utilizing his skill in arbitration, should the meeting reach an impasse. His religious prestige, mediating skills and neutral status (ethnically, he was an outsider) uniquely qualified him to serve as an arbitrator. My father ordered me to attend the meeting and to become thoroughly conversant with every facet of it, even requiring me to memorize the gist of the oratorical speeches. Assuming that I would some day forge out a career like his, my father was trying his best to prepare me. At the time, I resented what I regarded as his highhanded ways but, years later, came to appreciate, even be grateful for, his 'highhandedness'.

As a Social Science Research Council Fellow, I returned to Somalia in 1977 to do six months of field work (January–June) for my doctoral research. As I 'went native' with my pastoral kin for three months, I frequently sneaked across the Somali border into the disputed Ogaadeen. During one of these excursions, I visited my father's village of 'Eel Berde and had the good fortune of meeting there the main speaker of the Daaqato assembly, the man whom I identified by his nickname, Shivering Beard. With his and my father's help, I was able to refresh my mind on the specifics of the Daaqato assembly.

65 The Somali text of the taunt song:

Daaqato dagaaloo
Anaa shalay harkii dilay
Koodii u dooraa
Hilibkiisa duhurkii
Dugaagii u waray oo
Dadka uunku wada maqal.

66 Pastoral inter-clan raids are led by directors known as 'war leaders' (pl., *amaan-duuliyal*) who, in recognition of their leadership abilities, receive an extra portion of whatever stock their raiding parties succeed in carrying off.

67 For a scholarly discussion of *maq*-paying units, see Lewis, *A Pastoral Democracy*, *passim*.

68 Qamaan Ḍeere (Shivering Beard), Fieldnotes, 'Eel Berde, 25 May 1977.

69 Sheikh Samatar, Fieldnotes, 'Eel Berde, May 1977.

70 From Salaan 'Arrabay's poem, 'Hadaad ḍimato geeridu', alliterating in the letter **'ḍ'**.

71 I render the Somali word 'way' as 'alas'.

72 Pastoral Somalis believe that a man is haunted into manic sleeplessness by the spirits of his murdered kin if their deaths have not been avenged. This notion of the dead haunting the living serves to sustain the institution of reciprocal vendetta discussed above, pp. 23–7.

73 'Ḥabash': a pejorative Somali term for Amhara.

74 Lewis, *A Pastoral Democracy*, chapter 5.

75 Ibid.
76 The controversy is rooted in the verse's apparent affirmation of ethnic and national plurality, a notion which has the logical implication of undercutting a central theme in Islamic teaching: that of the Muslim community (*umma*) as *one universal* community. For further commentary on this matter, see 'Abdullah Yusuf 'Ali, *The Meaning of the Glorious Qur'an*, 3rd edn (2 vols., Cairo: Dar al-Kitab at-Masri, 1938), vol. 2, note 4933, p. 1407.
77 George Orwell, *Animal Farm* (New York: Harcourt Brace Jovanovich, 1946), p. 53.
78 In Somali: *qoore* (penis), *iyo ḥero* (testicles).

Chapter 2

1 Richard Burton, *First Footsteps in East Africa* (2 vols., London: Tylston and Edwards, 1894), vol. 1, p. 82.
2 Ibid., p. 81.
3 The observation comes from vol. 2, p. x of H. M. and N. K. Chadwick's monumental three-volume work, *The Growth of Literature* (Cambridge: Cambridge University Press, 1936), which is considered a major contribution to the subject.
4 Sheikh Jaama' 'Umar 'Iise, Fieldnotes, Mogadishu, 7 March 1977.
5 Sheikh 'Aaqib 'Abdullahi Jaama', Fieldnotes, Mogadishu, 6 March 1977.
6 Ibid.
7 B. W. Andrzejewski and I. M. Lewis, *Somali Poetry: An Introduction* (Oxford: The Clarendon Press, 1964), p. 44.
8 Aḥmad Faaraḥ 'Ali 'Idaajaa', Fieldnotes, Mogadishu, 1 February 1977.
9 J. W. Kirk, *A Grammar of the Somali Language* (Cambridge: Cambridge University Press, 1905), p. 173.
10 Maḥammad K. Salaad, Fieldnotes, Mogadishu, 7 February 1977. Cf. Andrzejewski and Lewis, *Somali Poetry*, p. 43.
11 Sheikh Jaama' 'Umar 'Iise, Fieldnotes, Mogadishu, 3 March 1977.
12 John Johnson, 'Recent contributions by Somalis and Somalists to the study of oral literature', in Hussein Adam, ed., *Somalia and the World: Proceedings of International Symposium* (2 vols., Mogadishu: Wakaaladda Madbacadda Qaranka, 1979), vol. 1, pp. 118–19.
13 John Johnson, 'The scansion of Somali poetry', in *Somalia and the World*, p. 132.
14 For the various theories proposed, see *Somalia and the World*, pp. 117–53.
15 Said S. Samatar, 'Gabay-Ḥayir: a Somali mock heroic song', *Research in African Literatures*, 11 (1980), 458–61.
16 Andrzejewski and Lewis, *Somali Poetry*, p. 46.
17 Enrico Cerulli, *Somalia: Scritti Vari Editi ed Inediti*, vol. 3 (Rome: Istituto Poligrafico dello Stato, 1964), pp. 1–40.
18 Ruth Finnegan, *Oral Poetry: Its Nature, Significance and Social Context* (Cambridge: Cambridge University Press, 1977).
19 From the Sayyid's poem, 'Ḥuseenow Ninkii Laable', alliterating in the letter **'l'**.
20 From Raage Ugaas' vowel-alliterated poem, 'Alleyl Dumay', a version of which appears in Somali Government (Wasaaradda Waxbarashada iyo Barbaarinta), *Suugaan, Fasalka Koowaad* (Mogadishu: Wakaaladda Madbacadda Qaranka, 1976), p. 8.
21 Andrzejewski and Lewis, *Somali Poetry*, pp. 116–17.
22 Margaret Laurence, *A Tree for Poverty* (Nairobi: Eagle Press, 1954), p. 40.

23 John 15.7.
24 From the Sayyid's poem, 'Ḥuseenow Ninkii Laable'.
25 B. W. Andrzejewski and Muuse I. Galaal, 'A Somali Poetic Combat', *Journal of African Languages*, 2, Part 1 (1963), 15.
26 Some of the poets who took part in these contests were Qowḍan Du'aale Suldaan and Aadan Ḥayd Suldaan 'Jaajaale' of the Isaaq clans and 'Abdi Gahayr of the Ogaadeen Daarood.
27 This theory receives comprehensive treatment from Albert Lord's classic work, *The Singer of Tales* (Cambridge, Mass.: Harvard University Press, 1964), pp. 30–67.
28 The Romantic evolutionist theories and their background are summarized by Ruth Finnegan, *Oral Poetry*, pp. 30–40.
29 Sheikh Jaama' 'Umar 'Iise (Aw Jaamac Cumar Ciise), *Diiwaanka Gabayadii* (Mogadishu: Wakaaladda Madbacadda Qaranka, 1974), pp. iv-v; Andrzejewski and Lewis, *Somali Poetry*, pp. 47–52; Samatar, 'Somali mock heroic', pp. 452–6.
30 For the genealogical relationship of the two clans, see fig. 1, p. 10.
31 Islaan 'Abdille, head of the princely house of the 'Umar Maḥamuud Majeerteen, says he got the story from his father who was a contemporary of the episode.
32 Sheeka-Ḥariir, Fieldnotes, Mogadishu, 25 January 1977.
33 Andrzejewski and Galaal, 'Poetic Combat', pp. 15–28.
34 Sheeka Ḥariir, Fieldnotes, Mogadishu, 3 April 1977.
35 Plains of the Ogaadeen with ideal pasturelands.
36 Andrzejewski and Galaal, 'Poetic Combat', p. 21.
37 Ibid., pp. 94–5.
38 Maḥammad Faaraḥ Maḥammuud 'Jaawali', Fieldnotes, Mogadishu, 7 April 1977.
39 From the poem, 'Khamra 'abitin mooyee hadaan 'aana laga ḍaaran', 'Abdi 'Iydiid, Fieldnotes, Nairobi, 10 June 1977.
40 See for example, *Richard III*, I.iii. 209–40 in *William Shakespeare*, *The Complete Works*, ed. Alfred Harbage (Baltimore: Penguin Books, 1969), pp. 561–2.
41 Cyrus Alder *et al.*, eds., *The Jewish Encyclopedia* (12 vols., New York, London: Funk and Wagnalls Company, 1901–12), vol. 4, 1903, p. 390.
42 Sheikh Jaama' 'Umar 'Iise, Fieldnotes, Mogadishu, 5 March 1977.
43 *Iqraan* are two angels in Islamic doctrine believed to be perching at all times on the shoulders of every human being to record his deeds, be they good or bad.
44 Shariif 'Aydaruus, buried in Aden, regarded by the pastoralists as saint of rain and milk.
45 Death rite and confession of faith refer to ritual phrases recited by a dying person which include the words, 'There is no god but God and Maḥammad is His Apostle', believed to be essential in preparing the dying for the hereafter.
46 'Light' here refers to children, the lack of whom is a horrible catastrophe in nomadic *weltanschauung*. The source of the poem is 'Ali Muumin Ismaa'iil, Fieldnotes, Mogadishu, 25 April 1977.
47 Sheikh Jaama' 'Umar 'Iise, Fieldnotes, Mogadishu, 5 March 1977.
48 The Ḍulbahante clan, as a result of their support for the Dervishes, were out of favor with the British for a while after the demise of the Dervish movement. They were allegedly made to pay for their part in the revolt by being forced to serve under Isaaq native administrators. 'Arab Ḍeere was one of these administrators, and while Police Chief of the Ḍulbahante town of Laas 'Aanood, he is alleged

to have used his new powers for clannish vendetta and score-settling. Ismaa'iil Mire, poet-spokesman of the Ḍulbahante, hence pronounced the curse on him.

49 'Ali Muumin Ismaa'iil, Fieldnotes, Mogadishu, 25 April 1977.

50 A Somali version of this poem appears in Sheikh Jaama' 'Umar 'Iise (Aw Jaamac Cumar Ciise), *Diiwaanka Gabayadii*, p. 63.

51 Richard Shelley, British Somaliland administrative officer at Bur'o.

52 From the poem, 'Duriyaadka Nabigaanunahay', Yuusuf Meygaag Samatar, Fieldnotes, Mogadishu, 26 March 1977.

53 The ninety-fifth Sūra of the Qur'an, called 'The Fig'.

54 Andrzejewski and Lewis, *Somali Poetry*, pp. 84, 86.

55 Alex Preminger, ed., *Encyclopedia of Poetry and Poetics* (Princeton: Princeton University Press, 1965), pp. 591–2.

56 B. W. Andrzejewski, Lecture, School of Oriental and African Studies, London, November, 1976.

57 Laurence, *A Tree for Poverty*, p. 36.

58 Ibid., p. 37.

59 Aḥmad Faaraḥ 'Ali, Fieldnotes, Mogadishu, 5 February 1977.

60 Koofil and Laaran: Somali corruptions of Richard Corfield and Mark (?) Lawrence, two British officers of the Somaliland Camel Corps, infamous for their rashness and ill temper.

61 Miira and Goglaa refer to the region of wife's kin. The poet is saying that his wife has the mistaken notion to suppose that the land of her people is a land of plenty.

62 Mortar used for grinding maize evokes land-tilling and other modes of peasant living which to the nomads signify a life of subservience and drudgery. Thus, the land of her kin, far from being a land of plenty, is in fact a contemptible place where men grind maize to eke out a livelihood.

63 The 'triple divorce oath' refers to a marital law in the Sharī'a in which a man solemnizes separation from his wife by uttering the third and final declaration of divorce in the presence of mature witnesses.

Chapter 3

1 A general account of the partition is given in I. M. Lewis, *The Modern History of Somaliland: from Nation to State* (London: Weidenfeld and Nicolson, 1965), pp. 40–62. For southern Somalia, see Robert Hess, *Italian Colonialism in Somalia* (Chicago: Chicago University Press, 1966).

2 Quoted in Somali Government, *The Somali Peninsula: New Light on Imperial Motives*, Revised (Shorter) Edn (London: Staples Printers, 1962), p. 76.

3 Quoted in B. W. Andrzejewski and I. M. Lewis, *Somali Poetry: An Introduction* (Oxford: The Clarendon Press, 1964), p. 57.

4 The statement is based on Sheikh 'Ali Sa'iid's estimate of the number of northern Somali *Ḥaj*-makers in the 1890s as opposed to those in the 1910s. Sheikh 'Ali is the head of the Saaliḥiya order in Bur'o and he has a reputation for knowledge on the history of Muslim orders in Somalia. His estimate that 5 percent of the male population of Berbera made the *Ḥaj* can be regarded a well-informed guess. He attributes the high proportion of *Ḥaj*-makers in the 1890s to an unusual prosperity of the clans during this time which enabled many to afford the cost of pilgrimage. Fieldnotes, Bur'o, 10 May 1977.

5 For African Islam, this theme receives a brief but provocative treatment in

B. G. Martin, *Muslim Brotherhoods in Nineteenth-Century Africa* (Cambridge: Cambridge University Press, 1976).

6 R. Coupland, *East Africa and Its Invaders*, 2nd edn (New York: Russell and Russell, 1965), pp..453–4.

7 E. Hertslet, *The Map of Africa By Treaty*, 3rd edn (London: Frank Cass & Co., 1967), pp. 304–8.

8 Ronald Robinson and John Gallagher, *Africa and the Victorians* (London: Macmillan Press, 1961), pp. 79–81.

9 The Qur'an, Sūra III, 110.

10 J. S. Trimingham, *The Sufi Orders in Islam* (Oxford: Oxford University Press, 1971).

11 Martin, *Muslim Brotherhoods.*

12 To be sure, belief in the millenarian, the notion of the coming Mahdi or prince – judge under whose government 'holiness', 'righteousness', and 'justice' will be triumphant as 'sin', 'wickedness' and 'oppression' are banished from the earth, is an underlying theme in Muslim eschatology, and the Mahdist figure frequently appears in the history of Muslim societies. See M. Th. Houtsma and A. J. Wensink eds., *The Encyclopaedia of Islam* (4 vols., Leyden: E. J. Brill, 1913–34), vol. 3, pp. 111–14.

13 Martin, *Muslim Brotherhoods*, pp. 5–6.

14 Robert L. Hess, 'The poor man of God – Muhammad Abdullah Hassan', in *Leadership in Eastern Africa: Six Political Biographies*, ed. Norman R. Bennett (Boston: Boston University Press, 1968), pp. 65–72.

15 H. G. C. Swayne, *Seventeen Trips through Somaliland* (London: Rowland Ward and Co., 1895), p. 202.

16 F. L. James, *The Unknown Horn of Africa* (London: George Philip & Son, 1888), p. 142.

17 Ibid., p. 129.

18 Harold Marcus, *The Life and Times of Menelik II of Ethiopia* (Oxford: Oxford University Press, 1975), pp. 136–9. Cf. F. B. Pearce, *Rambles in Lion-land* (London: Chapman & Hall, 1898), pp. 176–8.

19 Quoted in Hess, 'Poor man of God', p. 75.

20 Ibid., p. 75.

21 Martin, *Muslim Brotherhoods*, p. 2.

22 Aw: A Somali religious personage of slightly lesser stature than the *wadaad.*

23 Richard Burton, *First Footsteps in East Africa* (2 vols., London: Tylston and Edwards, 1894), vol. 1, p. 78.

24 His real name was 'Ali Muḥammad al-'Adali.

25 Martin, *Muslim Brotherhoods*, p. 2.

26 From the Qaadiriya *qasīda* 'Alla La Ilaha Illalah' popular with Sheikh Uways' followers. Uways Muḥiyadin Uways, Fieldnotes, Biyoolay, Somalia, 10–12 March 1977.

27 As an example of this, see Sheikh Jaama' 'Umar 'Iise (Aw Jaamac Cumar Ciise), *Taariikhdii Daraawiishta iyo Sayid Maxamad Cabdulle Xasan* (Mogadishu: Wakaaladda Madbacadda Qaranka, 1976), pp. 4–5.

28 'Abd as-Sabūr Marzūq, *Thā'ir min as-Sumāl* (Cairo: Dār al-Qowmiya, 1964), p. 13.

29 Students of the Dervish Movement almost to a man place the birth date of the Sayyid at 1864, a date which seems to have a single source: 'Abdirahmaan

Sayyid, the notably erudite son whose records give this date. Surviving Dervishes, however, unanimously reject this date and insist on the 1856 one. See Skeikh Jaama "Umar 'Iise (Aw Jaamac Cumar Ciise), *Taariikhdii Daraawiishta*, p. 4.

30 Better known by her nickname, 'Arro Seed.

31 Marzūq, *Thā'ir*, p. 14.

32 Muuse I. Galaal, Fieldnotes, Mogadishu, 21 April 1977.

33 Muuse I. Galaal and Aw Daahir Afqarshe, Fieldnotes, Mogadishu, 21 April 1977. Cf. Lewis, 1965, p. 65.

34 Marzūq, *Thā'ir*, p. 15.

35 Their names appear in Marzūq, *Thā'ir*, p. 16.

36 Although classical Islam has no clergy comparable to that of Christendom, appointment into Sufi khalīfships involves such regular rituals as to warrant the use of the term 'ordination'.

37 Muuse Galaal, Fieldnotes, Mogadishu, 21 April 1977. According to Mr Galaal, the thirteen sheikhs recognized in Sayyid Maḥammad qualities of leadership, and pleaded with Maḥammad Saliḥ to appoint him his spiritual envoy in Somalia as there was at this time a great need to counter the missionizing activities of the Roman Catholics in Berbera.

38 Muuse Galaal, Fieldnotes, Mogadishu, 21 April 1977.

39 Marzūq, *Thā'ir*, pp. 16–17. The same story is repeated by Muuse Galaal, a Saaliḥiya elder whose observations on the Sayyid form the chief source of the latter's stay in Mecca.

40 The incident allegedly took place at the Tuwahi quarters of the port of Aden. Sayyid Maḥammad, wearing resplendent robes and holding an umbrella over his head, attracted the attention of the officer who sought to accost him familiarly. But the Sayyid rebutted him with a casual indifference, whereupon the insulted officer rushed angrily after the Sayyid and pulled rudely on his umbrella. A scuffle followed in which, as the tale goes, the officer got 'pushed off the wharf' into the sea. The intervention of a Somali interpreter, named 'Ali Qaaje, saved the Sayyid from imprisonment for his misconduct. It is said the interpreter, wishing to explain to the port authority that the Sayyid was in spiritual ecstasy and thus could not be held responsible for his behavior, but not knowing how to describe such a concept in English, pleaded with the judge, 'Sir, pardon, he Mad Mullah' – thus giving rise to the epithet. Muuse Galaal, Fieldnotes, Mogadishu, April, 1977. Cf. Marzūq, *Thā'ir*, p. 17. Another version as to the possible source of the phrase relates to a tax incident. Upon arrival in Berbera, the Sayyid refused to pay the customs duties on his belongings and got away with the civil disobedience because the interpreter convinced the authorities of the Sayyid's insanity. See Sheikh Jaama' 'Umar 'Iise (Aw Jaamac Cumar Ciise), *Taariikhdii Daraawiishta*, p. 9.

41 John Drysdale, *The Somali Dispute* (London: Pall Mall Press, 1964), p. 28.

42 A. M. Brockett, 'The British Somaliland Protectorate to 1905', unpublished dissertation, Lincoln College, Oxford University, 1969, p. 266.

43 Brockett, 'British Somaliland', p. 286.

44 For further on *qaat*, see Samatar, 'Somali mock heroic', pp. 458–61.

45 Lewis, *Modern History*, pp. 65–66.

46 Sheikh Jaama' 'Umar 'Iise (Aw Jaamac Cumar Ciise), *Taariikhdii Daraawiishta*, p. 12.

47 Brockett, 'British Somaliland', p. 300.

48 Douglas Jardine, *The Mad Mullah of Somaliland* (London: Herbert Jenkins, 1923), p. 39.
49 Sheikh Jaama' 'Umar 'Iise (Aw Jaamac Cumar Ciise), *Taariikhdii Daraawiishta*, p. 12.
50 Jardine, *Mad Mullah*, p. 40.
51 A facsimile of the letter and the Sayyid's response faces p. 41 of Jardine.
52 Sadler to Salisbury, *Correspondence Respecting the Rising of the Mullah Muhammad 'Abd Allah Hassan in Somaliland and Consequent Military Operations* (hereafter referred to as *Correspondence*), No. 1, 12 April 1899, British Sessional Papers, Cmd 597, 1901.
53 Margery Perham, *The Government of Ethiopia* (Evanston, Illinois: Northwestern University Press, 1969), p. 161.
54 Isaḥaaq Maḥammad Daaḍi, brother of the late Sultan Nuuḥ Maḥammad Daaḍi, who is currently the hereditary chief of the princely house of the Aruusa Oromo in southern Ethiopia. Isaḥaaq, 78, is currently active in the Aruusa liberation movement at present fighting to gain autonomy from the central Ethiopian government. Fieldnotes, Mogadishu, 24 April 1977. For the history of the Ethiopian occupation of western Somalia, a knowledgeable person is Sheikh 'Aaqib 'Abdullahi Jaama' of the Bartire Daarood around Jigjiga. Fieldnotes, Mogadishu, 27 April 1977.
55 Perham, *Ethiopia*, p. 163.
56 Richard Pankhurst, 'The great Ethiopian famine of 1888–1892: A new assessment', Part II, *Journal of the History of Medicine and Allied Sciences*, 21 (1966).
57 See Richard Pankhurst's 'Assessment', in preceding note. Cf. Marcus, *Menelik II*, pp. 136–9.
58 Maḥammad Ḥaaji Ḥuseen 'Sheeka-Ḥariir', about 75, is one of two sources who provided this information. The other is Sheikh 'Aaqib 'Abdullahi Jaama', 65. Both men are from western Somalia. Sheeka-Ḥariir is from the Ogaadeen town of Ḍagaḥbuur and is renowned for his knowledge of western Somali history. He claims to have learned the above information from his father who was one of the Ogaadeen elders to work out a *modus vivendi* with the Ethiopian Governor of Harar.
59 Sheeka-Ḥariir, see preceding note.
60 Quoted in Somali Government, *The Somali Peninsula*, p. 37.
61 Jardine, *Mad Mullah*, pp. 285–6.
62 Sheeka-Ḥariir, Fieldnotes, Mogadishu, 6 February 1977.
63 Hess, 'Poor man of God', p. 75.
64 Tooḥyar Maḥammad, Fieldnotes, Taleeḥ, 7 May 1977.
65 Marcus, *Menelik II*, p. 138.
66 Sheeka-Ḥariir, Fieldnotes, Mogadishu, 6 February 1977.
67 Brockett, 'British Somaliland', p. 302.
68 Sadler to Salisbury, *Correspondence*, No. 2, Cmd 597, 1901.
69 Ibid.
70 Sayyid Maḥammad to Cordeaux, Foreign Office 78/5031, enclosed in Sadler to Salisbury, *Correspondence* No. 37.
71 For the names of the clans involved, see chapter 3 of my dissertation, 'Poetry in Somali Politics: The Case of Sayyid Maḥammad 'Abdille Ḥasan', Department of History, Northwestern University, Evanston, Illinois, 1979.
72 Sadler to Salisbury, *Correspondence*, No. 4, 16 July 1899, Cmd 597, 1901.
73 Ibid.

74 Sadler to Salisbury, *Correspondence*, No. 5, 16 July 1899, Cmd 597, 1901.
75 Harrington to Cromer, *Correspondence*, No. 6, 17 July 1899, Cmd 597, 1901.
76 Sadler to Salisbury, *Correspondence*, No. 7, 12 August 1899, Cmd 597, 1901.
77 Sheeka-Ḥariir, Fieldnotes, Mogadishu, 4 May 1977.
78 From the Sayyid's poem, 'Afbakayle'.
79 From the Sayyid's poem, 'Jiin' or 'Jiinley' alliterating in the letter 'j'.
80 This point was first brought out by Francesco S. Caroselli, *Ferro e Fuoco in Somalia* (Rome: Sindicato Italiano Arti Grafiche Editore, 1931), p. 8, and later developed by A. Brockett, 'British Somaliland', pp. 298–300.
81 Other imported terms include Hafildar, Jabidar and Resaldar, referring to designations in the army, and Memsahib (madam), Sahib (sir), and Brasahib (governor).
82 Sayyid Maḥammad to Sadler, *Correspondence*, No. 22, 9 September 1899, Cmd 597, 1901.
83 Jardine, *Mad Mullah*, p. 48.
84 Marzūq, *Thā'ir*, p. 36.
85 Martin, *Muslim Brotherhoods*, p. 182.
86 Sadler to Salisbury, *Correspondence*, No. 9, 31 August 1899, Cmd 597, 1901.
87 *Shariif* (Arabic) refers to a normally pious clan believed by Somalis to have descended directly from the Prophet.
88 'Sayyid' here refers to Sayyid Maḥammad. In one of its several meanings, the term 'Sayyid' connotes piety and holiness and this is one reason why both Maḥammad 'Abdille and his master, Maḥammad Saliḥ, assumed it as an honorific title.
89 A version of this poem appears in Sheikh Jaama' 'Umar 'Iise (Aw Jaamac Cumar Ciise), *Taariikhdii Daraawiishta*, p. 28.
90 Reference to Ḥaaji Suudi, a trusted lieutenant of the Sayyid.
91 'Iidagale clan, from the Sayyid's poem, 'War Suudow Dagaalka Anigu Doonimaayo'.
92 Sheikh Jaama' 'Umar 'Iise, Fieldnotes, Mogadishu, 4 February 1977.
93 The fullest and most detailed account is given by Douglas Jardine, *Mad Mullah*. For the official British view of the movement in its initial stages, see *Correspondence*, cited above in note 52. With respect to individual opinions, the following works are worth consulting: M. McNeill, *In Pursuit of the Mad Mullah* (London: C. Arthur Pearson, 1902); J. W. Jennings, *With the Abyssinians in Somaliland* (London: Hodder and Stoughton, 1905). The role played by the King's African Rifles in suppressing the Dervishes is recorded by Hubert Moyse-Bartlett, *The King's African Rifles: A Study in the Military History of East and Central Africa 1890–1945* (Aldershot: Gale and Polden, 1956), pp. 160–94, 419–33. For the treatment of the Dervishes in the modern period, see I. M. Lewis, *Modern History*; Robert Hess, 'Poor man of God', and B. G. Martin, *Muslim Brotherhoods*. For the Italian colonial view of the Dervishes, see Caroselli, *Ferro e Fuoco*. For the Somali nationalist view, see Sheikh Jaama' 'Umar 'Iise (Aw Jaamac Cumar Ciise), *Taariikhdii Daraawiishta*.
94 Jardine, *Mad Mullah*, p. 139.
95 Sir Charles Eliot, *The East Africa Protectorate* (London: Edward Arnold, 1905), chapter 7.
96 Sheikh Jaama' 'Umar 'Iise (Aw Jaamac Cumar Ciise), *Taariikhdii Daraawiishta*, pp. 74–5.

97 From Qaaje-Balas's poem, 'Raḥanraabkiyo Hawsha', Aw Daahir Afqarshe, Fieldnotes, Mogadishu, 6 March 1977.
98 'Yaos' refers to the Central African troops who, as members of the King's African Rifles, fought on the British side. Similarly, the Sudanese and Indians mentioned in the poem are imperial troops.
99 Quoted in Jardine, *Mad Mullah*, p. 122.
100 For vivid details of this visit, see Gustavo Chiesi, *La Colonizzazione Europea nell'Est Africa* (Torino: Unione Tipografico-editrice Torinse, 1909) p. 158.
101 The Qur'an, Sūra VIII, 55–8. For exegetic commentary on these verses, see 'Abdullah Yūsuf 'Ali, *The Meaning of the Glorious Qur'an*, 3rd edn (2 vols., Cairo: Dar al-Kitab al-Masri, 1938), vol. 1, note 1224, p. 429.
102 Quoted in Jardine, *Mad Mullah*, p. 185.
103 See Sheikh Jaama' 'Umar 'Iise (Aw Jaamac Cumar Ciise), *Taariikhdii Daraawiishta*, pp. 179–80.
104 Sheeka-Ḥariir, Fieldnotes, Mogadishu, 8 February 1977.
105 Ibid.
106 In Somali: ''Anjeel-tala-waa'. Literally, '*Anjeel* is the name for the genus *Mimusops*. See P. E. Glover, *A Provisional Check-List of British and Italian Somaliland Trees, Shrubs and Herbs* (London: The Crown Agents, 1947), p. 337. In this case, though, it metaphorically stands for a tree.
107 'Abdalla Qoriyow, the prestigious Islamic magistrate of the Dervish capital, who took part in the conspiracy.
108 Aḥmad Fiqi, also a conspirator, was the Dervish expert on Qur'anic exegesis.
109 Reference to the Sayyid's brother-in-law, Faaraḥ Maḥamuud Sugulle, whose involvement in the conspiracy was particularly bad news for the Sayyid.
110 Copies of this report are extant: Colonial Office 537/44 12 June 1909, and at the University of Durham Library: 'Special Mission to Somaliland', Box 125.
111 I will deal with these poems in a subsequent section on the impact of the Sayyid's poetry in the movement.
112 Jardine, *Mad Mullah*, p. 303.
113 Ibid., p. 247.
114 The document outlining the terms of the agreement is reproduced in Caroselli, *Ferro e Fuoco*, facing p. 224. Cf. Sheikh Jaama' 'Umar 'Iise (Aw Jaamac Cumar Ciise), *Taariikhdii Daraawiishta*, pp. 241–45.
115 Caroselli, *Ferro e Fuoco*, p. 224.
116 An English translation of it is enclosed in C. O. 535/42, Despatch No. 03286, 15 June 1916.
117 Mo 'alim 'Abdullaahi Ḥ. Rabaḥ, Fieldnotes, Machakos, Kenya, 7–15 January 1977.
118 Aw Daahir Afqarshe, Fieldnotes, Mogadishu, 6 March 1977.
119 AIR 5/1315 'Air History', 25 August 1919, The Public Records Office, London.
120 Jardine, *Mad Mullah*, pp. 290–302.
121 See Sheikh Jaama' 'Umar 'Iise (Aw Jaamac Cumar Ciise), *Taariikhdii Daraawiishta*, p. 298.
122 Jardine, *Mad Mullah*, p. 306.

Chapter 4

1 See, for example, Sheikh Jaama' 'Umar 'Iise (Aw Jaamac Cumar Ciise), *Diiwaanka Gabayadii Sayid Maxamad Cabdulle Xasan* (Mogadishu: Wakaa-

ladda Madbacadda Qaranka, 1974), p. 133. Cf. Tape Recording by same, 1974.

2 Sheikh 'Ali Sa'iid, current spiritual director of the Saaliḥiya community of Bur'o, Northern Somalia, Fieldnotes, 11 May 1977.

3 For details of the Dervish attack on Jigjiga, see chapter 3, p. 118.

4 Aw Daahir Afqarshe, Fieldnotes, Mogadishu, 6 March 1977.

5 The connotation of this line and following ones rests on the theme in Islamic theology that God in his generosity allows unbelievers to enjoy a brief material prosperity in this life and is based on such Qur'anic verses as in Sūra III: 196–7.

6 Aw Daahir Afqarshe, Fieldnotes, Mogadishu, 6 March 1977.

7 Ibid.

8 Yuusuf Meygaag Samatar, current member of the Language Committee, the Somali Academy, whose people on the whole opposed Dervishism, Fieldnotes, Mogadishu, 17 April 1977.

9 Sheikh Jaama' 'Umar 'Iise (Aw Jaamac Cumar Ciise), *Taariikhdii Daraawiishta iyo Sayid Maxamad Cabdulle Xasan* (Mogadishu: Wakaaladda Madbacadda Qaranka, 1976), pp. 63–4.

10 An apparent reference to the proposed marriage alliance which the Dervishes hoped would establish ties of kinship between them and the Majeerteen.

11 Aw Daahir Afqarshe, Fieldnotes, Mogadishu, 6 March 1977.

12 Iidoor: a variant name for Isaaq, many sublineages of whom were opponents of the Dervishes.

13 Bad-Eye: Lt. Colonel Swayne, commander of the British force, who was blind in one eye and received a minor wound in the battle.

14 An apparent reference to the proposed marriage alliance between the Dervishes and the Majeerteen.

15 Sheikh 'Ali Sa'iid, May 1977, see note 2 above.

16 The Sayyid required his followers to address him as 'Father' (Aabbe), clearly emphasizing the hierarchical authority he sought to impose on the egalitarian Somalis who normally address one another as 'Cousin' (Ina-adeer). Note also the servile humility with which the Dervish poet, Ḥirsi Diihaal Halanje, talks about the poverty of his 'poetic style' as opposed to the great talent of the 'father', in Sheikh Jaama' 'Umar 'Iise (Aw Jaamac Cumar Ciise), *Diiwaanka Gabayadii*, p. 175.

17 A version of this poem along with English translation appears in my 'Gabay-Ḥayir: a Somali mock heroic song', *Research in African Literatures*, 11, No. 4 (1980), 462–5.

18 Aw Daahir Afqarshe, Tape Recording, Mogadishu, n.d. but 1969.

19 Ibid.

20 For more details of this battle, see Hubert Moyse-Bartlett, *The King's African Rifles* (Aldershot: Gale and Polden, 1956).

21 Commissioner Swayne to Lansdowne, *Correspondence*, 6 October 1905, Cmd 2254, p. 477.

22 My translation of an excerpt from the Sayyid's poem, 'Ḥuseenow Ninkii Laable,' alliterating in the letter 'l'. tape recording by Aw Daahir Afqarshe, Mogadishu, October 1969.

23 Maḥammad Faaraḥ Maḥamuud 'Jaawali', Fieldnotes, Mogadishu, 25–30 April 1977.

24 Pp. 126–7.

25 One version of the 'Letter to the Biyamaal' appears in Somali Government,

Somaliya Antologia Storico-Culturale, No. 3 (Mogadishu: Ministero Publica Istruzione, 1967), pp. 7–26.

26 Aw Daahir Afqarshe, Fieldnotes, Mogadishu, 1 March 1977.

27 Maḥammad Ḥ. Ḥuseen 'Sheeka-Ḥariir', Fieldnotes, Mogadishu, 6 February 1977.

28 Ibid.

29 My translation of the Sayyid's poem, 'Ba'a E Yow Sheega', alliterating in the letter '**b**'.

30 The City of Infidels: Berbera, in the Somali coast which was then the administrative center of the Somaliland Protectorate.

31 The Somali texts of these proverbs came to me from 'Ali Mahdi of 'Eerigaabo, an inspector in the Somali army, Fieldnotes, 'Eel Berde, 25 May 1977.

32 Muuse Galaal, Tape Recording, n.d. A second Somali version of this poem is reproduced in Sheikh Jaama' 'Umar 'Iise (Aw Jaamac Cumar Ciise), *Diiwaanka Gabayadii*, pp. 264–6.

33 Reproduced in Sheikh Jaama' 'Umar 'Iise (Aw Jaamac Cumar Ciise), *Diiwaanka Gabayadii*, pp. 316–19.

34 Reer Ḥamar: Paternal lineage of the Sayyid.

35 My translation of portions of 'Ali Jaama' Haabiil's poem, 'Ma Talyaanigaasaa Mahdi Ah'.

36 Padre Giovanni Maria, *Grammatica Della Lingua Somala* (Asmara: Tipografica Francescana, 1914), p. 310. I am indebted to Dr B. W. Andrzejewski, who pointed this reference out to me.

37 A variant name of the Ḍulbahante.

38 B. W. Andrzejewski and I. M. Lewis, *Somali Poetry: An Introduction* (Oxford: The Clarendon Press, 1964), p. 4.

39 My translation of the Sayyid's poem, 'Ḥuseenow 'Aqligu Kaama Baḥo idim Ilaahaye', also called 'Afbakayle.'

40 Collected in Sheikh Jaama' 'Umar 'Iise (Aw Jaamac Cumar Ciise), *Diiwaanka Gabayadii.*

41 Andrzejewski and Lewis, *Somali Poetry*, p. 150.

42 Ibid., p. 68.

43 A Ḍulbahante lineage which defected from the Dervish ranks.

44 A variant name for Ḥiin Finiin, the Sayyid's favorite pony.

45 The Qur'an, Sura LXVIII, 10–16. The passage is based on an exegesis of six verses and not on a literal interpretation.

46 Andrzejewski and Lewis, *Somali Poetry*, p. 74.

47 Excerpt from the Sayyid's poem, 'Ḥirsow Naaqusnimo waa Waḥaad niiq la leedahay e', alliterating in the letter '**n**'.

48 As my informant, M. F. Maḥamuud put it, the Sayyid was wont to repeating the maxim, 'Gabyaaga waajib waḥaa ku ah inuu si sharaf leh waḥ u 'aayo' ('It is incumbent upon the poet to abuse with grace').

49 Yuusuf Meygaag Samatar, an Isaaq elder and a poet himself whose people for the most part remained either indifferent or hostile to the Dervish cause, referred to the Sayyid as 'one of the best reciters of provocative verse'. Fieldnotes, Mogadishu, 15 February 1977.

50 See preceding chapter, pp. 127–30.

51 Tooḥyar Maḥammad, Fieldnotes, Taleeḥ, 7 May 1977. Cf. Yaasiin 'Ismaan Keenadiid, Fieldnotes, Mogadishu, 23 April 1977. Tooḥyar, 86, born and

raised in Taleeḥ, was married to Sayyid Maḥammad's food-taster. She would not say which wife was involved in this incident for fear of present-day repercussions.

52 Ibid.

53 Muuse Galaal, Fieldnotes, Mogadishu, 25 April 1977.

54 Aw Daahir Afqarshe, Tape Recording, Mogadishu, n.d. but 1969. Cf. Sheikh Jaama' 'Umar 'Iise (Aw Jaamac Cumar Ciise), *Diiwaanka Gabayadii*, p. 57.

55 I. M. Lewis. *A Pastoral Democracy* (Oxford: Oxford University Press, 1961), p. 265.

56 'A Somali Poetic Combat', *Journal of African Languages*, 2, Part 1 (1963), 15.

57 The Sayyid's advisor and poem-memorizer, Ḥuseen Ḍiqle.

58 My translation. A Somali version of this poem appears in Sheikh Jaama' 'Umar 'Iise (Aw Jaamac Cumar Ciise), *Diiwaanka Gabayadii*, pp. 57–9.

59 'Sceptre' in the sense of authority.

60 Douglas Jardine, *The Mad Mullah of Somaliland* (London: Herbert Jenkins, 1923), p. 145.

61 Majeerteen coastal seas traditionally believed to be inhabited by evil spirits.

62 Fieldnotes, Mogadishu, 29 May 1977.

63 Ibid.

64 Jardine, *Mad Mullah*, p. 159.

65 Also called 'gudban'.

66 Sheikh Jaama' 'Umar 'Iise (Aw Jaamac Cumar Ciise), *Diiwaanka Gabayadii*, p. 30.

67 Jardine, *Mad Mullah*, pp. 170–5.

68 Andrzejewski and Lewis, *Somali Poetry*, p. 74.

69 In this line and the one following it, the poet is making reference to the commonness of genealogy between himself and the Warsangali, both of them belonging to the Daarood clan-family.

70 Andrzejewski and Lewis, *Somali Poetry*, pp. 79–80.

71 A Somaliland Protectorate coastal town.

72 A Somali version of the 'Bishaarooyinkii Eebahay' appears in Sheikh Jaama' 'Umar 'Iise (Aw Jaamac Cumar Ciise), *Diiwaanka Gabayadii*, pp. 31–3.

73 Andrzejewski and Lewis, *Somali Poetry*, p. 66.

74 The Somalis fear the hornbill as a bird of death.

75 The cluster of British-protected clans, a great many of whom opposed the Dervishes.

76 Muuse Galaal, Fieldnotes, Mogadishu, 3 April 1977.

77 See note 35 for this poem.

78 Thus the Sayyid's wife, Ḍiima, was tortured and executed for infidelity. After her death, the Sayyid composed the unkind taunt song gloating over her fate: 'Ḍiimaa god loo qoday, anaan laabta galinaynin'.

79 Sheikh Jaama' 'Umar 'Iise, Fieldnotes, Mogadishu, 1 February 1977.

80 Ibid.

81 Ibid.

82 The first three lines of the Somali version run:

Maanḍow i sii bahashanaan ku ahay waayeel e
Wab markaan ka siiyaa in ḍaha wahab ka duulaaye
I mana waasho naḥariishna waa kala wareegnaaye.

83 See, for example, his mock heroic parodying Ismaa'iil Mire's narrative poem,

'Annagoo Taleeḥ naal', reproduced in my 'Somali mock heroic', pp. 462–5.

84 An excerpt from the Sayyid's 'Ḥiin Finiin'.

85 Yuusuf Meygaag Samatar, Fieldnotes, Mogadishu, 4 March 1977.

86 Sheeka-Ḥariir, Fieldnotes, Mogadishu, 5 March 1977. Only 43 lines of the Sayyid's 99 proverbs alliterating in the letter '**b**' are extant.

87 Jardine, *Mad Mullah*, pp. 163–5.

88 Sheeka-Ḥariir, Fieldnotes, Mogadishu, 5 March 1977.

89 Reference to the disastrous Jidbaale defeat.

90 A Somali version of the 'This News' is reproduced in Sheikh Jaama' 'Umar 'Iise (Aw Jaamac Cumar Ciise), *Diiwaanka Gabayadii*, p. 27.

91 Sheeka-Ḥariir, Fieldnotes, Mogadishu, 5 March 1977.

92 Ibid.

93 My translation of the Sayyid's poem, 'Mahade Haw Sheego'.

94 One of these poems together with commentary appears in Sheikh Jaama' 'Umar 'Iise (Aw Jaamac Cumar Ciise), *Diiwaanka Gabayadii*, pp. 204–8.

95 Aw Daahir Afqarshe, Fieldnotes, Mogadishu, 1 February 1977. Cf. Muuse Galaal, Fieldnotes, Baltimore, Maryland, 5 November 1978.

96 Ibid.

97 Lt. Colonel E. Swayne, who carried the first two operations against the Sayyid and later on became Consul General of Somaliland.

98 My translation of the exchange between the Sayyid and Ḥuseen Ḍiqle, called 'Ḍurwaa Ariga Eebaa leh'.

99 A portion of the Somali version of this poem appears in Sheikh Jaama' 'Umar 'Iise (Aw Jaamac Cumar Ciise), *Diiwaanka Gabayadii*, p. 21.

100 The Sayyid's immediate family.

101 The sublineage of the Sayyid's Bah-Geri (Ogaadeen) lineage.

102 The versicle appears in Sheikh Jaama' 'Umar 'Iise (Aw Jaamac Cumar Ciise), *Diiwaanka Gabayadii*, p. 63.

103 Aw Daahir Afqarshe, Tape Recording, Mogadishu, n.d. but 1969.

104 Andrzejewski and Lewis, *Somali Poetry*, pp. 70–4.

105 H. F. P. Battersby, *Richard Corfield of Somaliland* (London: Edward Arnold, 1914), p. vi.

106 Sheikh 'Aaqib 'Abdullaahi, Fieldnotes, Mogadishu, 2 February 1977.

107 Aḥmad Faaraḥ 'Ali 'Idaajaa', and Sheikh Jaama' 'Umar 'Iise, Fieldnotes, Mogadishu, January 1977.

108 Andrzejewski and Lewis, *Somali Poetry*, p. 110.

109 Maḥammad Faaraḥ Maḥamuud 'Jaawali', Fieldnotes, Mogadishu, 15 April 1977. Cf. Sheikh Jaama' 'Umar 'Iise, 16 February 1977.

110 Sheikh Jaama' 'Umar 'Iise, Fieldnotes, Mogadishu, 7 February 1977.

111 Ibid.

112 The Shabeelle River across which remnants of the Dervishes were forced to flee, some drowning in the attempt.

113 A Somali version appears in Sheikh Jaama' 'Umar 'Iise (Aw Jaamac Cumar Ciise), *Diiwaanka Gabayadii*, pp. 124–8.

114 Iidoor: a variant name for the cluster of Isaaq clan families, a great many of whom opposed Dervishism.

115 Iimey: a small town on the headwaters of the Shabeelle River where the Sayyid retreated in his final days.

116 Literally, with his telegrams.

117 Mo'alim 'Abdullaahi Ḥ. Rabah, Fieldnotes, Machakos, Kenya, 2 January, 1977.

118 Fieldnotes, Mogadishu, 1 April 1977.

Chapter 5

1 The introductory portion of this chapter and a small section in the middle of chapter 4 appeared as part of 'Maḥammad 'Abdille Ḥasan: the Search for the Real Mullah' in *Northeast African Studies Journal*, 1, (1979), 60–76; two paragraphs from chapters 1 and 2 appeared in an article in *Research in African Literatures*, 11, (1980), 449–50.

2 Also referred to as the 'Sayyid' (master), Maḥammad 'Abdille Ḥasan is best known locally as Ina 'Abdille Ḥasan, 'Ina' meaning in Somali 'the son of', equivalent to the Arabic 'Ibn'.

3 For a representative sample of this kind of literature, see Great Britain, *Correspondence Respecting the Rising of the Mullah Muhammad 'Abd Allah Hassan in Somaliland and Consequent Military Operations*, British Sessional Papers, Cmd 597, 1901; R. E. Drake-Brockman, *British Somaliland* (London: Hurst and Brackett, 1912); Douglas Jardine, *The Mad Mullah of Somaliland* (London: Herbert Jenkins 1923); *The Times* of London, 1900–10.

4 For the Somalis, this view of the Sayyid was expressed by the main Somali historian of the Dervishes, Sheikh Jaama' 'Umar 'Iise, Tape Recording, Mogadishu, 21 May 1974.

5 Here, perhaps it would be helpful to point out that Sayyid Maḥammad was not the only leader in the modern history of Somalia to create an effective political organization. The two Majeerteen sultanates of Boqor 'Ismaan Maḥamuud and Yuusuf 'Ali Keenadiid of Hobyo both exercised a measure of centralized authority over relatively large territories. But unlike the Somali Dervishes, these Italian protectorates on the northeastern Somali coast lacked the supra-tribal, supra-regional identity enjoyed by Sayyid Maḥammad's movement.

6 Robert L. Hess, 'The Mad Mullah and Northern Somalia', *Journal of African History*, 3 (1964), 415.

7 Robert L. Hess, 'The Poor Man of God – Muhammad Abdullah Hassan' in Norman Bennett (ed.), *Leadership in Eastern Africa: Six Political Biographies* (Boston: Boston University Press, 1968), p. 100.

8 I. M. Lewis, *The Modern History of Somaliland* (London: Oxford University Press, 1965).

9 B. G. Martin, *Muslim Brotherhoods in Nineteenth-Century Africa* (Cambridge University Press, 1976).

10 The first to immortalize the epithet in poetic formula was the Isaaq opponent of the Sayyid, 'Ali Jaama' Haabiil. See p. 138.

11 Sadler to Salisbury, *Correspondence*, No. 8, Cmd 597, 1901.

12 Aḥmad 'Abdallah Rīrāsh, *Kashfi as-Suddūd fi Tārīkh as-Sumāl wa Mamālīikihim* (Mogadishu: Wakaaladda Madbacadda Qaranka, 1971).

13 Sheikh Jamma' 'Umar 'Iise (Aw Jaamac Cumar Ciise), *Taariikhdii Daraawiishta iyo Sayid Maxamad Cabdulle Xasan* (Mogadishu: Wakaaladda Madbacadda Qaranka, 1976).

14 Ibid., p. 4.

15 Sheikh Jaama' deleted six offending lines from the Sayyid's poetic diatribe, 'Corfield's Sister' ('Koofil Walaashi'), *Diiwaanka Gabayadii*, pp. 287–8; while

excluding from publication the Sayyid's malicious taunt song, 'Ḍiima', on his wife of the same name who was executed for alleged sexual misconduct, as well as the obscene attack, 'A Prince's Daughter', on Boqor 'Ismaan's daughter whom the Sayyid berated after she refused to marry him.

16 See notes 6 and 7 above.

17 Lewis, *Modern History*, pp. 70–1.

18 'Abd as-Sabūr Marzūg, *Tha'ir Min as-Sumāl* (Cairo: Dār al-Qowmiya, 1964).

19 J. S. Trimingham, *Islam in Ethiopia* (Oxford: The Clarendon Press, 1952), p. 133.

20 P. 120 above.

21 Jardine, *Mad Mullah*, p. 23.

22 Maḥammad Faaraḥ Maḥamuud 'Jaawali', Fieldnotes, Mogadishu, 5 May 1977. This elder, 76, took part in the last British operation against the Dervishes though the majority of his people were Dervish, from whom he was in a position to learn much about the life of the Sayyid and the day-to-day existence of the Dervishes.

23 Trimingham, *Islam in Ethiopia*, p. 34.

24 The observation comes from Tooḥyar Maḥammad. For a biographical note, see chapter 4, note 51.

25 Quoted in John Lee (ed.), *The Diplomatic Persuaders: New Role of the Mass Media in International Relations* (New York: John Wiley & Sons, 1968), p. xv.

26 Tooḥyar Maḥammad, see chapter 4, note 51.

27 Max Hayward and Leopold Labedz (eds.), *Literature and Revolution in Soviet Russia, 1917–1962* (Oxford: Oxford University Press, 1963), p. vii.

28 For this view of art, see Leo Tolstoy, *What Is Art? and Essays on Art*, trans. Aylmer Maude (Oxford: Oxford University Press, 1930), pp. 127–34.

29 Hayward and Labedz, *Literature and Revolution*, pp. xiv-xv.

30 See pp. 25–7 of chapter 1.

31 Maḥammad Faaraḥ Maḥamuud 'Jaawali', Fieldnotes, Mogadishu, 25 January 1977.

32 My translation of the Sayyid's poem, 'The Scourge of Infidels' ('Gaala-Leged').

33 Eyle: small village on the turbulent sea waters of eastern Somalia.

34 Igarray: Resaldar Major Ḥaaji Muuse Faaraḥ of the Habar Yoonis Isaaq was an important British collaborator and an implacable enemy of the Dervishes.

35 From the Sayyid's poem, 'Jidka Adari Loo Maro', a Somali version of which is reproduced in Sheikh Jaama' 'Umar 'Iise (Aw Jaamac Cumar Ciise), *Diiwaanka Gabayadii*, p. 15.

36 Maḥammad Faaraḥ Maḥamuud 'Jaawali', Fieldnotes, Mogadishu, 25 January 1977.

37 Sheikh Jaama' 'Umar 'Iise, Fieldnotes, Mogadishu, 25 March 1977.

38 Ibid.

39 See, for example, his letter of principles and policy declaration to the Biyamaal clan reproduced in Somali Government, *Somaliya: Antologia Storico-Culturale* (Mogadishu: Wakaaladda Madbacadda Qaranka, 1967).

40 There is no evidence that Greeks had done any harm to the Dervishes; possibly the Sayyid used the word 'Greek' because the alliteration of the poem in **'g'** forced the diversion on him.

41 This excerpt and following ones are my translation of portions of the Sayyid's poem, 'The Scourge of Infidels'.

42 Yuusuf Meygaag Samatar, Fieldnotes, Mogadishu, 26 March 1977.

43 From the Sayyid's poem alliterating in '**d**'. 'War Illeyn Doqone 'Alaf Ma Leh Dulbaaḥ Maḥaa Ka Baylahay'.
44 Fieldnotes, Mogadishu, 27 March 1977.
45 Sheikh Jaama' 'Umar 'Iise (Aw Jaamac Cumar Ciise), *Diiwaanka Gabayadii*, pp. vi, 263.
46 Margaret Smith, *Readings from the Mystics of Islam* (London: Luzac & Co., 1950), p. 1.
47 Ibid., p. 2.
48 Ibid., pp. 3–4.
49 Yaasiin 'Ismann Keenadiid, Fieldnotes, Mogadishu, 29 March 1977.
50 Jardine, *Mad Mullah*, *passim*.
51 Maḥammad Faaraḥ Maḥamuud 'Jaawali', Fieldnotes, Mogadishu, 3 February 1977. Cf. the Sayyid's poem, 'Waḥaa Tiraa Weeye', an English version of which appears in Andrzejewski and Lewis, *Somali Poetry*, pp. 82–6.
52 Andrzejewski and Lewis, *Somali Poetry*, p. 84, line 14.
53 Maḥammad Faaraḥ Maḥamuud 'Jaawali', Fieldnotes, Mogadishu, 3 February 1977.
54 'The Scourge of Infidels', lines 73–6.
55 Jardine, *Mad Mullah*, *passim*.
56 Ibid., p. 52.
57 Indeed in numerous periods in the history of Islam, Sufis found themselves accused by their orthodox fellow Muslims of the sin of *shirk* (setting up rivalry to God's sovereignty over his creation, one of the three worst iniquities in Islamic theological classification of sin) by claiming supernatural attributes. In one famous case Husayn Ibn Mansūr al-Ḥallāj reportedly declared: 'I am the Absolute Truth—ana al-Ḥaqq'. Al-Ḥallāj was tortured and ultimately put to death for his teachings and style of life which orthodox Muslims condemned as heretical. See Annemarrie Schimmel, *The Mystical Dimensions of Islam* (Chapel Hill, NC: North Carolina University Press, 1975), pp. 62–77.
58 Sheikh Jaama' 'Umar 'Iise, Fieldnotes, Mogadishu, 20 February 1977.
59 'Ali Muumin Ismaa'iil, Fieldnotes, Mogadishu, 1–2 May 1977.
60 Aw Daahir Afqarshe, Tape Recording, Mogadishu, n.d. but 1969.
61 Maḥammad Ḥ. Ḥuseen 'Sheeka-Ḥariir', Fieldnotes, Mogadishu, 1 April 1977.
62 Jardine, *Mad Mullah*, pp. 47–56, 308–15.
63 Sheeka-Ḥariir, Fieldnotes, Mogadishu, 11 April 1977.
64 Jardine, *Mad Mullah*, p. 315.
65 Quoted in T. O. Ranger, 'Connexions between "Primary Resistance" Movements and Modern Mass Nationalism in East and Central Africa', *Journal of African History*, 9, No. 3 (1968), p. 445.
66 From Shire Idaad's poem, 'Sayyidkaad Maqlaysaan Aduun Sababti Weeyaan e'.
67 Sheeka-Ḥariir, Fieldnotes, Mogadishu, 1 February 1977.
68 Jardine, *Mad Mullah*, p. 315.
69 Ibid., pp. 315–16.
70 A good summary of this series of incidents is provided by Somali Government, *The Somali Peninsula*, pp. 15–30, and I. M. Lewis, *Modern History*, pp. 33–6.
71 For the British officials' dislike of the Somalis and the general colonial opinion of the Somali peninsula as a hardship post, see Gerald Hanley's barely fictionalized autobiography, *Warriors and Strangers* (London: Hamilton, 1971).

72 Sir Charles Eliot, *The East Africa Protectorate* (London: Edward Arnold, 1905), p. 121.
73 Ibid., p. 122.
74 Lewis, *Modern History*, p. 90.
75 Maḥammad Khaliif Salaad, Fieldnotes, Mogadishu, 30 April 1977.
76 In Somali, 'Koofil Walaashi'.
77 Literally, 'He who has a faithful heart, does not lose my noble utterance', from the poem 'Ḥuseenow Ninkii Laable'.

Select bibliography

Archives

The Public Records Office, London, England: Chancery Lane Wing and Portugal Street Wing.
The India Office Library, London, England.
The British Museum Library (State Papers), London, England.
The Rhodes House, Oxford, England.
The University of Durham Library, Durham, England.
Archivio Storico dell'ex Ministero dell'Africa Italiana (ASMAI), Ministry of Foreign Affairs, Rome, Italy.
Istituto Italo-Africano (Via Aldrovandi, no. 16), Rome, Italy.
The Confidential Registry, Hargesia, Northern Somalia.
The Open Registry, Hargeisa, Northern Somalia.

Official publications

Great Britain. *Correspondence Respecting the Rising of the Mullah Muhammad 'Abd Allah Hassan in Somaliland and Consequent Military Operations.* British Sessional Papers, Cmd 597, 1901.
Official History of the Operations in Somaliland, 1901–4. 2 vols., London: War Office, 1907.
Correspondence Respecting Affairs in Somaliland. London: Darling and Son, 1910.
Somali Government. *The Somali Peninsula: New Light on Imperial Motives.* Revised edn, London: Staples Printers, 1962.
Somaliya: Antologia Storico-Culturale, No. 3. Mogadishu: Ministero Publica Istruzione, 1967.
(Wasaaradda Waxbarashada iyo Barbaarinta) *Suugaan: Fasalka Koowaad.* Mogadishu: Wakaaladda Madbacadda Qaranka, 1976.

Books and articles

'Abd ar-Raḥmān b. Sheikh 'Umar al-Qādiri. *Jalā al-'Aynayn fi Manāqib ash-Shaykhayn ash-Sheikh al-Wali Ḥajj Uways al-Qādiri wash-Sheikh 'Abd ar-Raḥman az-Zayli'i.* Cairo: n.p., n.d., c. 1954.

Jawhar an-Nafis fi Khawāss ash-Sheikh Uways. Cairo: n.p., 1383/1964.
'Abdullāhi Yūsuf Qutbi. *Al-majmū'at al-mubāraka*. 2 vols., Cairo: n.p., 1338/1919–20.
Abir, Mordechai. *Ethiopia: The Era of the Princes*. New York: Praeger, 1968.
'Aidrus ibn Sharif-'Ali. *Bughyat al-āmāl fi Tārikh as-Sumāl*. Mogadishu: Idārat al-Wasiya, 1954.
Alder, Cyrus, *et al.*, eds. *The Jewish Encyclopedia*. 12 vols., London: Funk and Wagnals Co., 1901–12.
'Ali, 'Abdullah Yūsuf. *The Meaning of the Glorious Qur'an*. 3rd edn, 2 vols., Cairo: Dar al-Kitab al-Masri, 1938.
Amery, L. S. 'Thought and Language.' The English Association, *Presidential Address*. London: n.p., 1949, pp. 3–19.
Andrzejewski, B. W. 'Poetry in Somali Society.' *New Society*, No. 25 (1963), 22–4.
Andrzejewski, B. W. and Muuse I. Galaal. 'A Somali Poetic Combat.' *Journal of African Languages*, 2, Part 1 (1963), 15–28; 93–100; 190–205.
Andrzejewski, B. W. and I. M. Lewis. *Somali Poetry: An Introduction*. Oxford: The Clarendon Press, 1964.
Battersby, H. F. P. *Richard Corfield of Somaliland*. London: Edward Arnold, 1914.
Bloch, Maurice, ed. *Political Language and Oratory in Traditional Society*. London: Academic Press, 1975.
Brockett, Andrew M. 'The British Somaliland Protectorate to 1905.' Unpublished diss., Lincoln College, Oxford University, 1969.
Burton, Richard F. *First Footsteps in East Africa*. 2 vols., London: Tylston and Edwards, 1894.
Caroselli, Francesco S. *Ferro e Fuoco in Somalia*. Rome: Sindicato Italiano Arti Grafiche Editore, 1931.
Cassanelli, Lee V. 'The Benaadir Past: Essays in Southern Somali History.' Diss. Ann Arbor, Michigan: University Micro-films, 1974.
Cerulli, Enrico. *Somalia: Scritti Vari Editi ed Inediti*. Vols. 1 (1957), 2 (1959), and 3 (1964), Rome: Istituto Poligrafico dello Stato.
Chadwick, H. M. and N. K. Chadwick. *The Growth of Literature*. Vol. 1 (1932), vol. 2 (1936) and vol. 3 (1940), Cambridge: Cambridge University Press.
Chaffee, Steven H. and Michael J. Petrick. *Using the Mass Media: Communication Problems in American Society*. New York: McGraw-Hill Book Co., 1975.
Chiesi, Gustavo. *La Colonizzazione Europea nell'Est Africa*. Torino: Unione Tipografico-editrice Torinse, 1909.
Corni, Guido. *Somalia Italiana*. Milano: Editoriale Arte e Storia, 1937.
Coupland, R. *East Africa and Its Invaders*. New York: Russell and Russell, 1965.
Doornbos, Martin R. 'The Shehu and the Mullah: The Jihads of Usuman Dan Fodio and Muhammad Abdallah Hassan in Comparative Perspective.' *Afrique*, vol. 14, No. 2 (1975), 7–32.
Drake-Brockman, Ralph E. *British Somaliland*. London: Hurst and Brackett, 1912.
Droandi, Ivo. *Il Cammello*: *Storia Naturale*. Florence: Istituto Agricolo Coloniale Italiano, 1936.
Drysdale, John. *The Somali Dispute*. London: Pall Mall Press, 1964.
Eliot, Sir Charles. *The East Africa Protectorate*. London: Edward Arnold, 1905.
Evans-Pritchard, E. E. *The Nuer: A Description of the Modes of Livelihood and Political Institutions of a Nilotic People*. Oxford: The Clarendon Press, 1940.
Finnegan, Ruth. *Oral Poetry: Its Nature, Significance and Social Context*. Cambridge: Cambridge University Press, 1977.

Galaal, Muuse and B. W. Andrzejewski. 'A Somali Poetic Combat.' *Journal of African Languages*, 2, Part 1(1963), 15–28; 93–100; 190–205.
Gallagher, J. and R. Robinson. *Africa and the Victorians.* London: Macmillan Press, 1961.
Giglio, Carlo. *L'Italia in Africa: Etiopia – Mar Rosse.* Rome: Editoriale Arte e Storia, 1958.
Glover, P. E. *A Provisional Check-List of British and Italian Somaliland Trees, Shrubs and Herbs.* London: The Crown Agents, 1947.
Greenfield, Richard. *Ethiopia: A New Political History.* New York: Frederick A. Praeger, 1965.
Hamilton, Angus. *Somaliland.* London: Hutchinson and Co., 1911.
Hanley, Gerald. *Warriors and Strangers.* London: Hamilton, 1971.
Harbage, Alfred, ed. *William Shakespeare: The Complete Works.* Baltimore: Penguin Books, 1969.
Hayward, Max and Leopold Labedz, eds. *Literature and Revolution in Soviet Russia, 1917–1962.* Oxford: Oxford University Press, 1963.
Hertslet, E. *The Map of Africa. By Treaty*, 3rd edn. London: Frank Cass and Co., 1967.
Hess, Robert L. 'The Mad Mullah and Northern Somalia.' *Journal of African History*, 3 (1964), 415–33.
Italian Colonialism in Somalia. Chicago: Chicago University Press, 1966.
'The poor man of God – Muhammad Abdullah Hassan.' Norman R. Bennett, ed. *Leadership in Eastern Africa: Six Political Biographies.* Boston: Boston University Press, 1968, pp. 65–108.
Hill, Richard. *Egypt in the Sudan.* Oxford: Oxford University Press, 1959.
Houtsma, M. Th. and A. J. Wensink, eds. *The Encyclopaedia of Islam.* Leyden: E. J. Brill, vol. 3, 1936.
Hussein M. Adam, ed. *Somalia and the World: Proceedings of International Symposium.* 2 vols., Mogadishu: Halgan, 1979.
Jaamac Cumar Ciise. *Diiwaanka Gabayadii Sayid Maxamad Cabdulle Xasan.* Mogadishu: Wakaaladda Madbacadda Qaranka, 1974.
Taariikhdii Daraawiishta iyo Sayid Maxamad Cabdulle Xasan. Mogadishu: Wakaaladda Madbacadda Qaranka, 1976.
James, F. L. *The Unknown Horn of Africa.* London: George Philip and Son, 1888.
Jardine, Douglas. *The Mad Mullah of Somaliland.* London: Herbert Jenkins, 1923.
Jennings, J. W. *With the Abyssinians in Somaliland.* London: Hodder and Stoughton, 1905.
Kirk, J. W. C. *A Grammar of the Somali Language.* Cambridge: Cambridge University Press, 1905.
Labedz, Leopold and Max Hayward. *Literature and Revolution in Soviet Russia, 1917–1962.* Oxford: Oxford University Press, 1963.
Labrouse, H. 'Le "Mad Mullah de Somaliland" Suite et Fin.' *Pount* (Djibouti, 1970), 15–28.
Laitin, David. *Politics, Language and Thought: The Somali Experience.* Chicago: Chicago University Press, 1977.
Laurence, Margaret. *A Tree for Poverty.* Nairobi: Eagle Press, 1954.
The Prophet's Camel Bell. London: Macmillan, 1963.
New Wind in a Dry Land. New York: Alfred A. Knopf, 1965.
Lee, John, ed. *The Diplomatic Persuaders: New Role of the Mass Media in International Relations.* New York: John Wiley and Sons, 1968.

Legesse, Asmarom. *Gada: Three Approaches to the Study of African Society*. New York: The Free Press, 1973.

Lewis, I. M. *A Pastoral Democracy*. Oxford: Oxford University Press, 1961.

The Modern History of Somaliland: From Nation to State. London: Weidenfeld and Nicolson, 1965.

Lewis, I. M. and B. W. Andrzejewski. *Somali Poetry: An Introduction*. Oxford: The Clarendon Press, 1964.

Lord, Albert B. *The Singer of Tales*. Cambridge, Mass.: Harvard University Press, 1964.

Low, D. A. 'The Northern Interior.' *History of East Africa*. Roland Oliver and Gervase Mathew, eds. Oxford: Oxford University Press, 1963, vol. 1, pp. 301–5.

Lytton, Lord. *The Stolen Desert*. London: Macdonald, 1966.

Maino, M. *La Lingua Somala – Strumento d'Insegnamento Professionale*. Alessandria: Ferrari, Occella and Co., 1953.

Marcus, Harold G. *The Life and Times of Menelik II of Ethiopia*. Oxford: Oxford University Press, 1975.

Maria, Padre Giovanni. *Grammatica Della Lingua Somala*. Asmara: Tipographica Francescana, 1914.

Martin, B. G. *Muslim Brotherhoods in Nineteenth-Century Africa*. Cambridge: Cambridge University Press, 1976.

Marzūq, 'Abd as-Sabūr. *Thā'ir min as-Sumāl*. Cairo: Dār al-Qowmiya, 1964.

McNeill, Malcolm. *In Pursuit of the Mad Mullah*. London: C. Arthur Pearson, 1902.

Morgan, William. *Population of Kenya: Density and Distribution*. Nairobi: Oxford University Press, 1966.

Mosse, A. H. E. *My Somali Book: A Record of Two Months of Shooting*. London: Sampson, Marston and Co., 1913.

Moyse-Bartlett, Hubert. *The King's African Rifles: A Study in the Military History of East and Central Africa 1890–1945*. Aldershot: Gale and Polden, 1956.

Nottingham, John and Carl Rosberg. *The Myth of 'Mau Mau': Nationalism in Kenya*. Cleveland: The World Publishing Co., 1970.

Orwell, George. *Animal Farm*. New York: Harcourt Brace Jovanovich, 1946.

Pankhurst, R. 'The Great Ethiopian Famine of 1888–1892: A New Assessment.' Part 2. *Journal of the History of Medicine and Allied Sciences*, 21 (1966), 294–310.

Pearce, F. B. *Rambles in Lion-land*. London: Chapman and Hall, 1898.

Perham, Margery. *The Government of Ethiopia*. Evanston, Illinois: Northwestern University Press, 1969.

Preminger, Alex, ed. *Encyclopedia of Poetry and Poetics*. Princeton: Princeton University Press, 1965.

Ranger, T. O. *Revolt in Southern Rhodesia: A Study in African Resistance*. Evanston, Illinois: Northwestern University Press, 1967.

'Connexions between "Primary Resistance Movements" and Modern Mass Nationalism in East and Central Africa.' *Journal of African History*, 9, Nos. 3 and 4(1968), 437–54; 631–42.

Rīrāsh, Sheikh Ahmad 'Abdallah. *Kashfi as-Suddūd fi Tārīkh as-Sumāl wa Mamālīkihim*. Mogadishu: Wakaaladda Madbacadda Qaranka, 1971.

Robinson, Ronald and John Gallagher. *Africa and the Victorians*. London: Macmillan Press, 1961.

Rosberg, Carl and John Nottingham. *The Myth of 'Mau Mau': Nationalism in Kenya.* Cleveland, Ohio: The World Publishing Co., 1970.

Samatar, Said S. 'Somalia.' Hassan S. Haddad and Basheer K. Nijim, eds. *The Arab World: A Handbook.* Wilmette, Illinois: Medina Press, 1978, pp. 157–164.

Sayyid, Muḥammad Mu'tasim. *Mahdi as-Sumāl: Batl ath-thowra min al-Isti'mār.* Cairo: Dar al-Qowmiya, 1963.

Schimmel, Annemarrie. *The Mystical Dimensions of Islam.* Chapel Hill, NC: North Carolina University Press, 1975.

Smith, Margaret. *Readings from the Mystics of Islam.* London: Luzac and Co., 1950.

Starkie, E. *Arthur Rimbaud in Abyssinia.* Oxford: The Clarendon Press, 1937.

Strayer, Robert W. *et al. Protest Movements in Colonial East Africa: Aspects of Early African Response to European Rule.* Syracuse, New York: Eastern African Studies Program, 1973.

Swayne, H. G. C. *Seventeen Trips through Somaliland.* London: Rowland Ward and Co., 1895.

Tolstoy, Leo. *What Is Art? and Essays on Art.* Trans. Aylmer Maude. Oxford: Oxford University Press, 1930.

Trimingham, J. Spencer. *Islam in Ethiopia.* Oxford: The Clarendon Press, 1952.

The Sufi Orders in Islam. Oxford: Oxford University Press, 1971.

Turton, Romilly. 'The Impact of Mohammad 'Abdille Hassan in the East Africa Protectorate.' *Journal of African History*, 10, (1969), 641–57.

Vecchi, Cesare Maria de. *Orizzonti D'Impero.* Milano: A. Mondadori, 1935.

Walsh, L. P. *Under the Flag and Somali Coast Stories.* London: Andrew Melrose, 1932.

Wensink, A. J. and M. Th. Houtsma, eds. *The Encyclopaedia of Islam.* Leyden: E. J. Brill, vol. 3, 1936.

Wolverston, Lord. *Five Months' Sport in Somaliland.* London: Chapman and Hall, 1894.

Yaḥya, Jalāl. *At-tanafus ad-Duwali fi Bilad as-Sumāl.* Cairo: Dar al-Qowmiya, 1959.

Index

Somali and Arabic names are indexed by first name, i.e. Aadan Gurray appears under A. When a name is commonly preceded by an honorific, it is indexed accordingly, i.e. Garaad 'Ali appears under G. All other names are indexed by surname.

Index

BOOKS IN THIS SERIES

3 Land Policy in Buganda *Henry W. West*

4 The Nigerian Military : A Sociological Analysis of Authority and Revolt 1960–1967 *Robin Luckham*

5 The Ghanaian Factory Worker: Industrial Man in Africa *Margaret Peil*

6 Labour in the South African Gold Mines, 1911–1969 *Francis Wilson*

7 The Price of Liberty: Personality and Politics in Colonial Nigeria *Kenneth J. Post and George D. Jenkins*

9 Dependence and Opportunity: Political Change in Ahafo *John Dunn and A. F. Robertson*

10 African Railwaymen: Solidarity and Opposition in an East African Labour Force *R. D. Grillo*

11 Islam and Tribal Art in West Africa *René A. Bravmann*

12 Modern and Traditional Elites in the Politics of Lagos *P. D. Cole*

13 Asante in the Nineteenth Century: The Structure and Evolution of a Political Order *Ivor Wilks*

14 Culture, Tradition and Society in the West African Novel *Emmanuel Obiechina*

15 Saints and Politicians: Essays in the Organisation of a Senegalese Peasant Society *Donal B. Cruise O'Brien*

16 The Lions of Dagbon: Political Change in Northern Ghana *Martin Staniland*

17 Politics of Decolonization: Kenya Europeans and the Land Issue 1960–1965 *Gray Wasserman*

18 Muslim Brotherhoods in Nineteenth-century Africa *B. G. Martin*

19 Warfare in the Sokoto Caliphate: Historical and Sociological Perspectives *Joseph P. Smaldone*

20 Liberia and Sierra Leone: An Essay in Comparative Politics *Christopher Clapham*

21 Adam Kok's Griquas: A Study in the Development of Stratification in South Africa *Robert Ross*

22 Class, Power and Ideology in Ghana: The Railwaymen of Sekondi *Richard Jeffries*

23 West African States: Failure and Promise: A Study in Comparative Politics *John Dunn*

24 Afrikaners of the Kalahari: White Minority in a Black State *Margo Russell and Martin Russell*

25 A Modern History of Tanganyika *John Iliffe*

26 A History of African Christianity 1950–1975 *Adrian Hastings*

27 Slaves, Peasants and Capitalists in Southern Angola 1840–1926 *W. G. Clarence-Smith*

28 The Hidden Hippopotamus: Reappraisal in African History: The Early Colonial Experience in Western Zambia *Gwyn Prins*

29 Families Divided: The Impact of Migrant Labour in Lesotho *Colin Murray*

30 Slavery, Colonialism and Economic Growth in Dahomey 1640–1960 *Patrick Manning*

31 Kings, Commoners and Concessionaires: The Evolution and Dissolution of the Nineteenth-century Swazi State *Philip Bonner*

32 Oral Poetry and Somali Nationalism: The Case of Sayyid Maḥammad 'Abdille Ḥasan *Said S. Samatar*

Books in this series

33 The Political Economy of Pondoland 1860–1930: Production, Labour, Migrancy and Chiefs in Rural South Africa *William Beinart*

34 Volkskapitalisme: Class, Capital and Ideology in the Development of Afrikaner Nationalism 1934–1948 *Dan O'Meara*

35 The Settler Economies: Studies in the Economic History of Kenya and Rhodesia 1900–1963 *Paul Mosley*

36 Slavery in Africa *Paul E. Lovejoy*

37 Amilcar Cabral: Revolutionary Leadership and People's War *Patrick Chabal*

38 Essays on the Political Economy of Rural Africa *Robert H. Bates*

LaVergne, TN USA
18 December 2009
167439LV00002B/2/P

9 780521 104579